Satisfy
YOUR
Soul

A Guide to African American,
African & Caribbean Restaurants

Satisfy YOUR Soul

A Guide to African American, African & Caribbean Restaurants

CARLA LABAT

IMPRESSIONS BOOKS

McLean, Virginia

Impressions Books
PO Box 9622
McLean, Virginia 22102-0622

Printed in the United States of America.

Library of Congress Catalog Card Number: 97-093896

ISBN: 0-9659204-0-2

First Edition: September 1997

Cover design by Carla Labat and RGM Graphics

Cover Photo Credits
Left: Caribbean Fusion Cuisine, courtesy of Bambou
        (New York); photographed by Jason Miccolo Johnson.
        Makeup by Dekar Lawson.
Center: Down home goodness from Mama Rosa's (Philadelphia);
        photographed by Jason Miccolo Johnson.
Right: Los Angeles Night Life; photographed by John Faulkner.
Author's Photo: Jason Miccolo Johnson.

Table of Contents

Acknowledgments

I would first like to thank all those who helped me identify some of the best eateries and clubs in the United States and those who opened their homes and took time out of their busy schedules to assist in any way they could with this project. I thank the restauranteurs, nightclub owners, and caterers I met across the country for having the perseverance to follow their dreams and do all they can to bring quality dining and entertainment to the public daily. Many thanks to my two biggest cheerleaders and best friends, Johnetta Boseman–Hardy and Dr. Judith Cothran. Thanks also to the entire Labat family, especially my sister Lori Labat–Scott and brother Yancey C. Labat.

Last but not least, special thanks to three important people without whose help this book would have never have come to fruition. I am grateful to my exceptional editor, D. Kamili Anderson, for hanging in there with me, and for adding clarity and polish to what was a very raw manuscript. To my parents—my mother, Dorothy M. Labat, who is more supportive than any mom should be, and my dad, Victor J. Labat, who has always encouraged me and my siblings to go out into the world, take risks, and truly enjoy life—thanks, I love you both.

Introduction

Finally, a guide that identifies and reviews African American, African, and Caribbean restaurants, nightclubs, and caterers across the United States! *Satisfy Your Soul* is the first comprehensive sourcebook of its kind, representing over 300 establishments primarily owned or patronized by Black people in more than 20 cities nationwide—and for good reason!

Satisfy Your Soul introduces you to places that are unfortunately unfamiliar to most Americans. Some of these establishments have been in operation for as long as 50 years, others are only a few months old. Many can be found on crowded inner-city avenues, others are situated in posh suburban neighborhoods. Some are located right in your back yard! What each has in common are dedicated, creative people committed to bringing you the absolute best in food, service, and entertainment. The goal of this guide is to recognize those establishments, many that would seldom receive national publicity otherwise. It's time to let the world know of their various accomplishments and offerings!

None of the establishments listed in *Satisfy Your Soul* paid to be included in this guide. They did have to meet certain criteria: the food has to be tasty and fresh, the dining areas presentable, and the wait-staff courteous and helpful. Information on each setting is broken down by cities, and descriptions of each establishment are arranged in alphabetical order by the following categories: fine dining, casual dining, cafeteria/buffet-style dining, take-out dining, nightclubs, and caterers.

New restaurants can emerge only when we begin to support the existing ones. My plans are to add three to five additional cities every year and expand and revise these listings as new establishments open and others fade. If you do not see your favorite dining or night spot listed in the guide, it could be that I was not made aware of its existence before going to press. **But you can help: Send your comments about your favorite African American, African, or Caribbean food establishment to me at *Satisfy Your Soul*, P.O. Box 9622, McLean, VA 22102-0622**. Include with your evaluation the name, address, and phone number of the establishment. Make sure you include your own name, address and daytime phone number, too. All entries will be considered for upcoming editions.

Carla Labat

Foreword

African Americans spent $30 billion in restaurants in 1996. Obviously, we know how to eat! We also know what good food is all about! Like other folks, we are constantly searching for establishments that cater to the type of cuisine and entertainment that we are accustomed to and enjoy. Dining out has become a convenient way to entertain, meet and greet, and see and be seen as well as take a break from the kitchen. Yet, in an arena that celebrates activities that are so strongly influenced by our culture, it is amazing that Blacks are so underrepresented in the world of culinary arts and entertainment.

Whether it's Creole, Cajun, Barbecue, Jamaican, Trinidadian, Ethiopian, Southern, Home-Style, Low-Country, or just plain Soul Food—the African American, African, and Caribbean Diaspora is a rich, spicy, colorful explosion of feel-good, taste-good, it's-all-good dishes. Adding to the excitement is the fact that each dish is so individual that across the country no one establishment prepares any one item the same way! Barbecue in Memphis is not the same as barbecue in Kansas City or St. Louis. Jerk Chicken has so many flavors and textures, you can never be disappointed, no matter how many times you eat it. This mouth-watering emphasis on variety all comes from our desire to please our taste buds and tempt our senses with all the exotic flavors and aromas they can stand! Our traditional foods also give us comfort, reminding us of mornings in the kitchen with our mothers and grandmothers, when we would offer our help in any way we could just to get close to whatever was so wonderful coming out of the oven!

The trends evident in today's African American, African, and Caribbean restaurants reflect these memorable meals of yesteryear while taking on both the challenges of the approaching millennium and the consumer orientation of modern business. The success of Nouvelle Soul Food as a response to these trends is confirmed by the recent openings of several major restaurants featuring this exciting new–old cuisine across the country. These establishments serve the foods many of us grew up with, but their culinary offerings are far more artistically presented and served and prepared with today's diners' health concerns in mind. Their dining environments much more upscale, and their wait-service certainly more commanding. At an average price of $16 a plate, is it worth it? Oh yeah!

Caribbean Fusion Cuisine is another hot food trend that has been quickly embraced by the American dining clientele. But is it just more Jerk Chicken and Oxtails? Not hardly! You won't be able to turn your nose up to these traditional island delicacies once you've tried dishes that reflect the marriage of European refinement and the Caribbean's carnival of spices. Truly a match made in gastronomic heaven!

Then, for those with little time on their hands or money in their hands, cafeteria/buffet-style dining is making a comeback in Black-owned food establishments across the country. This format has emerged as a way for many Black entrepreneurs to compete successfully in the volatile but flourishing food service industry. It's also an ideal way to enjoy great, hearty African American, African, and Caribbean meals without the wait.

There's no denying that more and more Black-owned food businesses are opening everywhere you turn, in cities across the U.S. Many of these ventures get their start without the help of traditional capital resources or business support. Many times, they begin simply as a dream in the minds and hearts of aspiring entrepreneurs or chefs with help from friends, family, and other individuals who understand both the pitfalls and the potentials of their dreams and the volatility of the industry. *Satisfy Your Soul* was written to give credit to and inform consumers of these establishments, and to provide insights on the inspirational people who make them happen.

It's now *our* turn to give back to these establishments by acknowledging their existence and supporting them with our patronage and support. The restaurants, caterers, and nightclubs listed in this guide proudly embrace the rich diversity of the food and entertainment that is their cuisine and culture. They eagerly wish to share it with us all, in generous portions and repeat performances. This book gives these establishments, their owners, chefs, and staff a chance to say, "You're welcome." It gives you, the reader, the information you need to seek them out and say, "Thank you," for great service, great ambiance, and most of all, great food. *Satisfy your soul!*

Explanation of Classifications and Symbols

Cities and restaurants are listed in alphabetical order. Each restaurant is classified as either a fine dining, casual dining, cafeteria/buffet-style dining or take-out dining establishment. My definition of each is as follows:

Fine Dining: Sophisticated menu featuring the highest quality cuisine, handsome decor, as well as courteous and knowledgeable wait-service.

Casual Dining: Comfortable surroundings with an uncomplicated, reasonably priced menu. Casual dining is the broadest classification and may range from an upscale and trendy eatery to a family-style restaurant or a simple fast-food establishment.

Cafeteria/Buffet-Style Dining: Self-serve or cafeteria-line service in an informal dining environment.

Take-Out Dining: Minimal to no seating available; short-order, inexpensive menu.

Following each review are symbols that indicate the amenities applicable to each establishment described.

The dollar cost indicated reflects an average cost per person for a dinner with one drink and tip. A dinner is an entree; this does not include à la carte items such as salads or appetizers. A drink equals a soft drink or a glass of wine where alcohol is served. Tips are calculated on 15% of the average meal price where wait-service is available.

Price ranges are in bold type. For example, a price reference of **$10** suggests an average cost of up to $10 per person; **$20+** suggests an average cost of over $20 per person.

Key to Symbols

Reservations Suggested ------ ☎   ✓C ------------ Catering Available

Full Bar ---------------------------- 🍷🍾   🔊 ----------------Outdoor Seating

Live Entertainment ---------- ♫   ❏ ------- Credit Cards Accepted

Valet Parking -------------------- V   ☕ ------------------ Sunday Brunch

Banquet Facilities Available

for Private Parties------------- 🎁   ☆ ------- Highly Recommended

Please note restaurant days and hours of operation are not included as these times are subject to change. Menu selections described in this guide, as well as any specific prices indicated, are also subject to change at the establishment's discretion. Before visiting any of the listed restaurants or nightclubs, I strongly suggest you call first to confirm times, location, cover charges, menu, nightly special events, and any other changes that may occur.

ATLANTA

Fine Dining

**The Abbey   163 Ponce de Leon, Atlanta, Georgia
404.876.8831**
**☆The Mansion 179 Ponce de Leon, Atlanta, Georgia
404.876.0727**
Two of Atlanta's most elegant restaurants are located just
across the street from each other, yet they maintain totally different
personalities. George Gore, director of operations and managing
partner of both The Mansion and The Abbey, started his association
with the two restaurants in 1971. Under his management, both have
received so many culinary awards and acknowledgments that wall
space for displaying them is at a premium.
The Abbey is situated in a old Methodist Episcopal Church,
which provides a formal, almost-medieval setting for its renowned
Continental cuisine. The Mansion is located in a former Victorian
home, complete with a wedding gazebo, open-air courtyard, a lily
pond filled with Japanese *koi*, and all the charms one would expect
such an elegant setting to possess. Indeed, The Mansion is perfect
for private functions large or small; up to 400 people can be
accommodated in its quadrangle area. During the 1996 Olympics,
this restaurant hosted the German Olympic team, whose several
hundred members heartily enjoyed many of the southern specialties
it is known for.
The first course at the Mansion offers a choice of **Stuffed
Quail with Okra and Red Chile Whiskey Sauce; Southern
Fried Grits with Shrimp, Ham, and Red-Eye Gravy;** and
Savannah Crab Cakes. Main courses consist of **Potato-Crusted
Snapper, Duet of Duck Confit with Ratatouille, Haricot Vert
with Cherry Sauce,** and **Herb-Roasted Rack of Lamb**.
$25+ ☎ ☐ 🍴 🎁 ♨ ☕ V

**☆Hairston's   1273 South Hairston Road, Stone
Mountain, Georgia   770.322.9988**
When two seasoned nightclub owners decided to open a
supper club in the upscale Stone Mountain suburb of Atlanta the
outcome was bound to be a success. Brothers Bob and Frank

Williams opened Hairston's in April 1994. The end result: a sophisticated restaurant/bar/nightclub that attracts a professional, over-30 crowd comprised of local politicians, corporate executives, celebrities, athletes, and other well-heeled area residents.

Complimentary valet parking is at your service upon arrival. The big, soft, pink leather bar stools at Hairston's central marble-top bar offer the ultimate in comfort. The main dining room is spacious yet intimate, seating up to 300 people, and its layout is conducive to either a quiet dinner for two or a larger group. All parties can enjoy **Live Jazz** from the restaurant's center stage. The lovely New Orleans Room is perfect for private parties seating up to 50 people. Summer dining *al fresco* on the rooftop deck is a refreshing option.

Hairston's specializes in "delicious New Orleans-style cuisine." Start with appetizers ranging from **Oysters, Crab, Andouille Sausage, and Shrimp Gumbo, Creole Catfish Bites**, and **Fried Crawfish Tails**, to **Bayou Oyster Salad with Warm Creole Mustard Dressing**. Yum! But wait, that's only the beginning! Main course selections include **Cajun Shrimp Platter, Chicken Etouffee**, and a **Chicken Tenders Platter**, all of which come with **Dirty Rice** or **Cajun Fries** to round out your meal.

$20+ ☎ ☐ ✓ 🍷 🎵 🚗 ♿ v

"**Beautiful Restaurant serves the best home-cooked breakfast I've ever had—you can taste the love that goes into preparing each meal.**" *Michael Perch, President Corporate Presentation Services*

Casual Dining

☆Chelsea Place   405 Lee Street, West End, Atlanta, Georgia 404.752.6700

"Welcome to our melting pot of vibrant and exotic flavors cooked with love and inspired by the culture, warmth and excitement of the Caribbean." This greeting welcomes every diner to Mike Thelwell's Chelsea Place, a colorful restaurant located near the historically Black Spelman College campus. After 17 years of working in corporate America, Thelwell journeyed to Europe to learn the art of Italian and French cooking. Taking what he had learned of European cuisine, he merged his favorite American and Caribbean recipes to create what he calls "fusion" cooking: a blend of festive, saucy New–Old World dishes with enough zing to make them sing!

Start your meal with **"Fiya"** (spicy, fiery wings of chicken with cool cucumber–yogurt sauce) or a **Jamaican Jerk Caesar Salad**. Chelsea's favorites include the **"Kiss Mi Bac Foot" 8-ounce burger, Bacardi Under the Sea Jumbo Scallops with Shrimp-in-a-Shrimp Satay Sauce, Jerk Snapper**, and the **Rose Hall Strip Steak** (a 10-ounce New York strip sirloin marinated in Jamaican rum). The #1 lunch item is the **Bob Marley Burger**, a hefty grilled eggplant, zucchini, tomato, onion, and Fontina cheese sandwich, served with the best **Sweet Potato Fries** to be had in Atlanta. After a lunch like that, you *know* the rest of the day is going to be good!

$10–$15 ☐ ✓₵ 🍴

Paschal's   830 Martin Luther King Jr. Drive, S.W., West End, Atlanta, Georgia   404.577.3150

Paschal's is arguably the most famous African American-owned restaurant in Atlanta. Legend has it that brothers Robert and James Paschal left their home of Jackson, Georgia, in 1946 with all of three dollars between them and headed to Atlanta to make their fortune. They opened Paschal's restaurant in 1947 with Robert cooking the meals and James running the business. Little did they realize that their humble restaurant would one day serve fried chicken to every president of the United States from Kennedy to Clinton. Martin Luther King, Jr. used Paschal's as a frequent meeting place and is said to have organized the march on Selma from one of its booths. Today, the restaurant is owned by Clark–Atlanta University, which is committed to continuing the tradition of good food and service established over 50 years ago. The legacy of the Paschal brothers is carried on by Ms. Oran Sherman, a hostess at the restaurant for over 30 years. At 80 years young, Ms. Sherman shows no sign of slowing down and has become just as famous as the restaurant she has so faithfully served.

Paschal's menu features traditional southern-style family meals, which include all the favorites. Like its **Fried Chicken**, the restaurant's **Peach Cobbler** is nationally known; it can also be shipped anywhere in the U.S.. Breakfast at Paschal's is also a popular favorite with local folks.

$10 ☐ ✓₵ 🍴

☆Showcase Eatery 5549 Old National Highway, College Park, Georgia 404.669.0504

Samuel Simmons has combined all of the energies that have shaped his life over the years—running, music, culinary appreciation—to create the Showcase Eatery.   As he originally envisioned it, the Showcase Eatery would be an upscale restaurant that not only paid tribute to African American heritage, but one where people from all walks of life would feel welcome. That dream-come-true is a delightful, eclectic restaurant that rivals any of the downtown restaurants in decor, quality, and creativity of cuisine.

As you walk pass the showcases that display Black rag dolls, vintage photos, and assorted memorabilia, you cannot help but notice the attention Simmons has devoted to creating just the right ambiance. Musical instruments hang from the ceiling. Cherrywood dining tables call up memories of grandma's parlor and provide a feeling of at-home comfort.   Simmons has made sure that his re⁻ᵗᵃurant is not only a feast for the eyes but for the palate as well. The international menu is extensive and full of original, freshly prepared, health-conscious dishes. (Showcase Eatery does not serve fried foods.) Every dish is artistically presented and seasoned to your taste.   Start off with **Pinkie's Palate Pleasures** (sautéed mushroom, chicken, or shrimp appetizers).   The Chef's Fantasy dishes include **Champagne Chicken, New Orleans-Style Colossal Shrimp, Sassy Salmon, Crab Leg Feast, Whole Maine Lobster**, and **Greek-Style Mahi Mahi**.

$20+ ☎ ▢ ⛾

☆Soul Vegetarian Restaurant
> **879 Ralph D. Abernathy, Southwest, Atlanta, Georgia 404.752.5194**
> **652 North Highland Avenue, Midtown, Atlanta, Georgia 404.875.0145**

Best of Atlanta **voted Soul Vegetarian "Best Vegetarian Restaurant" five years in a row from 1989 to 1994.** For any restaurant to be in existence for over 20 years, it must be doing something right! Soul Vegetarian specializes in **Vegan-Style Dishes** "guaranteed to please your palate, satisfy your appetite, and add to your life and longevity." The menu features "Soups from Jerusalem," including a **tasty Split Pea Soup** spiced with fresh garlic. *Megedeem* (sandwiches) range from the **Lentil Burger** to the crunchy **Battered Tofu Filet with Tartar Sauce**. *Saleem* (lunch baskets) are served with a choice of **Fried Battered**

Mushrooms, Tofu, or Cauliflower or Soul Vegetarian's **famous Onion Rings** and **Salad. Dinner Specials are Posted Nightly** and are served with hot cornbread, a fresh garden salad, and "the finest hospitality."
$10 ☐ ✓ ⓒ

☆**Sylvia's of Atlanta   241 Central Avenue, Downtown, Atlanta, Georgia   404.529.9692**
Opened January 1997. See New York write-up for menu details.
$10–$15 🖥 ☐ ✓ ⓒ ♟ 🎼 📷 ☕

"The opening of Sylvia's Restaurant here in Atlanta reminds me of the times back home in New York when my family and I would go downtown from Mt. Vernon to Sylvia's in Harlem for that good, down-home cooking. Now, I can re-live those fond memories and once again enjoy that delicious, Southern-style food." *Anthony Fulton, Advertising/ Marketing Consultant, ABF Beck Communications*

Youngblood's R&B Café   Rio Mall 595 Piedmont Avenue, Atlanta, Georgia 404.249.6666
As a kid washing dishes at the old Atlanta Playboy Club, Kenneth Sharpe learned the art of fine cooking from the club's old retired Navy chef. In college, he switched from the kitchen to the sound studio, working in a local radio station and gaining popularity as a deejay. When the opportunity to open a restaurant came, Sharpe envisioned a setting in which his love for cooking could be combined with his passion for music. The concept of playing the best of Motown and old R&B favorites while serving up the best of an all-American menu was exactly what Sharpe knew his customers would enjoy.
At Youngblood's, the sweet sounds of the Temptations floating through the air starts one immediately reminiscing and finger-popping. The menu is equally entertaining: start with **Etta James's Cheese Trio Taco** ("At Last!"), **Bobby Womack Wings** ("Don't Talk, Just Eat"), or the **Sam Cooke Spinach Nachos** ("You Send Me"). Main courses include the **Aretha Franklin "Do Right" Catfish, Big O** (Otis Redding) **Baby Back Ribs**, and the **Gene**

Chandler T-Bone Steak. All meats and fish are marinated for 24 hours for ultimate flavor. And don't even *think* of leaving without trying the **Apple Walnut Pie with Cinnamon Ice Cream** or the **Homemade Banana Pudding**. Like the song says, "Ain't nothing like the real thing"!

$10–$15 ☐ 🎁🍴

Cafeteria/Buffet-Style Dining

☆**Beautiful Restaurant**
      2260 Cascade Road, S.W., Atlanta, Georgia
         404.223.0080
      397 Auburn Avenue, Downtown, Atlanta,
      Georgia 404.223.0080

In 1979, when the elders of The Perfect Church were seeking a suitable name for the restaurant they had created to feed their growing congregation, they decided upon one that called up images of the biblical temple referred to in Acts 3:2. Although the restaurant was originally opened for members of the church only, others in and outside of the local community heard of the delicious food and were welcomed. Under the professional guidance of Lenore Reese, Beautiful Restaurant has served Atlantans of every race, creed, and color, from the humble to the high up. Scores of local and national business executives, celebrities, and politicians, including Vice President Al Gore, have made breakfast at this Atlanta institution a must before attending important events in the city.

The casual interior of Beautiful Restaurant is clean and provides a friendly, Christian-oriented dining atmosphere. "Soulfully southern" is how Sister Reese describes the food. "Prepared with lots of love and healthy ingredients, we use only the best," she proclaims proudly, "We take pleasure in serving our customers." The dinner menu features such favorites as **Baked Chicken, Stuffed Fish, Smothered Meats**, and **Beef Ribs**. There are also several delectable side dishes to choose from and excellent **Apple Cobbler, Homemade Cakes**, and **Banana Pudding** to satisfy your sweet tooth.

$10 ☐ ✔🍴

☆Chanterelle's   646 Evans Street, West End, Atlanta, Georgia   404.758.0909

As a kid growing up, becoming a chef was the last thing Al Bridges ever imagined he would do. Yet, as an adult, he received formal training in international cuisine from an accomplished German chef. After years of working as an executive chef in other people's establishments and making them successful, Bridges decided it was time to branch out on his own. Today, his restaurant, Chanterelle's, is one of Atlanta's more popular dining spots.

Chanterelle's interior is not fancy as its name suggests. The restaurant is modest but clean and seats approximately 100 people. The menu reflects a unique marriage of Old and New World cuisines, or as Bridges claims, "country French with a southern flair." That means this is *not* the place for fried catfish! Everything is sautéed, broiled, or steamed, and no pork is added to the vegetables. The menu changes daily, and according to locals, the food is consistently good. Specialties of the house include **Baked Rosemary Chicken**, **Curried Turkey**, a wide variety of **Sautéed Vegetables**, and **Homemade Cheesecake** and **Carrot Cake** for dessert.

$10 ◻

Domiabra Vegetarian Palace   2329 Cascade Road, S.W. Atlanta, Georgia   404.753.2008

Trinidad-born Ras Lumumba, proprietor of Domiabra Vegetarian Palace, moved to Atlanta from New York City in 1991. He brought his concept of "quality vegetarian food" first to the trendy Little Five Points area, where the reception was lukewarm at best. Ras then moved to the Cascade area next to a health food store. The community welcomed him with open arms and Ras found a home.

Domiabra specializes in **Vegan-Style Food**—that is, according to Lumumba, "no fins, fur, or feathers." He mixes recipes from his homeland with spices and dishes from all over the world. **Lasagna**, **Peas and Rice**, **Curried Dishes**, **Barbecue Tofu**, **Mixed Vegetables**, **Yams**, and **Collard Greens** are just a few of the selections available daily. The specialty of the house is **Roti-Dhall Puri**, a burrito-like, East Indian-style sandwich stuffed with curried potatoes and channa (chick peas). **Live Music** is featured on weekends, and **Lectures on Healing, Wellness, and Other Health Topics** are held weekly.

$10 ◻ ✓ℂ

☆Patti Hut Café   595 Piedmont Avenue, Downtown, Rio Mall, Atlanta, Georgia   404.892.5133

John and Carol Burrows started out selling their delicious homemade Jamaican meat patties out of the back of a truck. The demand became so great that they opened a small carry-out in the Rio Mall. Business grew steadily, and a full menu of Jamaican cuisine was soon added. With the Patti Hut's increasing popularity (*Atlanta* and *Creative Loafing* magazines rated it the #1 Jamaican restaurant in the city), the Burrows recently renovated it to make room for more tables, a full bar, and a huge, colorful mural depicting the free and easy life of the islands.

Patti Hut chef Stedman Broderick is locally recognized for fixing the best **Oxtails** in the city as well as the best **Jerk Chicken**. Both are tender and moist and of excellent quality. But it's the **Jamaican Meat Patties** that put the Patti Hut Café on the map and that continue to make its reputation stick. The crust is flaky, the filling thick and spicy. In addition to great food, the Café sponsors **Poetry Readings** every Thursday evening and **Live Reggae** on Friday and Saturday nights.

$10 □ ✓ ℂ ⴵ ♫

☆Satterwhite's Restaurants
   851 Oak Street, S.W., Atlanta, Georgia
      404.756.0963
   3131 Campbellton Road, Atlanta, Georgia
      404.344.6401
   590 Cascade Avenue, Atlanta, Georgia
      404.758.9825

Bernie Satterwhite's career in food service began at the tender age of 14 when he got a job washing dishes and flipping burgers at a roadside diner. He later formalized his culinary training during his military service, finishing third in his class. After 20 years with the Marriott Corporation in various executive chef/management positions, Satterwhite took his expertise and opened his first restaurant in 1990. Several more restaurants soon followed, each offering what the proprietor calls "American food with a southern touch" that is sure to "tickle the taste buds, fit the pocket, and be heart smart."

The #1 item on the menu is Satterwhite's legendary **Baked Chicken and Dressing**. According to Bernie, approximately 10,000 orders of this delicious entree are sold each week, and that many patrons *cannot* be wrong! Other favorites

include the **Stir-Fried Shrimp, Stuffed Trout, Meat Loaf, Pot Roast**, and **Macaroni and Cheese**. À la carte entrees includes **Rack of Lamb**, **Chateaubriand**, a 16-ounce **Prime Rib of Beef**, and **Lobster**.
$10 Buffet menu/ $10–$25 à la carte menu/ ❑ ✓ ℂ

Take-Out Dining

Carifesta Caribbean Restaurant   2440-R Wesley Chapel Road, Decatur, Georgia   770.987.0688
When Yvonne Belle moved to the Decatur area from New York several years ago, there were no Caribbean restaurants at all in the vicinity. Having previously owned a bakery in New York, it was inevitable that the small take-out restaurant she opened in Decatur would offer a wide variety of pastries and breads baked on the premises. Belle named her restaurant after the annual festival held in many of the Caribbean islands and Guyana to celebrate their cultural diversity and showcase their unique art and cuisine.

The Carifesta Restaurant specializes in traditional Caribbean cuisine, including such favorites as **Stewed Oxtail, Curried Goat, Jerk Chicken, Roast Pork with Mango Sauce,** and **Steamed Snapper**. **Chicken, Goat, or Shrimp Roti (Dhall Puri)** are also popular items. Desserts range from **Butter Flap (Coco Bread), Plait Braid, Cheese Rolls, Pineapple Tarts,** and **Passion Fruit Cheesecake** to **Bread Pudding**. Traditional island thirst quenchers like **Sorrel, Ginger Beer, Ting,** and **Mauby** are also available.
$10 ❑ ✓ ℂ

"**Jazzmin's is the trendy, upscale gathering spot in downtown Atlanta where you can have a nice meal, listen to smooth jazz, and then go downstairs and dance the night away.**" *Pamela G. Howell, Atlanta Entertainment Journalist*

Yasin's
>   736 Ponce de Leon Avenue, Midtown, Atlanta,
>   Georgia   404.873.9971
>   5340 Old National Highway, College Park,
>   Georgia   404.765.9823
>   3045 Buford Highway, Atlanta, Georgia
>   404.634.3440
>   387 Cleveland Avenue, College Park, Georgia
>   404.559.0336
>   3541 Martin Luther King Jr. Drive, West End,
>   Atlanta, Georgia   404.696.3277
>   2969 Campbellton Road, Atlanta, Georgia
>   404.349.0177
>   4856 Memorial Drive, Atlanta, Georgia
>   404.294.6022

Enough with hamburgers already! Arguably one of the largest Black-owned independent fast-food chains in the South, Yasin's offers **Fried Fish and Chicken** prepared *your* way! No little squares of what usually passes for fish filets at those other places, Yasin's serves real **Catfish**, **Whiting**, or **Trout Sandwiches**, **Fish Tacos**, **Jumbo Shrimp**, **Clams**, and lots of **Chicken Wings**. Home-style **Lemon Meringue, Pineapple Cream Cheese, and Pecan Pies,** along with their famous **Bean Pies** make Yasin's a unique place to eat quick!
$10 Up to $15 for Family-Pack Boxes

Nightclubs

☆Café Echelon   5831 Memorial Drive, Stone Mountain, Georgia   404.292.5539

Thomas and Cheri Dixon opened Café Echelon in 1994, then later partnered up with Cleveland Davis and Raymond "R.J." Jones. Named "**Best Urban Contemporary Dance Club in Atlanta**" by *Atlanta* magazine in 1996, their nightclub lives up to its reputation every night of the week. Café Echelon deejays pumps out the very best in contemporary R&B, house, hip-hop, and old-school music to a young crowd that *knows* how to party. In addition, the club features nationally known acts like Howard Hewitt, Silk, SOS Band, The Whispers, and CeCe Peniston, just to name a few. And the crowded bar is a great place to meet and mingle, or to take a break and enjoy

White Fish Nuggets or the **World's Largest Burger** from the bar menu. Better keep it light while the night is still young, though, 'cause the lighted dance floor at Café Echelon pumps with the party people 'til the wee hours of the morning!
Cover charge/ 25+ crowd / ☐ ♬ 🎵

☆Café Jazzmin's 571 Peachtree Street, N.E., Atlanta, Georgia 404.817.2286

"Finally, the formula for all your entertainment needs." This is indeed an appropriate slogan for *the* new hot spot in downtown Atlanta. Numerous local politicians and entertainers have discovered this upscale nightclub, which features **Live Jazz and Comedy, Ladies' Nights, After-Work Social Hours** (from 5–8pm weekdays), and a **Top-Notch Restaurant**. Downstairs is where the party is going on: Jazzmin's boasts a large private dance room, separate from the mellow scene upstairs, so as not to disturb the wining and dining guests above.

Café Jazzmin's international menu includes such delights as the **Jazz Sampler** (chicken wings, ribs, and catfish nuggets), **Soft Shell Crabs on a Bed of Caesar Salad, Teriyaki Chicken**, and **Seafood Pasta**. There's also a **Kid's Menu** and a **Sunday Brunch**.
Cover charge/ 25+ crowd / ☐ ♬ 🎵 🎁 V

The Crow's Nest 5495 Old National Highway, College Park, Georgia 404.767.012

The Crow's Nest is southside Atlanta's most elegant nightspot, hosting a range of events nightly from black-tie affairs to get-down-and-dirty, throw-down parties. The club is large enough to accommodate huge crowds and has showcased big-name acts such as Regina Belle, Pieces of a Dream, George Howard, Roy Ayers, and others. It also has a sports bar for catching the game and a large dance floor for the party crowd. For late night bites, the Crow's Nest has got all your cravings covered with menu selections ranging from **Grilled T-Bone Steak** and **Sautéed Grilled Chicken** to **Salmon Caesar Salad**.
Cover charge/ 25+ crowd/ ☐ ♬ 🎵 🎁

BALTIMORE

Fine Dining

☆**La Tesso Tana   58 West Biddle Street, Baltimore, Maryland   410.837.3630**

Hailed by *The Best of Baltimore* as "the Most Romantic Restaurant in the City," La Tesso Tana ("The Badger's Den") is chef/owner Ed Rogers's first restaurant. Like many chefs, Rogers started out in the business as a teenage dishwasher, when his only interest was in making a little spending cash. Well, as the story so often goes, one day the cook quit and Rogers was somewhat reluctantly promoted to that position. He didn't take his new responsibilities seriously until a fellow worker, noticing his lackadaisical attitude, nudged the budding young chef to take more pride in what he was doing and to do it right—or not at all. After that, Rogers began concentrating on his culinary skills, over the years developing a flair for gourmet international cuisine and later receiving citywide recognition as one of Baltimore's premier chefs. In 1995, ready to strike out on his own, he acquired La Tesso Tana.

Located beneath the lovely, Victorian-style Abercrombie Badger Bed & Breakfast and across the street from the Myerhoff Symphony Hall and the Lyric Opera House, La Tesso Tana's sophisticated decor and first-class menu blends nicely with its high-brow neighbors. Despite its fine-dining classification, La Tesso Tana offers a comfortable, unpretentious dining environment in two separate rooms connected by a spacious cherrywood bar. The setting is perfect for after-work or post-concert cocktails.

La Tesso Tana specializes in **Italian Cuisine**, and all of its recipes were developed by Rogers himself. Start your meal with an **Antipasto of Frutti Di Mare** (a sampler of assorted seafood), **Gorgonzola Pane** (bread and cheese), or **Insalata La Tesso Tana** (fresh greens tossed with a raspberry vinaigrette). Entrees like **Shrimp Fra Diavola** (jumbo shrimp sautéed in a spicy marinara sauce), **Vittello Alla Saltimbocca** (veal sautéed with mozzarella cheese and proscuitto ham served over a bed of spinach), **Pollo Alla Ashley** (chicken sautéed with artichoke hearts, sundried tomatoes, toasted pine nuts, and vermouth), and **Linguini Alla Tesso Tana** (jumbo shrimp and sea scallops in a lobster cream sauce) are just a few of the distinctive dishes Rogers prepares for your dining pleasure. A choice from the delicious array of **Italian Desserts** completes a memorable meal.

$20+ ☎ ☐ ✓ (♆ ✉🏠

Casual Dining

Larry Stewart's Place   21 South Calvert Street, Downtown Baltimore, Maryland   410.752.5253

Larry Stewart, former Washington Bullets basketball player now with the Seattle SuperSonics, and his boys Phil Booth and Ron Finney grew tired of making the national franchise eateries rich on Friday nights after the games. So, the three came up with the concept of a restaurant where patrons could watch sporting events, meet new people, eat good food, and enjoy great entertainment any night of the week. Opened for business in August 1996, Larry Stewart's Place is the "Cheers" of B'more—a great place to fall into anytime!

Larry Stewart's features **Four TVs,** an **Extra-Long Bar,** and a **Casual Dining Room Upstairs,** but it's more than just a sports bar. It also offers nightly entertainment ranging from serious **Live Jazz and R&B on Saturdays** and **Karaoke Night on Wednesdays,** to lively **Dance Parties on "Phat Fridays."** Menu selections include traditional American favorites like **Wings, Potato Skins, New York Steak, Crab Cakes,** and tender **Baby Back Ribs.**

$10–$15 ☐ ♆ 🎼

☆The Redwood Grill   12 South Calvert Street, Downtown Baltimore, Maryland   410.244.8550

Three blocks away from the tourist trappings of the Inner Harbor, where waiting for a table on a Saturday night can take up to 45 minutes, is a lively, tasteful setting offering everything you really want and more: The Redwood Grill. Proprietors A. R. Wolmack and Cleveland Jerrett opened their restaurant in May 1996 on the site of what used to be the showroom of Baltimore's first Cadillac dealership. (The dealership's tile emblem still graces the entrance way.) The building's lofty cathedral ceiling, with its classical moldings and ornate plaster reliefs, marries beautifully with the burgundy booths and contemporary paintings that are the heart-and-soul of the Grill's decor scheme. The long marble-and-wood bar is the spot to meet and greet Baltimore's hip young professionals for drink and conversation.

The Redwood Grill is **Open for Lunch and Dinner** and features **Classic American Fare.** Appetizers of **Backfin Crab Dip with Pita Points** and **Baltimore's Best Buffalo Wings** are great for starters. **Stuffed Pork Chops, New York Strip Steak, Grilled Sausage and Roasted Red Pepper Pasta,** and **Blackened Red Snapper** are just a few entrees on its extensive menu. The Redwood Grill offers the best in **Live Jazz Thursdays through Saturdays,** and **Happy Hours Weekdays.** Already, its **Large Banquet Hall** has been the site of several corporate affairs.

$15–$20 ☐ ✓ ♦ ♦ ♫ ♦

> **"Nouvelle Italian Cuisine, classic surroundings, and first-class service makes La Tesso Tana one of Baltimore's premier dining experiences!"**
> *Aaron J. Allen, Law Student*

Take-Out Dining

The Caribbean Kitchen   218 North Liberty Street, Downtown, Baltimore, Maryland   410.837.2274

It has always been Shirley Lewis's dream to own a restaurant, so with her entire life's savings and the help of family members, she opened the Caribbean Kitchen. And although her take-out has been open less than a year, it has received rave reviews and plenty good customers. The oldest of 11 children, Lewis is thrilled with the success of her venture: "God is good to me!" She attributes her strength and "stick-with-it-ness" to God and to her mother, without whose help, she claims, she would have folded up shop a long time ago. Today, however, Lewis brags that her restaurant's **Peas-and-Rice Dishes** are so popular that customers ask to come back into the kitchen with her so they can peek over her shoulder and learn how she prepares the dish so just right! No such luck, folks, you'll just have to come in to the Caribbean Kitchen and try it for yourself!

The Caribbean Kitchen offers an extensive **Breakfasts and Lunch Menu of American Classics** from **Scrapple and Eggs** to **Cheesesteak Subs** and **Chicken Salad Sandwiches,** but it is best known for its **Caribbean Dinners.** **Jerk Chicken, Red Snapper, Brown Stewed Chicken, Curried Goat,** and **Oxtail** are just a few of the island specialties Lewis serves daily.

$10 ✓ ♦

Nightclubs

The New Haven Restaurant & Lounge
1552–1554 Havenwood Road, Baltimore, Maryland
410.366.7416

Located 10 minutes from downtown Baltimore in a sleepy suburban strip mall, the New Haven Restaurant & Lounge wakes up the neighborhood on Wednesday nights with **Live Down-Home-and-Dirty Blues**. Located near Morgan State University, "the Haven" is a dark, funky little club where every seat is part of a cozy booth and whose walls feature original murals depicting scenes from the classic movie *Stormy Weather*. But the club itself is the real star of the show, with music and an ambiance that will remind you of a real southern roadside juke joint. For the past 10 years, the Haven has drawn a racially mixed crowd of young and old, students and neighborhood folk, Baltimoreans and out-of-towners seven nights a week, all in appreciation of the **Good Live Jazz, Blues, and R&B** served up nightly, along with large helpings of soul food on the side. **Chicken Gravy 'n Biscuits, Lake Trout, BBQ Ribs**, and **Jumbo Fried Shrimp** are just a few menu items to choose from. **Cover charge/ $10–$15 Dinner menu/** ☐ ⌖ 🎵

Cigar Bar

The Havana Club   600 Water Street, Downtown, Baltimore, Maryland   410.468.0022

Steve de Castro, a native of Cuba and owner of the Ruth's Chris Steak House franchise in downtown Baltimore, recognized the need for an after-work or dinner destination when too many of his patrons asked for a recommendation and he couldn't offer a suitable suggestion. Until now. De Castro established The Havana Club in 1997—a sophisticated, 6,000-square-foot lounge that seats up to 200 and features piped-in jazz, blues, and Latin music. The club offers **More than 60 Brands of Cigars,** and a full bar featuring premium wines and liqueurs. The impressive **Light-Fare Menu** emphasizes savory appetizers and decadent desserts. **$20+** ☐ ⌖

CHARLOTTE, GREENSBORO, RALEIGH/DURHAM

CHARLOTTE

Casual Dining

Anntony's Caribbean Café   2001 East 7th Street, Charlotte, North Carolina   704.342.0749

Dr. Anntony Martin, nutritionist, found it difficult to get people into his office to educate them on proper diet and low-fat cooking. So, one day he figured that if he opened a restaurant that served the type of cuisine people are familiar with but prepared in a healthier way, his goals to educate and inform would be accomplished. Drawing upon the culinary influences of his West Indies upbringing (he was born in Guyana and raised in Trinidad/Tobago), he opened Anntony's Caribbean Café.

As you walk in the door to Dr. Martin's place, the exotic aromas, coupled with the sea-green walls, island motifs, and steel drum music whisk you off to another land far away. The best-selling dish at Anntony's Caribbean Café is the **Caribbean Chicken**, prepared rotisserie-style with just the right blend of spices to make it unique. Charlotte's *Creative Loafing* magazine voted Dr. Martin's **Greens #1 in the City**. Other popular dishes include traditional island fare as well as healthily prepared southern favorites.

$10 ☐ ✓ ℂ ⚑

Georgia On Tryon   9th & Tryon Street, Charlotte, North Carolina   704.334.1108

Located in the Days Inn, Georgia On Tryon gets its name from its proprietor's home state. When owner James Bazzelle (who hails from Athens, Georgia) first visited Charlotte years ago, he liked what he saw in terms of potential business opportunities in this bustling southern city. So Bazelle moved his family and took a job as a chef at a local hotel. He soon left to start a catering business out of his home, eventually securing a couple of corporate accounts, and all the while looking for a restaurant of his own. Although the

Days Inn setting wasn't his first choice, after numerous obstacles with other sites, Bazelle decided that it was meant to be.

Georgia On Tryon features southern-style cooking with special attention to low-fat preparation and seasoned to bring out the best in flavor. **Sauteed Turnip Greens and Pasta with Cayenne Pepper, Fried Chicken, Fried Croaker, Red Beans and Rice with Smoked Turkey Sausage, Tia Chicken,** and **Chicken Pasta Alfredo** are a few of the restaurant's favorite entrees, served with plenty of refreshing **Sweet Tea** ("We are in the South, you know," claims Bazelle). Breakfast is served daily.

$10 ☐ ✓ ℂ

McDonald's Inn & Cafeteria 2810 Beatties Ford Road, Charlotte, North Carolina 704.399.2378

John McDonald had a vision: it involved gas, food, and lodging. Born in Charlotte, he grew up in Brooklyn, New York, where he opened his first restaurant in 1955. McDonald moved back to Charlotte in 1981 and opened McDonald's Cafeteria. Three years later, he opened McDonald's Inn, with its 96 rooms and **Three Large Banquet Halls**. Soon after, he opened Fun City, a small amusement park, across the street, which features putt-putt golf and other family recreational activities. When Mr. McDonald passed away in 1995, his wife and family experienced a series of management problems keeping his visionary empire together but have since regained control and are back at the helm.

McDonald's Cafeteria is legendary in Charlotte. Home cooking is its specialty, with selections like **Roast Chicken and Dressing, BBQ Ribs, Liver and Onions, Country-Style Steak over Rice, Virginia Ham, Roast Duck,** and **Lamb**. Their **Oven-Baked Yeast Rolls** and **Bread Pudding with Lemon Sauce** are worth the trip alone! After all that good eating, you'll need to get a room—for a nap! Their famous Sunday Brunch is also highly recommended, but be sure to get there early to beat the crowds!

$10 ☐ ✓ ℂ ☕ ☕

staurant   516 North Graham Street,
rth Carolina   704.334.6640

alkboard at Simmons' Restaurant lists Bible verses James 1:12 and James 1:19 as the day's specials. Giant-sized bottles of hot sauce sit on each table, most of them well used. The teal green walls are all but hidden by signed posters and photos of famous and local celebrities who have eaten there. And who hasn't eaten at Simmons'? From Patti Labelle to Doc Severinson, from the hip-hop group Black Street to Marie Osmond—the list goes on and on. Dot and Robert Simmons have established quite a business for themselves in the form of a small, comfortable eatery specializing in good-ol' home-style cooking and lots of it.

If you weren't hungry before you ordered your meal at Simmons', you will be starving by the time you receive it. But it's worth the wait for tender **BBQ Ribs, Baked Chicken and Dressing, Smothered Pork Chops, Meatloaf,** and crispy **Fried Chicken,** served with mounds of **Collard Greens, Potato Salad, Squash Casserole,** or **Candied Yams. Breakfast** served daily. **$10**

Take-Out Dining

Austin's Caribbean Cuisine   345 South Kings Drive, Charlotte, North Carolina   704.331.8778

Craig Martin wanted this restaurant; he wanted it bad. Though he didn't have any formal background in restaurant management, he saw the potential for a good take-out Caribbean place in Charlotte. Armed with an extensive business plan and his home as collateral, Martin approached every loan office in town. Totally frustrated by all the banks' red tape and run around, he decided to borrow money from the only person who truly believed in his dream: his father, Austin Martin.

Taking its name from its financier and with Martin's mother Yvonne as chief cook, Austin's Caribbean Cuisine opened in early 1997. Word of the take-out's deliciously authentic West Indian cooking spread quickly throughout Charlotte. **Jerk Chicken, Ackee and Saltfish, Curried Goat, Curried Shrimp, Pineapple Chicken, Oxtails,** and **Roti** are just a few of the choice meals that are ready to go at Austin's. And don't forget to get a slice

of Yvonne's homemade **Marble Cake** or her **Pineapple Cake**—they're both a cake lover's dream!
$10 ✓ ₵

Tropical Goodies   2020-A Beatties Ford Road, Charlotte, North Carolina   704.399.6001

Dennis Grant's Caribbean take-out, Tropical Goodies, is an establishment that pays daily tribute to the proprietor's favorite cook, his grandmother. As a young man, Grant's love of food and his fondness for the influences it has had in his life led him to pursue a career in restaurant management. While visiting a friend in Charlotte one year, he noticed that the city didn't have any Caribbean restaurants. Recognizing a golden opportunity, Grant relocated to the area and opened Tropical Goodies in 1982.

Fresh wholesome foods are the standard at Tropical Goodies. **Jerk Chicken, Curried Goat, Curried Chicken, Oxtails, Peppered Steak, Cajun Shrimp, Escoveitch Fish, Fried Plantains, Rice and Beans**, and delicious **Whole Wheat Vegetarian Patties** are just a few of the menu choices at this health-conscious take-out.
$10 ✓ ₵

Nightclubs

Excelsior Club   921 Beatties Ford Road, Charlotte, North Carolina   704.334.5709

Established in 1944, the Excelsior Club is arguably one of the oldest Black-owned nightclubs in the United States. For decades, the club's first-floor **Dance Floor** has been crowded with folks "gettin' their groove on" to classic R&B. For those who prefer to watch, **Two Large Bars** on the upper level provide perfect perches for surveying the scene from above. There's also plenty of **Bar Food** and **Live Music (Jazz and R&B)** in the evenings from Tuesday through Sunday.
Cover charge/ Mature crowd/ ☐ ♆ 𝄞 🎷

☆Harvey's Garage   516 North Graham Street, Downtown, Charlotte, North Carolina   704.337.8090
    Balrie Parks, a community executive consultant by day and jazz singer by night, wanted a spot where she and her friends could get together, hold jam sessions, invite their friends, and have a good time. (This is my kind of crowd!) When the opportunity came to take over Harvey's Garage and move it to Charlotte's Four Points area, Parks jumped on it. Harvey's Garage is everything a jazz club should be: intimate without being cramped and featuring **World-Class Jazz**, both straight-ahead and contemporary. There's even a comfortable **Outdoor Seating Area** for cool listening under the stars. Harvey's also offers an **Extensive Dinner Menu** featuring classic American dishes and specials nightly.
No Cover Charge/ Dinner menu $10–$15/ ☐ ⛄ 🎼 🏧

Caterers

Affairs to Remember   631 North Tryon Street, Charlotte, North Carolina   704.333.8899
    Charlotte native Ron Goodwin had the pleasure of starting his career in food service working "with the best cook that ever existed": his mother. While in the 10th grade, he started helping his mother, a popular cook in a private household, with the various catering jobs her employer "loaned" her out on. Over the years, Goodwin built his own reputation as an excellent cook, working in various cities across the country. In the Sixties, he started Metro Foods in Washington, D.C., one of the first Black-owned food services in the country. In 1991, Goodwin returned to Charlotte, where he opened Affairs to Remember.
    "Prepared to Pamper" is Goodwin's company motto. Located in the Renaissance Restaurant, with its sunny, circular dining room that holds up to 150 people, Affairs to Remember is a **Full-Service Catering** service offering **On-Site Banquet and Reception Facilities**. Servicing events ranging from weddings to business meetings, from 50 to 5000 people, Goodwin and his staff can prepare almost any type of cuisine desired. They also service the restaurant's weekday lunch and Sunday brunch crowd. Buffet-style dining favorites at those meals include Goodwin's crispy **Fried Chicken**, delicious **Peach Cobbler**, and refreshing **Peach Punch**.

GREENSBORO

Casual Dining

☆**East Market Seafood Restaurant 1905 East Market Street, Greensboro, North Carolina   910.379.1311**

Located down the street from the North Carolina A&T campus, the East Market Seafood Restaurant is the site of many a spirited discussion between the long-time neighborhood regulars and young college students who flock to its tables. The restaurant is simple in its decor, but the people and conversations you may encounter in it are worth more than any expensive wallpaper or fancy frills. Their talks usually center around current events, sports, and the state of Black America—then and now. Voices may rise, and there are plenty of "in my day" or "we really had it hard" testimonials, but it's all in good fun.

Seafood items featured at East Market can be prepared either fried or broiled, but this is *the* place for the flakiest, non-greasiest fried fish in Greensboro. Earl Washington, proprietor of East Market Seafood Restaurant, is not giving out any secrets but claims that his batter is the key. He also notes that he is careful not to drown his fish in oil but rather to prepare it in a healthy, kosher manner. **Flounder, Perch, Trout, Whiting, Red Snapper, Jumbo Shrimp** and **Scallops** are just a few of the seafood varieties available on the menu. **Perfect Fries** and **Hushpuppies** accompany each meal.

$10 ❒ ✓ C

☆**Madison Kitchen/United House of Prayer for All People   101 South Dudley, Greensboro, North Carolina   910.574.2596**

Located in the basement of Greensboro's United House of Prayer for All People is the Madison Kitchen, the busiest lunchtime spot in the city. Serving cafeteria home-style meals during the week and breakfast on weekends, this establishment's large dining room is modern with pretty purple tables and chairs and a diligent staff that clears off tables with lighting speed. The cafeteria attracts a broad customer base that bridges racial and professional lines. Everyone eats here! Why? It's simple: the food is really good, really fast, and really reasonable! **Fried or Baked Chicken, BBQ Ribs,**

Neck Bones, **Pork Chops**, **Pigs' Feet**, **Meat Loaf**, **Cabbage**, **Green Beans**, **Rice and Gravy**, and an assortment of **Cakes** and **Pies** are a few of the items featured daily.
$10

☆Robinson's Restaurant   438 Battleground Avenue, Greensboro, North Carolina   910.272.6854

May 2, 1997, will mark the 20th year that Roosevelt and Freida Robinson have owned and operated Robinson's Restaurant. The idea to open a restaurant can be credited to Freida, who wanted something to do while her husband was on the road as a labor representative. (As if raising seven children wasn't enough work! God bless her.) When the opportunity came for the family to move, Roosevelt said to his wife, "You pick the state and I'll pick the city." They settled on Greensboro, opened the restaurant, and put the kids to work in it. Twenty years later, they have many proud moments and accomplishments to celebrate.

Breakfast at Robinson's ranges from **Country Ham and Eggs** to **Steak and Biscuits**. Lunch and dinner feature dishes that taste like good ol' home cooking, including **Oyster Stew**, **Squash Casserole**, **T-Bone Steaks**, **Pork Chops**, **Fried Chicken**, and **Jumbo Shrimp**. There are also usually a number of daily specials to choose from. The main reason to eat at Robinson's, however, is to meet Mr. Robinson, with his gregarious personality and love for story telling. If you're lucky, he'll take time out of his busy schedule to sit and chat with you for a while. Perhaps that's why President Bill Clinton and Vice President Al Gore and their families stopped to dine at Robinson's during the last campaign tour. You can rest assured that Mr. Robinson entertained and fed them well.

$10 ☐ ✓ ⅃ **/Beer served**

The Summit Café   1050 Summit Avenue, Greensboro, North Carolina   910.272.8377

Once out of the Marines, Roderick Wright started his career in restaurant management at Sambo's (Sambo's! Now you're telling your age, Mr. Wright!) He worked his way up through the ranks, then went to Taco Bell as a district manager. When the opportunity came to open his own place in 1989, Wright knew everything about running the restaurant but nothing about cooking. What he really needed was a chef! After securing one, he opened the Summit Café serving an extensive down-home-style breakfast and super sandwiches for lunch.

Today, the Summit Café is known for its **All-Day Breakfast**, which includes **Salmon Cakes and Eggs**, **Corned Beef Hash**, **Pork Brains and Grits**, **Pecan Waffles**, and **Ribeye Steak and Potatoes**. Lunch offerings include the **One-Third-Pound Super Chili Burger**, **Grilled Steak Salad**, "**The Boss**" **Bologna Burger**, and the **Tuna Melt**, to name a few. With its short counter, minimal number of tables, and friendly, fun-loving staff, this small hometown restaurant is where folks can meet, hang out all day, enjoying good food and lively conversation.
$10 □

Nightclubs

Q–TTIP'S Night Club 120 North Davie Street, Greensboro, North Carolina 910.379.8689
Quick Chicken Restaurant 120 North Davie Street Greensboro, North Carolina 910.275.1515

Proprietor Walter Johnson's Q–TTIP's Night Club showcases **Comedy**, **Jazz**, **Live Bands**, **Nationally Renowned Acts,** and the **Hottest Deejays** playing the best urban contemporary and dance music Wednesdays through Sundays nights. The club caters to the young, college crowd, holds up to 500 people, and is open until the wee hours of the morning. The take-out restaurant downstairs, Quick Chicken, provides **Late Night Eats** of **Fried Chicken**, **Hot Wings**, **Fries**, and down-home sides like **Macaroni and Cheese**.
Cover charge / 21+ crowd / □ ♬ 🎼 🎁

RALEIGH/DURHAM

Casual Dining

☆**Rock 'N Reggae Jamaican Café 2109–110 Avent Ferry Road, Raleigh, North Carolina 919.832.3577**

Move over Hard Rock Café, the Rock 'N Reggae Jamaican Café is the future, with food and music that caters to global unity. Indeed, Jamaica's national motto, "Out of Many, One People," is featured on the bottom of this restaurant's menus and is quite possibly the inspiration behind this successful business venture. The brainchild of Donovan Carless, the Rock 'N Reggae is a festive eatery that attracts a diverse clientele—from the young, hip crowd to old-school connoisseurs—but mainly anyone who enjoys good ethnic foods. Friday nights feature **Live Deejay Music**, and on Saturday nights, **Live Reggae Bands** take the floor. Carless's own band, Jam–Rock, gigs here twice a month, and internationally known reggae groups like Christafari have also performed.

OK, we all know about Jerk Chicken, but the Rock 'N Reggae's jerk chicken is "all that," on account of its chef hailing from the parish in Jamaica where "jerking" originated. He makes his own seasonings, and **Jerk Chicken**, **Wings**, and **Pork** are this restaurant's most popular dishes. Other delights include **Curried Goat, Curried Shrimp, Oxtail, Escoveitch Fish, Brown Stew Fish, Roti,** and **Callaloo Stew**.

$10–$15 ☐ ✓ 🍷 🍸

Cafeteria/Buffet-Style Dining

☆Dillard's Bar B Q Restaurant & Catering
3921 Fayetteville Street, Durham,
North Carolina 919.544.1587

Samuel D. Dillard, known to most as "Sam" or "S. D.", is a local icon for building the business empire that is Dillard's Bar B Q. Fifty years strong, Dillard's is, if not the oldest, one of the oldest African American-owned restaurants in Durham. Originally, Sam wanted to open a grocery store, but he fell in love with the art of preparing perfect barbecue. His early years in the business were not easy ones, and he had to rely on his outgoing personality and the help of his family and community to pull him through. Over the years, however, Dillard established a successful restaurant and catering businesses as well as made and marketed his own line of barbecue sauces, the "North Carolina's Famous" brand, sold in grocery stores statewide. Though he passed away in January 1997, he left a proud legacy that continues with his daughter Wilma, her mother, and siblings, who are steady growing the family business and carrying on a name they and their community are mighty proud of.

The unpretentious interior of Dillard's Bar B Q reflects the proprietors' deep roots in the Durham community. Colorful banners from area colleges hang upon the walls. Local groups make frequent

use of the cozy community room that seats up to 45 for luncheons or other meetings. Dillard's specializes in **Pork and Beef BBQ**, **Ribs**, **Chitterlings**, and **Fried Chicken**. **Bone Fish Trout**, **Collard Greens**, **Candied Yams**, **Cabbage**, **Fried Okra**, **Apple Cobbler**, and **Banana Pudding** are a few of the other selections available.
$10 ❏ ✓ ₵ 🖼🎁

☆Jamaica Jamaica   4853 Highway 55, Durham, North Carolina   919.544.1532

During lunchtime, the buffet line at Jamaica Jamaica wraps around the front of the restaurant to reveal a diverse group of customers eagerly anticipating their turn at the plate (pun intended!). Indeed, this Durham hot spot attracts the most racially and professionally mixed clientele outside of a major metropolitan city. Its patrons include technicians and chemists from nearby Research Triangle Park, construction workers, professors and students from the area's several educational institutions, Whites, Blacks, locals, visitors—you name 'em, you'll see 'em at Jamaica Jamaica. The restaurant's prime location near a thriving, rapidly expanding business hub has a lot to do with it, but the main reason why Jamaica Jamaica is so well received and successful is that it offers beautifully presented Caribbean cuisine buffet and generous portions. What's more, according to proprietor Fernando Von Rainford, the food at Jamaica Jamaica is served up quick and "prepared with your health in mind."

The interior of Jamaica Jamaica almost explodes with color and sound: sunny yellow walls, vivid multicolored posters, and throbbing reggae music. The lunch buffet features the best of the West Indies: **Jerk Chicken**, **Jerk Pork**, **Curried Goat**, **Stir Fried Shrimp**, **Trout Filet**, and **Oxtail Stew**—and there's plenty of homemade **CoCo Bread** and **Carrot Cake** to top off your meal. In the evenings, the restaurant offers wait service, a more extensive menu, and **Live Jazz** on Thursdays, with **Contemporary African Disco** and **Reggae** on Saturday nights. Not bad for sleepy Durham, eh?
$10 ❏ ✓ ₵ /Beer & Wine served

LeCount's Family Cafeteria & Restaurant   1214 Lenoir Street, Raleigh, North Carolina   919.821.4388

With 23 years of restaurant experience behind them, William and Queen LeCount enjoy knowing that all those years of hard work have paid off. LeCount's is one of Raleigh's more popular restaurants, frequented by everyone from business executives to neighborhood regulars alike. The LeCounts started their business with a hot dog and fries stand inside a record store. They eventually moved to the space next door and expanded their menu. In 1993, the LeCounts moved the restaurant to its current location.

Simply decorated in red and white, LeCount's Cafeteria is spacious enough to accommodate the crowds who rush to the popular **All-Day, All-You-Can-Eat Sunday Buffet. BBQ Ribs, Baked and Fried Chicken, Chitterlings, Pork Chops, Candied Yams, Collard Greens, String Beans, Banana Pudding,** and **Assorted Cakes** are a few of the items found on the buffet line at LeCount's. No time to sit down? LeCount's **Take-Out** offers the same good food found at the buffet, and then some. A **Community/ Banquet Room** is also available for larger groups or special events. $10 ✓ 🅲 📠

Mae's Country Kitchen   610 West South Street, Raleigh, North Carolina   919.821.5884

"Keep your knees in good shape so you can pray!" Mae Perry, proprietor of Mae's Country Kitchen, offers this advice to anyone thinking of going into the restaurant business, and obviously the praying helped because she has endured in the restaurant business for over 30 years. A self-taught cook, Perry started out years ago preparing home-style meals when she realized people were turning away from fast foods. "Home cooking away from home" is her restaurant's slogan, and just like most of us at home, she doesn't decide what will be on the next day's menu until the night before. "Whatever is fresh is what the people want," she claims. **Baked or Fried Chicken, Fried Shrimp, BBQ Pork, Chitterlings, Butter Beans, Neck Bones, Turnip Greens**, and **Candied Yams** are just a few of the old-fashioned dishes served up at Mae's rustic and homey restaurant. And don't leave her Country Kitchen without one of her famous **Apple Jacks** or a slice of the very tasty **Lemon Pie.** Have Mercy!
$10

Mama's Country Cooking & Catering
2008 New Bern Avenue, Raleigh, North Carolina
919.231.3611

Ethel Chapman, "Mama" to you and me, started selling dinners out of her house years ago, then realized she could do more business if she had a restaurant to cook out of. With the help of her son Ivan, she opened Mama's Country Cooking & Catering in 1990. It's a small, folksy place with Chapman still doing the cooking. The menu changes daily, but the cuisine is pure soul food—**Ham Hocks**, **Pigs' Feet, Pork Chops, BBQ Ribs, Salisbury Steak, Short Ribs of Beef**, and the daily must-haves of **Rice and Cabbage**—or else Mama Ethel wouldn't open the doors! What's lunch without a delicious slice of Mama's own **Pig Pickin' Cake** made with pineapple, coconut, and walnuts? Yummy!

$10 ✓ C

The Know Deli 2520 Fayetteville Street, Durham,
North Carolina 919.956.KNOW

Located inside The Know Book Store is The Know Deli, a small but lively enterprise that came about when proprietor/manager Bruce Bridges realized he could put empty space to good use. Bridges wanted to do something that would benefit the community. He decided on a deli that specialized in healthy foods: **No Fried Foods or Pork.** The Know Deli offers a full range of sandwiches including **Smoked Turkey Breast, Veggie, Baked Fish**, and **Mama Bridges' Special Homemade Chopped Chicken BBQ. Bean Soup, Fresh-Squeezed Lemonade**, and the Deli's famous **Bean Pies** round out the menu.

$10

CHICAGO

Casual Dining

Addis Abeba   3521 North Clark Street, Chicago, Illinois   312.929.9383

Addis Abeba, named after the capital of Ethiopia, is a lovely restaurant that celebrates the culture of that African nation with its unique cuisine and exotic decor.   The restaurant's proprietor, Tensaye Gizaw, arrived in Chicago from Ethiopia in 1981 to attend college.   He opened the restaurant in 1987 with a group of friends and became sole owner in 1992.   Since then, Gizaw has turned Addis Abeba into Chicago's premier Ethiopian restaurant.

Moms may hate this place because eating with one's hands is a must at Addis Abeba.   Diners are seated around large, colorful woven baskets, upon which large plates of colorful and highly seasoned dishes are placed within easy reach of everyone's hands. **Vegetarian Meals are the Specialty** at Addis Abeba, so try some **Inqoudai** (fresh mushrooms and yellow split peas seasoned with garlic and ginger) or **Fosolia** (string beans, onions, and carrots cooked in tomato sauce).   Meat dishes include **Yebeg Alitcha** (lamb cooked in spiced butter, onions, and turmeric), **Siga Tibs** (beef tenderloin stir fried with onions and jalapenos), and **Doro Wot** (chicken simmered in red pepper sauce, honey wine, and spiced butter).   The food is meant to be shared and large parties are encouraged, so bring your adventurous friends along to experience the ultimate in culture and dining—the Ethiopian way.

$10–$20   ☐ ⛾

☆Army & Lou's   422 East 75th Street, Chicago, Illinois   773.483.3100

Arguably the most famous African American-owned restaurant in Chicago, Army & Lou's was established in 1945 by William and Luvilla Armstrong.   The restaurant has changed owners several times over the years and weathered many storms, but in the capable hands of current owner Dolores Reynolds and her associates at In Good Taste, Inc., Army & Lou's is ready for the next 50 years. Since its beginnings, local politicians and business-men have used Army & Lou's as a meeting place. Former mayor Harold Washington is said to have conducted much of the city's business in the **Banquet Room** next door. The restaurant's reputation for superb food and service is renowned. During the summer of 1996, the *New York Times* recommended only four restaurants for conventioneers attending the Democratic convention held that year in Chicago, and Army & Lou's was among them!

Reputation aside, the cuisine at Army & Lou's is nothing fancy. According to Reynolds, it's "southern-style cooking—comfort food, good and well-prepared, like what one's mother or aunt would make." Nonetheless, she claims that a visit to Army & Lou's "will give you a look into the true flavor of what Chicago and it's people are all about." Specialties of the house include **Homemade New England Clam Chowder, Army & Lou's Award-Winning Fried Chicken**, **Short Ribs of Beef,** and **Blackberry Cobbler** (the best!).

$10–$20 ☎ ❏ ✓ ℂ 🍽 🎥 ☕

☆Bazzell's French Quarter Bistro   215 West North Avenue, Downtown, Chicago, Illinois   312.787.1131

Named after and dedicated to owner John Moultrie's grandmother Juanita Bazzell, this cozy, contemporary bistro brings a little of the Vieux Carre to the Windy City. Bazzell's is decorated with exceptional art work ranging from grand portraits of jazz greats in the main dining room to softer watercolors hanging in the courtyard. The exposed wine racks over the bar and rear courtyard dining area give the restaurant what Moultrie calls its "European/French Quarter savoir faire."

Indeed, Moultrie's years of expertise in restaurant and nightclub management culminate and are well represented at Bazzell's, which specializes in **Cajun and Creole cooking**. **Acadienne Crawfish, Fried Lobster,** and **BBQ Shrimp** are perfect appetizers to start with. **Fried Red Snapper, Crawfish Etouffee, Smothered Chicken Bazzell's,** and **Shrimp and Blackened Catfish Acadienne** are a few of the specialties featured. Bazzell's also boasts an extensive champagne and wine list. Pipe and cigar smoking are permitted in the courtyard only.

$20 ☎ ❏ ✓ ℂ 🍽 🎥

> **"The Retreat serves rolls like the ones my grandmother made; light, airy, and just a hint of sweetness. Absolutely wonderful!"**
> *Judith A. Cothran, M.D.*

Capt.'s Hard Time Dining   436–440 East 79th Street, Chicago, Illinois   312.487.7210

Josephine Wade has been in the food service business all her life, and she says she just loves the creativity it brings. She also loves working with the people involved. With her husband Rupert Smith, she opened Capt.'s Hard Times Dining in 1989 in the community she is so proud of. In turn, the community is very proud of her and her restaurant. In Wade's view, dining out is "a form of entertainment," and to keep her customers coming back for more, she and her very capable staff have but one motto: "Your Satisfaction is our Goal."

With its lovely interior accented in mauve tones, Capt.'s Hard Times Dining specializes in international cuisine suitable to everyone's palate. Sample entrees include **Gumbo–Louisiana Style**, **Long Island Duckling**, **Roasted Chicken with Dressing**, **Braised Short Ribs**, and **Oriental Stir-Fry**. **Diet Delights** and **Seafood Pasta** specialties are refreshing light-fare additions to the menu. There is also a full bar and an impressive list of after-dinner drinks.

$20+ ☐ ✓ 🇨 ⛾ 🦺

☆C'est Si Bon! 5225 South Harper, Hyde Park, Chicago, Illinois   312.536.2600

Renee Bradford was just looking for a place to continue her successful **Full-Service Catering** business. When she came across her present location, she decided to combine her catering company with a deli and a small restaurant. Under the umbrella of C'est Si Bon, Bradford's customers enjoy the variety of cuisine and services she has to offer.

Muffuletta (grilled chicken breast sandwiches) and **Sweet Potato Cheesecake** are two items well worth the drive to C'est Si Bon's deli. For a sit-down early dinner, try the restaurant's **Cajun - Fried Catfish Nuggets**, **Grilled Salmon Steak**, and other tasty entrees, and sample the **Bread Pudding with Whiskey Sauce** for dessert. Make it a "C'est Si Bon Sunday" with the restaurant's superb **Sunday Brunch**, which features an international menu as well as a **Breakfast Bar** elegantly presented behind gold lamée curtains. The **Sweet Potato Biscuits** are divine! And don't forget, C'est Si Bon's catering staff offers **Full-Service Event Planning** to ensure that your next affair is a memorable one.

$15–$20 ☐ ✓ ℂ ☕

☆Chez Delphonse French–Caribbean Restaurant
2201 North Clybourn, Chicago, Illinois   312.472.9920

The *Chicago Sun–Times* awarded three-and-a-half stars to Chez Delphonse for its superb cuisine, yet Haitian-born Marc Delphonse, chef and proprietor, claims he still has a difficult time attracting new clientele. "Most people are not familiar with Caribbean food," he laments. "They look at the menu, it sounds good, but they are not sure what to expect." All doubts aside, however, there is only one thing to expect when dining at Chez Delphonse: delicious food, low in calories and loaded with flavor!

Chef Delphonse brings the spirit of Haiti to Chicago by decorating his restaurant in a carnival-like motif. Assorted madras tablecloths with lace skirts cover the tables, palm trees made of Christmas lights grace the dining area, and Haitian artwork adorns the festive pink and green walls. **Patio Dining** is available in the summertime, and Chez Delphonse offers a semiprivate dining area for parties. Specialties of the house include **Conch** (cooked in a jalapeno–pimento sauce), **Jerk Chicken** (a little sweet, not spicy like Jamaican-style), **Filet of Salmon, Skirt Steak with Tomato–Cilantro Sauce,** and **Samba Shrimp Sautéed with Vegetables in a Light Coconut Sauce**.

$10–$20 ☐ 🍷 🎨

☆Gladys' Luncheonette   4527 South Indiana Avenue,
Chicago, Illinois   773.548.4566

Recognizing the need for a nice, clean place for folks to eat in Memphis, Gladys Murrell, formerly a waitress at the Greyhound bus station in that city, opened the Loop Café in 1935. She sold dinners for 15 cents and pies for 5 cents. There she met her future husband, Kinnard Holcomb, whom she married in 1945. The two later moved to Chicago, where they opened Gladys' Luncheonette, which soon became a favorite with the pullman porters who stopped there to eat on their trips through Chicago. Once these grateful men spread the word about Gladys', the entire Midwest flocked to its doors! Gladys and Kinnard Holcomb run the place to this day, but their current clientele is comprised of diverse diners ranging from college students and blue-collar workers to business executives, all of whom swear by Gladys' for its good, home-cooked meals and hearty breakfasts, pleasant atmosphere, and bright, busy decor.

While the dinners no longer cost less than two bits, the original recipes are still used today. **Breakfast** is a tradition at Gladys', and the **Biscuits** are legendary. The **Lunch** and **Dinner** menus change daily, but you can count on Gladys' for excellent **Smothered or Fried Chicken** and **Short Ribs of Beef**.
$10

Infinity Restaurant 9156 South Stony Island, Chicago, Illinois 312.375.1800

New to the Chicago scene, Infinity is a contemporary restaurant that will most likely be the next hot "see-and-be-seen" spot in the Windy City. The spacious dining area is attractive and informal, with splashes of color that lend a Caribbean flavor. Infinity also offers a **Banquet Room** that seats 150-plus. On weekends, the tables are pushed back, and the **Dance Floor** comes alive with a **Deejay** spinning today's most popular tunes. Or cool out in the **Sports Bar** area to watch the Bulls play or just check out the scene.

Infinity offers a mixture of familiar **Southern and Caribbean Cuisine**. **Caribbean Chicken**, **Fried Buttermilk Catfish**, **Shrimp Etouffee**, and **Roasted Pork Loin with Garlic Mashed Potatoes and Fried Corn** are just a few of the entrees awaiting its diners. Desserts range from a tantalizing **Spice Cake** to **Cherry Cheesecake** to **Strawberry Shortcake**.
$10–$20 🚬 ✓ 🍷 🍸 🎁

☆Izola's 522 East 79th Street, Chicago, Illinois 773.846.1484

"Izola's—The most popular place in town, where you meet the nicest people." This is the slogan for Izola's Restaurant, and truer words were never spoken. For over 41 years, proprietor Izola White has welcomed Chicago to her namesake eatery. As a waitress in the South Chicago area in her early years, her goal was to own her own restaurant. When a seafood place on East 79th Street became available in 1956, she jumped on the opportunity. Since then, Izola's has served **Home-Cooked Meals, 24 Hours a Day, 6 Days a Week**! And like Ms. Izola says, "If you can't find anything on this menu, you weren't hungry when you came in!"

Pictures of former mayor Harold Washington, state and national legislators, police personnel, family, and friends—loyal customers all—surround the walls of Izola's. The dining area is divided into two sections. On one side is a long lunch counter, reminiscent of days gone by. The other side is devoted to casual seating and has been the site of many a meeting of local city officials and law enforcement groups. The reasons why Izola's has become such a popular place for these meetings can be attributed to the food and to the woman herself. Ms. Izola is as proud of her community as she is of the restaurant for which she is known. As one regular patron summed it up, taking a moment from his daily breakfast, "It's all about the food here at Izola's. Everything she serves comes from the heart."

Breakfast at Izola's is an all day affair, and offerings range from **Pork Chops and Eggs** to the **Denver Omelet**. The lunch and dinner menus seem to go on and on forever, but some of the house favorites include **Stewed Chicken and Dumplings, Grilled Liver and Onions**, and Izola's famous **Apple Cobbler**.
$10 ☐

"Army & Lou's is a South Side tradition. My favorite dishes are the smothered chicken with dressing (so tender, the meat falls off the bone!), and the porkchops. When you go, however, be prepared to wait because the service is polite but slooow! P.S., it's worth it!" *Adrienne Ray, M.D.*

Michael Jordan's Restaurant 500 North La Salle Street, Downtown, Chicago, Illinois 312.644.386

Michael Jordan's Restaurant is *the* theme restaurant in Chicago. Attracting Bulls fans, tourists, suburbanites, locals, and celebrities alike, most come to Michael Jordan's in hopes of getting a glimpse of the Great One himself. The restaurant consumes three levels, each one heavily sprinkled with MJ memorabilia. The Fast Break Bar & Grill on the first level is the quintessential **Sports Bar**, with a 20-by-6-foot video wall and its own menu of burgers, generous sandwiches, and salads. Located on the second tier is the main dining room, tastefully decorated and accented with murals inspired by the 1992 summer Olympics. The third level offers **Banquet Facilities** accessed by private elevators and is available for parties of from 20 to 250.

The menu at Michael Jordan's is as All-American as its namesake. **Spicy Shrimp Cakes, Fried Housemade Mozzarella,** and **Crispy Onion Rings** are great starters. **Michael's Crispy Fried Shrimp, Fusilli with Garden Vegetables, Home-Style Pot Roast, Baby Back Ribs**, and a **10-ounce Cheeseburger with Handcut Fries** are just a sampling of what's in store. And speaking of stores, don't forget to stop by the gift shop for those all-important, must-have, official MJ logo golf balls!

$20 ☎ ☐ ✓ (⚱ 📷 ✓

☆The Retreat Restaurant   605 East 111th Street, Chicago, Illinois   773.568.6000

The **Best Brunch in Chicago** is found in the most handsome restaurant in town: The Retreat. This establishment is located in a lovely restored mansion whose origins date back to 1881. Formerly owned by the first general superintendent of the Pullman Palace Car Manufacturing Company, it was at one time the largest and finest single-family residence in the then-Chicago suburb of Pullman. Today, John S. Meyer, his wife Hope, his mother Juanita Gibson, and his father Henry Meyer own the restaurant housed within this stately mansion and maintain its elegance by providing exceptional cuisine, good service, and fine dining to South Side Chicago. One visit to The Retreat Restaurant and it's obvious that John Meyer's formal training and experience as a chef at the University Club of Chicago prepared him well to meet the ultimate challenge: to satisfy the discriminating taste of Chicago's local diners and its thriving tourist trade—and keep them coming back for more.

Nationally known for its **Sunday Brunch** (more like Sunday dinner!), the menu at The Retreat offers some choice "must-haves." The **Fresh-Baked Rolls** served to each table may tempt you to eat the whole basket, but save room for the following delectables among the entrees: succulent **Pork Loin**, **Mustard-Fried Catfish**, **Spicy Chicken Wings**, and **Sweet Barbecue Ribs**. **Fresh Vegetables** and **Old-Fashioned Potato Salad** (made the way no one makes it anymore!) are only two of the many exceptional side dishes served. Desserts include an assortment of cakes, pies, and cobblers—all to die for!

$20+ ☎ ▢ ✓ 🍴 🥂 🎦 ☕

☆Salaam Restaurant & Bakery   700 West 79ᵗʰ Street, Chicago, Illinois   773.874.8300

Owned and operated by the Nation of Islam, the service and organization at this **Multifaceted Food Establishment and Banquet Facility** are most impressive. The first floor is shared by four different operations: The Salaam Bakery, the Blue Seas Take-Out Counter, Elijah's Garden Restaurant, and The Atrium Restaurant. Named after Nation of Islam founder The Honorable Elijah Muhammad, Elijah's Garden is decorated with emerald-green columns and wrought-iron chairs and boasts a fountain centerpiece. The Atrium Restaurant, furnished with white wicker chairs, wraps around the perimeter of the room and offers an international buffet dinner nightly. **Tandoori Chicken**, **Fish Curry**, **Baked Whiting with Garlic Butter**, **Chicken Teriyaki**, an assortment of **Fresh Vegetables** and **Soups,** and **Peach Cobbler** are just a few of the selections from The Atrium's menu.

The gem of the entire operation can be found upstairs in the Salaam Grand Ballroom, where the word "grand" is an understatement. Outside the main ballroom is a lovely, intimate piano nook called Alvan's Corner, named after current Nation of Islam leader Minister Louis Farrakhan's brother. Inside, crystal chandeliers, rich heavy velvet drapes, tastefully upholstered high-back chairs, a bandstand, and center dance floor are just a few of the amenities featured in this magnificent hall, which is available for banquets, weddings, receptions, and business functions.

$10–$15 ▢ ✓ 🍴 🎦 ☕

☆**The Shark Bar   212 North Canal Street, Chicago, Illinois   312.559.9057**
    Opened March 1997. See New York listings for menu and ambience details
$20 ☎ ☐ ✓ 🍴 🍶 ☕

Take-Out Dining

☆**Lem's**
    5914 South State Street, Chicago, Illinois
        773.684.5007
    311 East 75ᵗʰ Street, Chicago, Illinois
        773.994.2428
    "If you want the best, you would want to come to Lem's," says William Lemons, proprietor of Lem's Barbecue on South State Street. If you don't believe him, just ask anyone in Chicago which restaurants have **Great Ribs** and Lem's will be one of the first names mentioned! People from all over the state come to this hole-in-the-wall take-out joint, and what brings them? Lemons says it's his grandmother's barbecue sauce, a recipe passed down to his uncle and father who started Lem's 45 years ago. The taste is a little sweet and vinegary, and it's pure perfection! Lem's also makes its own **Hot Links** and sprinkle mix, but the main attraction here are the **Rib Tips**—thick and tender. Need I say more?
$10

☆**Mississippi Rick's**
    Lake Meadow Shopping Center, Chicago, Illinois   312.791.0090
    101 East 47ᵗʰ Street, Chicago, Illinois 312.624.3474
    From the music industry to the trucking business to the barbecue pit, entrepreneur Richard Williams's goal is to establish Mississippi Rick's as the **"Home of the Gourmet Rib Tip."** As Willie Jones, special events coordinator for Mississippi Rick's, explains: "A rib tip is the top piece of the rib, cut and prepared in a certain way, topped with our mumalicious sauce." Wait a minute, did he say "mumalicious"?!?—'splain, please! Unfortunately, Mr.

Jones is not divulging any secrets, so whatever it is that makes their sauce so tongue-twisting good will have to remain just that. So let's let the name speak for itself!

Rick's also makes and sells **Hot Links, Fried Fish,** and **Chicken**. Its catering clients include Chaka Kahn's concert tour, the DuSable Museum of African American History, Operation PUSH, and numerous others. In the summertime, outdoor music and seating is provided at the Lake Meadow location.

$10 ☐ ✓℃ 🐟

☆Mojava Coffee Bar 1617 East 55th Street, Hyde Park, Chicago, Illinois 312.324.5335

Located in the Hyde Park section of town, Mojava Coffee Bar is the hippest place in Chicago these days. Order a **Café Breve** (espresso and steamed half-and-half) and relax in the cozy yet ultra-chic lounge area. Admire the revolving art gallery, which showcases local talent, or start up a game of chess with a willing patron. Mojava takes the concept of the coffee shop one step further by providing an upscale, laid-back atmosphere where one can kick back while enjoying a **Vegetable Melange Sandwich** and an **Iced Cappuccino**. Some evenings, Mojava features **Poetry Readings, Live Jazz or Blues,** and **Game Nights** that include a variety of board and card competitions. Mojava is also available for private parties.

$10 ☐ 🖾🍴

Nightclubs

☆Buddy Guy's Legends 754 South Wabash Avenue, Downtown, Chicago, Illinois 312.427.0333

This spacious, comfortable nightspot, owned by legendary Chicago blues man Buddy Guy celebrated eight years of hosting the blues on June 9, 1997, and the crowd in attendance that night was treated to the very best in great music, food, and fun. The club boasts a **State-of-the-Art Sound System** and **Four Pool Tables**, and is a great place to host a private affair. The kitchen serves a **Full Dinner Menu of Cajun Louisiana-Style Food**, including **Baby Back Ribs** and **Hoppin' John**. But best of all, it presents **Live Blues Seven Nights a Week**, featuring some of Buddy's famous friends like King Floyd, Johnny Adams, Junior Wells, and Earl King, to name a few.

Cover charge/ $10–$20 Dinner menu/ ☎ ☐ ♉ 🎼 🎁

The Clique   2347 South Michigan Avenue, Downtown Chicago, Illinois   312.326.0247

The proprietor of The Clique, attorney Dwain Kyles, describes his club as having "a one-stop-shopping format." Indeed, the club is a **Full Entertainment Center**. Under one roof, one can enjoy **Live Jazz** in the downstairs lounge, **Stand-Up Comedy** in the back room, and **Dancing** upstairs to music that shakes with the pulsating beat of urban contemporary sounds. This place is huge—it's the **Largest Dance Club in Chicago**—and all venues marry well without disturbing each other. On off nights, the club is available for private parties, community meetings, and political gatherings, and Kyles is committed to making The Clique available for any events that serve to enhance the neighboring community and its growth.

Cover charge/ 21+ crowd/ ☐ ♉ 🎼 🎁

☆The Cotton Club   1710 South Michigan Avenue, Downtown, Chicago, Illinois   773.341.9787

Cool jazz up front and the hottest vibes out back are terms that aptly describe one of Chicago's most sophisticated nightspots: The Cotton Club. This club, which caterers to the 25-and-over crowd, has a split personality. The large front room has a **Great Bar Scene**, and showcases terrific **Local Jazz Talents** like Panther or Ray Silkman. There is ample seating, and bar food is available so you can lounge and enjoy the smooth vibes being laid down on stage. If you feel yourself becoming a bit too mellow, pass through the double doors and enter The Cotton Club's "alter ego": the dance room. Here, the walls sweat with energy from the music and from the dancers gettin' their "groove" on.

Cover charge/ 25+ crowd/ ☐ ♉ 🎼

Milt Trenier's Lounge 610 North Fairbanks, Downtown, Chicago, Illinois 312.266.6226

In the heart of downtown, Milt Trenier continues to entertain Chicago's audiences as he did 40 years ago. Upon entering the club, one is greeted by a wall of photos, each telling the history of the proprietor's career in entertainment. Over the years, Trenier has sung with all the greats and appeared in scores of clubs and other venues across the country, including Las Vegas. He has also performed with his brothers as the R&B group "The Treniers." Today, the lounge that bears his name offers **Live Jazz and Blues, Cocktails**, and **Dancing**. When the house band, featuring Trenier, is performing songs from yesteryear, he totally charms the crowd with his cornball jokes and "too much drinking" bit. At that point, all one can do is smile, sit back, and enjoy the show!

Cover charge/ Mature Crowd/ ☐

DALLAS

Casual Dining

☆Cajun Blues   3701 West Northwest Highway, #173, Dallas, Texas   214.350.3234

Once you step out from your car under the awning built to shield Cajun Blues patrons from Dallas's infamous summer evening thunderstorms, pass through the large wooden doors, and enter the spacious dining area, you know you are in for one relaxing and enjoyable evening. Cajun Blues's sophisticated Vegas-style decor is designed to entertain—starting, on stage left, with **Live Jazz, R&B, and Blues** performances Thursday through Saturday evenings, as well as a host of events other nights of the week.

The menu is pure Cajun, and fun reading, too. While you linger over the details, order some **Fried Crawfish Tails, Down-Home Blues Pies** (stuffed jalapenos), or a cup of **Chicken & Andouille Sausage Gumbo**. For your main course, there's the fried **WEE-Z-ANA Platter** (catfish, oysters, shrimp, and crawfish), the **Whole Thang Platter** (whole catfish butterflied), **Voo Doo Baby Back Ribs** (now you see 'em—now you don't!), **Shrimp Etouffee** (mama knows best, mmm!), or **Barbecue Shrimp** (a dirty finger dish that's so good!) to choose from on this extensive menu. And please, don't even mention desserts! Well, OK, ask your waiter to bring a little of that delicious **Bread Pudding** over while you listen to that good ol' down-home blues.

$15–$20 ☎ ❒ ⍾ 🎵 🚗

Famous Smokey John's Bar-B-Q & Home Cooking Depot

6412 Lemmon Avenue, Dallas, Texas   214.352.2752

110 Preston Royal Shopping Center, Dallas, Texas 214.368.2494

Jude 1:2—"May mercy, peace, and love be multiplied to you." After over 20 years in business, Smokey John's proprietor John Reaves continues to extend that passage and his good wishes to each of his customers, personally and through his food. This is the kind of place you expect to see in Dallas. The rustic interior showcases many of the authentic western antiques that Reaves has picked up here and there over the years. The Lemmon Avenue location features an absolutely fabulous curio case with stained-glass panel doors. The **Banquet Room**, perfect for small private gatherings, is straight out of saloon scenes from the wild, wild West.

While barbecue plates of **Beef**, **Ribs**, **Ham**, **Hot Links**, and **Chicken** are what Smokey John's is known for, there are also plenty of **Daily Home-Style Specials** to chose from. Tons of vegetables and side salads add to the feast.

$10 ☐ ✓ℂ 🖼

Hardeman's BBQ   2901 South Lancaster, Dallas, Texas 214.371.7627

Olivia Hardeman married into a Texas barbecue family. Her father-in-law was a great barbecue man whose secret recipes were proudly passed down to his son. When her family moved to Dallas in 1955, they opened Hardeman's BBQ. Over 40 years later, Hardeman's is still family-owned and managed by Mrs. Hardeman, along with her five children. **Beef Brisket** (smoked for eight hours), tender **BBQ Pork Ribs, Links, and Chicken** are just a few of the reasons people continue to go to Hardeman's. As Mrs. Hardeman contends: "We take the time to prepare our food as if we were eating it ourselves." Amen!

$10 ☐ ✓ℂ

☆Queen of Sheba Café and Restaurant 3527 McKinney, Dallas, Texas 214.521.0491

This is quite a story: Berhane and Elsa Kiflom fled the province of Eritrea, northern Ethiopia, for the United States in 1982. Their country was engaged in civil war and the Kiflom's lives were in danger. Their American sponsors smuggled them safely to Amarillo, Texas. While in Amarillo, Elsa befriended the owners of an exclusive Italian restaurant. An excellent cook in her own right, Elsa learned the art of preparing many Italian dishes. When the Kifloms moved to Dallas, she took a job working in one of the city's Ethiopian restaurants. When the opportunity to buy the restaurant presented itself, Elsa and her husband became the owners of Texas's oldest Ethiopian restaurant and certainly one of its best. Exotic yet cozy, Queen of Sheba's goal is to provide a most enjoyable dining experience. States Elsa: "Hospitality is our way of life. It is our family tradition to serve you any way we can!" This philosophy, along with excellent food and staff, makes Queen of Sheba the quality restaurant that it is.

Queen of Sheba offers diners lovely, semiprivate bamboo "huts" for their meal (seating up to four people), re-creating the setting in a traditional Eritrean village. Meals start with a special "washing of the hands" ceremony. Handpainted murals and skins tell the story of the Queen of Sheba on the restaurant's walls. Beautiful Eritrean women's hairstyles are also displayed, as are many ancient Coptic crosses and musical instruments.

The restaurant's **Award-Winning Menu** is filled with dishes that tantalize the tastebuds and encourage sharing. The **Lunch Buffet** provides an excellent chance to sample many authentic Eritrean foods. The **Queen's Dinner** is a complete meal from appetizer to dessert, including an aperitif, a glass of wine, and coffee or tea. A feast truly fit for a queen or king!

$10–$20 /Queen's Dinner $30+/ ☎ ▢ ✓ 𝄪 🍴 🎦

"**Elaine's Kitchen** certainly follows the old adage that 'good things come in small packages.' This Jamaican fare is as good as any I've had and small enough to provide a personal touch."
Linda English, Investor Relations, Texas Industries

Red's BBQ   2021 North Hampton Road, DeSoto, Texas
972.298.5580

Reginald Dorsey felt the sting of the entrepreneurial bug when he was lured away from his corporate job to manage Smokey Joe's BBQ Restaurant in Oak Cliff, Texas. After nine years of learning the ups and downs of the barbecue business, Dorsey set out to make his own mark, opening Red's BBQ in February 1995. Boasting an attractive rustic western decor, Red's is located in a mostly White neighborhood, and Dorsey, who is Black, has found attracting a African American clientele harder than he imagined. Still, he says, "I want to see my people in here—even though I'm here not only to serve Blacks—I'm here to serve customers. I wanted to prove that Blacks could have a nice restaurant. It doesn't always have to be a joint."

And nice Red's is, with excellent barbecue. The secret? Dorsey is quick to share: "We put our feet, toes, and knees in everything we cook!" His restaurant specializes in tender **BBQ Ribs**, **Brisket**, **and Chicken**, **Baked Beans**, **Chili**, and **Homemade Cobblers**. The menu changes, its owner says, to keep things interesting and to keep the customers coming back. Don't worry, Reginald, the food will do that for you!

$10/ Slabs of Ribs slightly more / ❒ ✓ℂ

Take-Out Dining

☆DC's Café   8224 Park Lane, Dallas, Texas
214.363.4348

"**Best Overall Restaurant in Dallas**"—that's pretty big praise for a small take-out spot like DC's Café. But the only thing small about DC's is the eating space (six tables). The food portions are generous, the staff is friendly, and owner Damon Crow has lots and lots of personality. When asked why he went into the restaurant business, Crow offered the following enthusiastic response: "When God made man, He created only a few things that was necessary. You don't have to have clothes, but you do have to eat!" His take-out career began in 1992, when he was preparing and delivering homecooked meals out of his apartment. On the first day, he claims, "We sold 63 lunches...and never looked back." Today, located next to North Park Shopping Mall, more than 200 people stop by for lunch at DC's Café daily. And Damon attributes his establishment's success and growth to faith: "Strictly faith, that's all there is."

Pork Chops, **Fried Catfish,** and **Daily Down-Home Specials** are featured items on DC's mouth-watering menu, but this café's real claim to fame is its desserts. People line up for Crow's homemade **Chocolate Cakes**, **Pineapple Cake** and **Fried Sweet Potato Pies** (yes, fried!). Made to order by his mother, these tempting sweet potato turnovers are hot and flaky, stuffed with a delicious filling, and topped with powdered sugar, cinnamon, and vanilla ice cream! Ahh, things that make you go, "May I also order one to go, please!"

$10 ❒ ✓ℂ

☆Elaine's Kitchen   1912 Martin Luther King Jr. Boulevard, Dallas, Texas   214.565.1008

When Elaine Campbell first visited Dallas, she just couldn't find a good Jamaican restaurant. Thank goodness her brother decided to open one—even if it is only a take-out! When he asked her to take a leave of absence from her corporate job in New York City to help get his new venture off the ground, Elaine moved to Dallas, rolled up her sleeves, and pitched right in. Her brother was so grateful, he named the restaurant after her! Elaine eventually took over the reins of ownership, and has since turned Elaine's Kitchen into an eatery that has earned a reputation as *the* place for authentic Caribbean food in Dallas. It has been hailed **"Best Caribbean Place"** and **"Best for $5"** by the local press. Indeed, the line for lunch starts forming early in the morning, and that many people can't be wrong!!

The menu at Elaine's Kitchen is arranged by entree sizes (small, medium, and large) and priced accordingly. **Oxtail**, **Curried Goat**, **Curried Chicken**, **Jerk Chicken**, **Stew Peas**, **Cow Foot**, **Ackee**, and **Red Snapper** are a few of the selections. Elaine's also provides **Full-Service Catering** and sells Jamaican spices and other products.

$10 ✓ ℂ

Nightclubs

GG's Jazz   5915 East Northwest Highway, Dallas, Texas   214.207.7436

Nancy Wilson, Howard Hewitt, and lots of great local talent have appeared at GG's Jazz. Opened in 1993, GG's is an upscale nightclub, perfect for special occasions, with tons of amenities. The club features **Two Bars**, a large **Dance Floor**, cozy corner sofas for really private parties, and a **Pool Room** accented with Tiffany lamps and heart-shaped chairs. It also hosts **"T.J.'s Open Mike Night"** for the talented and nervy, **Ladies' Nights**, **Live Bands**, **Dancing**, **Specially Priced Drinks**, and a **Complimentary Buffet** on certain evenings. Call for a calendar of events.

Cover charge/ 25+ crowd/ ☐ ♟ ♫ ♫

Lakeside   3100 West Northwest Highway, Dallas, Texas   214.904.1770

With its featured **Urban Contemporary, Rap, Hip-Hop, and R&B Music**, Lakeside caters to a crowd that *knows* how to party! Laid back, with **No Dress Code**, this club can fill to 1,800 people on a Saturday night. **Nationally Known Bands** such as The Barkays, and Lakeside, as well as local greats pack the house regularly. Lakeside also offers **Male Dancers on Ladies' Nights**, and a **Buffet on Friday Evenings**.

Cover charge/ 21+ crowd/ ☐ 🎷 🎼 🎁

Park Avenue Nightclub   9100 North Central Expressway, Dallas, Texas   214.739.5548

The Park Avenue is a large, sexy nightclub where Dallas's 25-and-over professional crowd goes to see and be seen. As the word around town goes: "At Park Avenue, everyone is a V.I.P." Designed by Charles Bush, nightclub designer/owner extraordinaire, the club features **Three Bars**, a huge **Dance Floor**, animal-print bar stools, a private area for parties, 1,500-person capacity, and a great sound system that cranks out **R&B** and **Old-School** favorites. Additionally, **Big-Name Bands** such as Morris Day, Solo, and Groove Theory have performed at the Park Avenue.

Cover charge / 25+ crowd/ Dress Code/ ☐ 🎷 🎼 🎁

DENVER

Casual Dining

☆Bocaza Mexican Grille   1740 East 17th Avenue, Denver, Colorado   303.393.7545

African American entrepreneurs Edward Hughes and Reggie Smith noticed a strong trend moving toward **Mexican/ Southwestern Cuisine** in the Denver area. Recognizing a golden opportunity, they opened an upscale, contemporary Mexican restaurant near Denver's high-traffic hospital district.

The first thing one notices upon entering Bocaza is the handsome decor: adobe colors accented against copper/brick walls. The intoxicating aroma of the grill mixes with the pungent freshness of salsa spices. The restaurant's Mexican American chef and staff are quickly at your service to ensure that you enjoy an authentic Southwest dining experience. Bocaza offers a healthy alternative to traditional Mexican food by not using any animal fats or lard in their cooking processes. The salsas are all homemade and come in various degrees of spiciness from mild to salsa inferno! Menu selections include **Green Chile Pesto Burritos with Chicken and Poblano Pesto**, **Vegetarian Fajitas Popular** (a blend of marinated vegetables, cheese, lime cilantro rice, and salsa) and **Steak Tacos**. Bocaza is quality food at great prices and highly recommended. Watch out, Taco Bell!

$10 ☐

☆Brown Sugar's Burgers & Bones   2415 Welton Street, Denver, Colorado   303.292.4177

George Brown, proprietor of Brown Sugar's Burgers & Bones, has more on his mind than simply selling hamburgers and chili; he has a vision for his people and his community. As a result, Brown Sugar's Burger & Bones is not your typical burger joint. Through it, Brown is helping to bring his vision to reality. First, he employs people from Denver's African American community to work in his restaurant. Brown Sugar's Burgers & Bones also offers positive images of Black people in its decor. An impressive collection of Black art graces the restaurant's walls.

Third, Brown is working to establish work–study programs on college campuses in Denver to teach Black youth entrepreneurial skills and food service management.

According to Brown, Brown Sugar's serves great "semi-fast" food. Everything is fresh, prepared to order, and, well—different. Featured burgers include **The Andi** (topped with green peppers and fried onions) and **The Cheesey George** (topped with chili and cheese). Other sandwiches include **The Crack Brown** (hot polish sausage with chili), **The El Cheapo** (grilled cheese), and **The Ty-Ty Tender** (breaded pork tenderloin). And don't forget the **Ribs** at Brown Sugar's, which are sold "by the bone" or as a combo with your favorite burger.

$10 /Slabs of Ribs slightly more/ ◻

Ethel's House of Soul   2622 Welton Avenue, Denver, Colorado   303.295.2125

Watching her mother manage a restaurant in Chicago while she was growing up, Ethel Allen dreamed of owning her own food establishment one day. Her dreams were realized after she moved to Denver and opened Ethel's House of Soul in Denver's predominantly Black Five Points neighborhood in 1971. To this day, Allen still does all the cooking using a time-honored formula: "No measuring, just cook!" She is also very active in the Five Points community, participating in its annual Juneteenth celebrations and serving over 300 meals to the homeless every Christmas.

Allen's slogan for her restaurant is simple, like the place itself: "In the mood for good food? Visit Ethel's House of Soul." The mural on the wall at Ethel's is a classic, featuring a caricature of an old cook and a few of his favorite dishes from bacon and eggs to fried chicken. The food is nothing fancy, but it's all down-home good. House specialties include **Pork Chops, Smothered Steak, Neck Bones, Chitterlings, Hog Mauls, Chicken and Dressing**, and, of course, **Peach Cobbler** for dessert.

$10 ✓ ℂ

"**I'm a big guy and I never really liked burritos before, but the delicious chicken burritos at Bocaza are more than enough to satisfy my healthy appetite!**" *Earl T. Conway, Insurance / Investment Advisor*

☆Kal'line's Café   2736 Welton Avenue, Denver, Colorado 303.292.9717
Crown Food Full-Service Catering   303.576.0303

The newest entree to Denver's historic Five Points district is Kal'line's Café, a friendly restaurant that makes you feel like you're sitting in your mama's kitchen. Kal'line's is indeed a tribute to brothers John, Mac, and William Watts's mother, Minnie Lee, affectionately called "Kal'line" by her father-in-law. Clarence "Buck" Watts, Kal'line's husband, was a log cutter with a hearty appetite, and Kal'line had eight children to feed as well. Today, her delicious recipes and dishes live on, "served with kindness" by her appreciative restauranteur/caterer sons.

Kal'line's is a bright and cheery place with good service and some of the freshest-tasting food in town. Sundays after church are the restaurant's busiest times. If you come for breakfast, Mama's Specials include **Bologna and Eggs**, **Biscuits and Gravy**, **Corned Beef Hash**, and **Grilled Pork Chops**. Dinner serves up **Ole Homeboy Ribs**, **Aunt Josie's Meatloaf**, and **Big "K" Pan-Fried Kat Fish**. **Kal'line's Succotash**, made with green peppers, lima beans, okra, tomatoes, and ground beef, is just one of the simmering side dishes that can complement your meal. Don't leave home without your appetite!

$10–$15 ❑ ✓ ℂ

Kapre Fried Chicken   2729 Welton Avenue, Denver, Colorado 303.295.9207

From serving in the segregated Army to working 15 years with the Union Pacific railroad to running a lounge in a notorious gambling joint, Wilford Thomas, proprietor of Kapre Fried Chicken, has lived an interesting life. In 1957, he opened The Kapre Lounge in a building across the street from his present location. After noticing that the various other places on the block were serving mostly soul food, Thomas, who claims to enjoy cooking only as a hobby, decided that his specialty would be fried chicken.

Today, however, Thomas states that his **Fried Chicken "is the Best in Town."** It is good, too—just spicy enough, with a nice, crispy skin. Other specialties include his **Fried Shrimp, Whiting, and Catfish, Hot Links,** and the **Gizzard, Liver,** and **Giblet** dinners. Actually, that's the whole menu at Kapre Fried Chicken, but with chicken this good, what else do you need?

$10 ☐ ⛟

☆M&D's Café   2004 East 28ᵗʰ Avenue, Denver, Colorado   303.296.1760

When Mack Shead retired from 25 years of military service, he knew it was time to go to work. Armed with over 35 years of family barbecue history and recipes, Mack, his wife Daisy, and family moved to Denver, where he opened two fish-and-rib houses. In 1977, Shead opened M&D's to continue serving the great barbecue and fried fish Denver had grown to love. Since then, M&D's has been voted **"Best BBQ Restaurant"** in 1986, '87, '89, '90, and '91 by *Westworld*, Denver's news and arts weekly, and **"The Best in Town"** by the *Denver News* in 1994. The restaurant has won numerous other awards, too many to mention, but for the most part, they all say the same thing: M&D's is *the* place to eat in Denver!

From M&D's smoker come serious **Ribs**, **Chicken**, **Sliced Beef and Pork,** and **Hot Links**. (The restaurant's **Award-Winning Sauce** is sold at local grocery stores throughout the Denver area.) Its deep fryer offers **Catfish**, **Buffalo Fish**, **Ocean Perch**, **Red Snapper,** and **Shrimp**. Everyone's favorite ending to a meal at M&D's is the famed **Peach Cobbler à la Mode**: "a mountain of vanilla ice cream atop a sunset of steaming hot delicious peach cobbler." Start the diet tomorrow...unless of course, you come back to M&D's the next night for more!

$10–$15 Slabs of Ribs slightly more/ ☐ ✓ ℂ

☆Pierre's Supper Club   2157 Downing Street, Denver, Colorado   303.861.8231

Located in a spacious townhouse close to downtown for the past 30 years, Pierre's Supper Club is *the* spot for entertainment in Denver.   The first level features a **Huge Bar** where the networking among the professional after-work crowd starts around 5pm and continues into the late evening. Upstairs, the back area doubles as overflow seating for the main dining room and turns into a lively **Dancing** area when the deejay starts spinning everyone's favorite R&B records. One more short set of stairs takes you to the restaurant that boasts it is the **"Home of the World-Famous Catfish."**

What makes Pierre's catfish so good? It has a lot to do with the chef's gourmet batter and homemade spicy seasoning mix, all exclusive to Pierre's and available for sale downstairs. Other items featured on the dinner menu include the **Seafood Platter** (catfish, jumbo shrimp, and oysters), **Bar-B-Que Ribs**, **T-Bone Steaks**, **Fried Chicken,** and **Grilled Pork Chops**.

$10–$15 ☐ ✓ ℂ ⚷🍴

"**Being originally from Kentucky, I had never eaten catfish before in my life. It wasn't until my second visit to Pierre's Super Club when I was encouraged to try their famous fried catfish. Well, after that delicious experience, I haven't ordered anything else since!**" *Shelia Harris, Assistant Housing Director Francis Heights-Clare Gardens*

☆Sam Taylor's Bar-B-Q   435 South Cherry Street, Denver, Colorado   303.388.9300

Diehard Denver golfers live for 40-degree weather during the winter months and will gladly tee off on small mounds of stubborn snow if they have to! And after 18 holes have been played, everyone heads to Sam Taylor's for a beer from one of the 25 available (including Sam Taylor's own brew) and a slab of what many Denverites consider the **Best Barbecue Ribs in Town**—or the best in America, according to proprietor Sam Taylor. Taylor moved his restaurant from the golf course to its new location in January 1997, and while the digs are a little fancier than the old place, the food's still just as good.

Gotta warn you, though: you'll need plenty of napkins to handle the food at Sam Taylor's. Its **"Sammiches"** are famous and come in several varieties. **Rib, BBQ Poke, Hot Links,** the **Chicago Big Weenee** (it's a man thang!), and **Maxwell Street Polish Sausage sammiches** are just a few of the items on the menu. **The Works Slab,** which includes a **Slab of Ribs with Baked Beans, Potato Salad,** and **Texas Toast**, will feed three hungry golfers. Just make sure they're not far from their recliners!
$10 Slab Dinners $20+ / ☐ 🍸

Take-Out Dining

Horne's Catering Restaurant   2861 Colorado Boulevard, Denver, Colorado   303.320.8571

At 9 years old, chef Jim Horne started his career in food service, standing on Coca Cola crates in order to reach the sinkfuls of dirty pots he had to scrub day in and day out. At age 12, Horne was promoted to fry cook. At 17, he entered the military, and after his tour of duty, he finished culinary school and worked for a while at a country club. By that time, Horne had decided it was time to go into business for himself. For years, he ran his own top-flight catering concern, providing food for events hosted by local government, weddings, and corporate parties. He also owned a first-class restaurant and inn in Atlanta. And if that's not enough, Chef Horne has also served as Pastor Horne, presiding over his church for 15 years.

Today, Horne's Catering Restaurant prepares and delivers dinners to hospitals and nursing homes in the Denver area as well as offers delicious take-out soul food. **Catfish**, **Bar-B-Q Ribs**, **Roast Duck**, **Neck Bones**, **Liver and Onions**, **Pigs' Feet**, and **Oxtails** are just a few of the items featured daily, and Horne claims that his establishment sells 180 pounds of **Chitterlings** a week! Plenty of freshly prepared side dishes are also available.
$10 ❑

Sweet Surprise Bakery & Café   1514 17th Street, Denver, Colorado   303.572.7772

Akwe Oseye's 20 years of experience in the catering and retail business prepared her for the ultimate challenge: opening her own bakery and café right in downtown Denver. When Sweet Surprise first opened, Oseye only served sandwiches and bakery items. Ever the smart retailer, she listened to what her customers told her they wanted and decided to add an **Espresso/Cappuccino Bar**. (You mean Starbuck's missed a corner? How can that be?)

Sweet Surprise's rosy interior offers a comfortable, relaxing environment for downtowners seeking refuge from the stress-filled workday. Oseye has combed the Denver area to bring her customers the best in baked goods, which include **Scones**, **Lemon Bars**, **Bagels**, **Donuts**, and **Muffins**. Her take-out also specializes in **Health-Conscious Sandwiches** like **Cashew**

Chicken or Turkey prepared with low-fat mayo and served on multigrain bread, available individually or boxed as part of a lunch-to-go.

$10 ☐ 🦷

Catering

Fanciful Foods 2267 Kearney Street, Denver, Colorado 303.321.6802

According to Regina Friend, owner of Fanciful Foods Catering, "The focus at Fanciful Foods is not what *we* want, it's what *you* (the customer) want." Friend started catering on a small scale in 1986. She quickly went from running a home-based business to managing a retail catering shop to operating a **Full-Service Catering/Event Planning** business. Today, whether the cuisine desired is Caribbean, southwestern, or international, Fanciful Foods can provide a custom menu, first-rate service, and upscale presentation to fit every client need. Typical catering jobs range from weddings, corporate parties, and nonprofit functions to small private affairs. Available event planning services include finding the perfect facility to hold an affair, arranging musical entertainment, and locating valet service. As the proprietor proudly proclaims, Fanciful Foods "treats you as if you were our only customer!"

DETROIT

Fine Dining

☆Edmund Place Restaurant   69 Edmund, Downtown, Detroit, Michigan   313.831.5757

Only a visionary like Joseph Thompson would resurrect a first-class restaurant on an otherwise deserted noncommercial block. With only a thousand dollars in hand, Thompson purchased a shell of a building and transformed it into a showpiece that pays homage to good ol' down-home cooking. With all the ambience associated with fine-dining establishments, coupled with a familiar and extremely reasonably priced menu, Edmund Place is indeed a triumph.

The cozy bar area is the first stop on your tour of this restaurant. Next visit the semiprivate dining rooms, some with working fireplaces, their entrances framed by graceful silk floral arrangements. All of these features indicate that a special evening is in store. But what makes this restaurant truly unique is that for all its upscale attributes, the meals are priced so that almost anyone can enjoy all that Edmund Place has to offer. It boasts an extensive **International Menu featuring Salads, Pastas, Stir-Fry Dishes, and Southern Specialties. Beef Satay in Honey Soy Sauce, Seafood Pasta, Chicken and Pinched Dumplings, Orange Roughy, Smothered New York Sirloin**, and **Baby Back Ribs** are just a sampling of some of the savory offerings.

$20 ☎ ▯ ♟ ☕

☆Harlequin Café   8047 Agnes, Detroit, Michigan   313.331.0922

There are several reasons to dine at the Harlequin Café: the lovely dining room, the **Live Piano Playing**, the **Most Extensive Champagne List in Detroit**, and, of course, the terrific food. But the main reason is to meet the owner and chef, Sherman Sharpe. To hear Sharpe reciting the evening's menu, replete with his romanticized descriptions of each dish and elaborate hand gestures, is nothing short of grand theater! Sharpe started his professional career as an attorney, which explains how he can expertly summarize the menu and deliver it with such eloquence. So entertaining is each recounting, many diners have a difficult time deciding what to order!

Harlequin Café specializes in **French-Inspired Cuisine**. Appetizers include the **Caviar Potatoes, Champagne Oysters,** and **Bay Scallop Florentine**. Recommended entrees include the **Shrimp Pesto, Tilapia with Citrus Madeira Sauce, Lamp Chops, Wilshire Sweetbreads, Veal Marsala "Don Corleone,"** and **Whiskey Peppercorn Steak**. Each dessert is an artistic creation onto itself. Indeed, the Harlequin Café is one of Detroit's premier dining experiences. Bon appetit!

$25+ ☎ ☐ ⛊ 🎵 📦 V

Casual Dining

☆The Blue Nile Restaurant 508 Monroe Street, Greektown, Detroit, Michigan 313.964.6699

Located in the heart of Greektown is the charming Blue Nile, an Ethiopian restaurant that's charming and cozy. Ethiopian dining is too much fun for just two, so bring the gang! Once seated in front of a roaring fire on low, ornamented chairs, you'll be greeted by a hostess offering warm, moist towels. This is because you will be eating with your hands! According to owner Seifu Lessanework, "Eating with one's hands and feeding each other is a custom of Ethiopia. It shows caring and loving." And it's obvious Seifu practices what he preaches because you can just feel the love and caring he has put into making The Blue Nile a most enjoyable dining experience—from the wide-eyed, stained glass angels that watch over patrons as they enjoy cocktails at the bar, to the pleasing, authentic cuisine served Ethiopian-style.

For adventurous diners, the Blue Nile offers its **Ethiopian Feast,** made up of almost a dozen chicken, beef, lamb, and vegetable dishes. This generous sampling is placed before guests in a colorful round basket, making reaching for the food easy for everyone. Instead of forks, a spongelike bread called *Injera*, native to Ethiopia, is used to scoop up the food, even when eating salad! So dig in, don't be shy, and bring a partner—after all, what's a little finger licking among friends?

$20 ☎ ☐ ✓ ₵ ⛊ 📦

"Jada is a great, upscale barbecue restaurant with smooth jazz, terrific food and a variety of tasty sides to complement it all." *Glenda Gill, Owner, Special Projects*

The Brown Bag and Eatery   15070 Hamilton, Highland Park, Detroit, Michigan   313.869.6668

Six years ago, The Brown Bag and Eatery's proprietor Joanne Grear took her 20 years of experience as a caterer and parleyed it into a successful neighborhood spot. Instead of heading to the downtown areas, Grear and her associates elected to stay their neighborhood and support their community. Located in the Highland Park area approximately 20 minutes north of the city, this restaurant has become a favorite of savvy locals who come from all over Detroit to dine there.

The daily specials at The Brown Bag and Eatery are recited by the professional and attentive staff. Sample entrees include **Smothered Pork Chops, Fried Catfish, Chili Mac,** and **Baked Chicken.** Po' Boy Sandwiches, **The Brown Bag's Special Salad** (grilled chicken breast, feta cheese, and seasonal greens with ranch dressing), **Vegetable Stir Fry with Rice Shrimp,** and **Creole Gumbo** are just a few other selections from this varied menu. Portions are more than generous, but room for dessert is a must since most of the cakes are made from scratch by Grear's mother!
$10 ☐ ✔ ℂ /Closed on Saturdays

☆Dempsey's Place   3000 East Jefferson Avenue, Downtown, Detroit, Michigan   313.259.9806

Alan Jackson, proprietor of Dempsey's, envisioned a restaurant where people could meet, exchange ideas, and enjoy fine dining in an upscale environment, and he brought in the man he claims is "the best chef in Michigan" to deliver on that dream: Keith White. In Chef White's view, the food at Dempsey's Place ranges "from the simplistic to the extraordinary." Call it international cuisine, or continental cuisine with what White calls "African rootage," or whatever—it is his way of contributing to "keeping the tradition alive." According to White, "We view cooking as an art...to have a specialty would be a limitation." Regardless of how you classify the cuisine at Dempsey's, make sure you try the **Homemade Rolls, Chef White's Secret Fresh Italian Salad Dressing, Marinated Shrimp,** and **Chicken à la Champagne.** Dempsey's also features **Evening Jazz Sets on Fridays** to ease patrons into the weekend.
$20+ ☎ ☐ ✔ ℂ 🍴 🍷

☆East Franklin Restaurant   1440 Franklin, Downtown, Detroit, Michigan   313.393.0018

Enter through massive brass double doors to a large foyer leading to a busy, modern dining room. View the proudly displayed works by local artists on the exposed brick walls. You have just joined those who enjoy the pleasures of the upscale dining environment that is the East Franklin Restaurant! Drawing upon his knowledge of the construction industry, John Thompson, proprietor and creative director, and his sister Joanne turned an old shell of a building into a place the community is proud to call "African-American owned." As the two Thompsons maintain, when you come from a family of 10 children, you quickly learn that a positive attitude, a sense of togetherness, and a belief in hard work contribute to the success of any project. And as their restaurant demonstrates, the family that works together, makes good together!

Located in the up-and-coming Detroit neighborhood of Rivertown, East Franklin offers a reasonably priced menu of dishes we all know and love—the best in down-home, "soul" cooking. **Fried Chicken** and **Fried Catfish** are the house specialties, and according to Joanne, the recipes for both are closely guarded family secrets. Other favorite entrees include **Orange Roughy**, **Smothered Steak, Baby Back Ribs,** and **Fancy Chops.** $10–$15 ☐

☆Jada   546 Larned, Downtown, Detroit, Michigan   313.965.1700
Vicki's BBQ   3845 West Warren, Detroit, Michigan   313.894.9906

Armanda Herbert, the brains behind Jada, the newest addition to Detroit's revitalized and thriving downtown area, comes from a barbecue family. Her parents have owned and operated Vicki's BBQ, where Armanda received her basic education in the art of preparing barbecue, for over 40 years. Named after an old jazz song performed by saxophonist Sydney Bechet back in the day, Jada offers barbecue and other favorites in a modern, loft-like environment. Keeping with the Motor City theme, its decor has a slightly industrial appearance to it: lead pipe barstool legs, high-tech lighting, exposed brick walls, and floor-to-ceiling windows for watching folks walk by. But the food is pure "down-home," the product of Herbert's years of comparative research and experimenting with recipes. As she explains, "Our barbecue is a combination of three cooking styles: oven, hickory-smoked, and charcoal-grilled. Our sauce is a unique blend of 26 ingredients resulting in a caramelized concoction with a sweet and tangy flavor." Yumm! Lead the way!

Aside from terrific barbecue, Jada offers **Marinated Fried Catfish, Hand-Dipped Fresh Batter Shrimp, Chicken and Waffles,** hearty **Black-Eyed Peas** (with a hint of curry), and **Macaroni and Cheese** (made with four gourmet cheeses). **Bread Pudding** with a drizzle of chocolate sauce just adds to the inevitable destruction of your diet. (Get over it, already!) **Live Music** livens things up on Tuesday, Thursday, Friday, and Saturday evenings.

$15–$20 ☎ ❏ ✓ ₵ ♫

☆New Detroiter Fine Food Restaurant
7339 East Jefferson Avenue, Downtown, Detroit, Michigan 313.822.2642

Charles Braggs, proprietor of the New Detroiter, claims he has always loved to cook. So, when the opportunity to obtain his current site presented itself in 1988, he grabbed the brass ring and turned a former Chinese restaurant into a great soul food place. Don't expect a fancy interior at the New Detroiter, but do expect good service and good food. Famous for **its $2.00 Wow Breakfast** and its **All-Day Breakfast Service**, this restaurant is best known for its **Ribs**. According to owner Braggs, the New Detroiter serves up "the best barbecue in the world!" (The world!? A little biased, isn't he?) Nevertheless, check out the **Ribs, Fried Chicken**, great **Macaroni and Cheese**, and the fabulous **Seven-Up Cake**. Then judge for yourself, and see if you don't agree with Braggs, who proudly proclaims that the food at his restaurant "makes your stomach smile!"

$10 ❏ ✓ ₵

☆Sauce   225 East Jos Campau, Downtown, Detroit, Michigan 313.567.7766

New on the scene in the growing Rivertown area is a funky little place called Sauce that is big on ambience, great food, and cocktails. The patrons at this restaurant are on display, seated as they are in front of its huge picture windows surrounded by red hot walls and shiny, lacquered chairs. The bar scene at Sauce is alive as well.

Its international clientele can be found wiling away the hours, nursing martinis and nibbling on the featured **Dragon Eggs**, a spicy little appetizer consisting of chicken breast meat stuffed with cheese and dipped in fiery hot sauce.

Sauce's judiciously priced menu is very focused and a **Steak Lover's Delight**. House specialties **Stuffed Filet Mignon**, **Porterhouse**, and **New York Strip** are all under $18. On the light side, sandwiches are also available, as are **Cajun-Spiced Buffalo Wings** and **Sauce's Caesar Salad**. **Live Entertainment Thursday through Saturday** ranges from straight-ahead and Latin jazz groups to sultry vocalists. In the summer months, the whole neighborhood comes alive when Sauce's patio opens and all the good vibes flow out onto the street.

$20 ☐ ⛾ 🌐

"**Chef Glenn Williams is the top caterer in the area. His presentations and menus are just wonderful!**"
Patrice L. Green, Marketing Consultant

Cafeteria/Buffet-Style Dining

Bush's Garden of Eating   3955 Woodward Avenue
Downtown, Detroit, Michigan   313.831.6711

Bush's Garden of Eating may be almost 40 years old, but its owner, James Bush, continues to draw new clients as well as loyal regulars to his humble eating establishment. Looking around the dining area, one sees friends of the owner coming in with their grandchildren, introducing them to one of their favorite Detroit traditions. The fact that Bush's has not changed after almost a half-century of providing service and comfort to its neighboring community is a tribute to its success. Bush's daughter Janice continues to bring forth from the Garden of Eating's kitchen the same delicious food that started this restaurant's traditions in 1959. **Open for Breakfast, Lunch, and Early Dinner**, each meal offers hearty portions and daily specials. Favorites include Bush's **Short Ribs and Dressing**, **Pork Chops**, **Porterhouse Steak**, and **Fried Chicken**. Not to be forgotten, **Homemade Pies** and **Peach Cobbler** are available to top off any meal.
$10

Steve's Soul Food   8443–47 Grand River Avenue, Detroit, Michigan   313.894.7978

When he opened up Steve's Soul Food in 1986, president Steve Radden felt there was no place like his for the locals to eat. As one regular customer proudly told me, "You will know when you're getting close to Steve's Soul Food. Just look for all the cars in the parking lot." Sure enough, Steve's is typically packed by 11:30am on weekday mornings, and it usually stays that way throughout the afternoon!

What's the attraction? Cafeteria-style service, a large, pleasant dining area, and good food at prices that can't be beat. On any day, **Chicken** (baked, fried or barbecued) served with **Greens** and **Macaroni-and-Cheese** is one of many meals that can be served up hot and quick. Steve's also offers plenty of daily specials, along with cakes, pies, and other goodies galore.

$10   ☐

Take-Out Dining

☆Milt's Gourmet Bar "B" Que   10223 Whittier, Detroit, Michigan   313.521.5959

A while back, when a friend of Milt Goodson asked him where she could get some good barbecue, his response was "his house." This led to him being asked to cook a similar meal for his church's picnic, to his selling barbecue on the corner of his block, to his opening up the location that has been Milt's Gourmet Bar "health benefits and a B" Que since 1989. Milt's has been recognized as the **Best Rib Pit in Detroit** by most of the area's major publications. The dining area at Milt's may be small and the decorations minimal, but love and caring emanate from every square inch. Indeed, the owner claims that his restaurant is more a "ministry" than anything else—offering quality food, a clean, smoke-free environment, and jobs that provide his employees with sense of self-worth. Keep spreading that good word, Mr. Goodson!

Besides **Ribs**, Milt's Gourmet specializes in **Fish Dinners**, **Hickory-Smoked Turkey Breast**, **Homemade Clam Chowder**, and **Chicken Noodle Soup**. Its showcase of desserts will make you want to skip the main course and head straight for the **German Chocolate Cake** or **Turtle Cake**, but don't, even though all the cakes are made on the premises. Milt's continues the tradition of his mother, whom he claims baked a cake or pie every evening when he was a child. There is *no way* you can leave without at least a slice!

$10 Slabs of Ribs slightly more/ ☐ ✓ ℭ

Mr. FoFo's 8902 Second, Detroit, Michigan 313.873.4450

There really is a Mr. FoFo at Mr. FoFo's! His real name is Otis Knapp Lee, and he is the proprietor of this popular establishment that offers a virtual assembly line of take-out treats. The deli counter serves up **Huge Sandwiches** piled high with **Corned** or **Roast Beef, Turkey**, and **Hot Pastrami**. Mr. FoFo's **Fried Fish Sandwiches and Dinners** can be prepared with **Orange Roughy, Perch, Buffalo, Whiting**, and, of course, **Catfish**. **Ribs** and **Chicken** round out the menu in the form of **Short Ribs of Beef, Slabs**, and **Whole Barbecued Chickens**. There are lots of sides to chose from, and Mr. FoFo's bakery features delicious **Deep-Dish Cobblers, Pineapple Upside-Down Cake, Donuts**, and **Banana Pudding**. There's also a cheery seating area for those who can't wait 'til they get home to dig in!

$10 Slabs of Ribs slightly more/ ☐ ✓ ℭ

☆The Turkey Grill 8290 Woodward Avenue, Detroit, Michigan 313.872.4624

In his many trips throughout the South, George Lyles noticed that turkey was offered on menus more often in that part of the country than it was in Detroit. He also noticed that diners were becoming more health-conscious.   Given these insights, Lyles recognized an opportunity in the restaurant market and jumped on it, opening The Turkey Grill in February 1996. According to Lyles, his place is "the **Most Unique Concept in Carry-Out to Hit Detroit**."

But don't most people associate turkey with Thanksgiving dinner or with the humble turkey-and-mayo sandwiches afterwards? Think again, and get ready for The Turkey Grill's **Cajun-Fried Turkey Wings** (so tasty and tender, who knew?), its famous **Turkey Burgers** (with sautéed onions, green peppers, tomatoes, garlic, and spices), and **Turkey Kabobs**. Along with sandwiches, **Whole Turkeys, Smoked or Fried**, are also available. And there are lots of traditional side dishes to choose from. Weekends are for **Homemade Ice Cream** and **Lemon Cake** made on-site. All entrees are prepared upon ordering, so allow some time for your meal to arrive. Rest assured, however, that it *will* be worth the wait

and so well seasoned that you'll be ordering a second helping before finishing the first! Don't miss out!
$10 Whole Turkeys $20+

> **"Flood's is a nice, relaxing place with good food and great music. You can relax and be comfortable with your friends."** *Marcia and Frank Hayden, Educational Consultant / Contracts & Grants Manager*

Coffee House

Café Mahogany   1465 Centre, Downtown, Detroit, Michigan   313.963.6886

Whether you stop in for a game of chess, an **Espresso Wake-Me-Up** and a newspaper, or simply wish to check out the local arts and music scene, Café Mahogany guarantees a relaxed atmosphere, an international crowd, and plenty of cool vibes. Situated in Detroit's trendy Harmonie Park area, this trendy coffee shop is a must-stop for the restaurant-weary.   Plop into the overstuffed settees and indulge in an **Almond Joy Cappuccino**. By day, Café Mahogany serves up **Cappuccinos**, **Lattes**, **Deli Sandwiches,** and **Fresh-Baked Bagels**. By night, they serve up even more.   **Acid Jazz and Poetry on Tuesdays,** a **Comedy Showcase on Thursdays, Live Jazz on Fridays and Saturdays**, and **Hip-Hop After Hours from 2am–until? on Fridays**.
$10 ❒

Nightclubs

All Jokes Aside   2036 Woodward Avenue, Downtown, Detroit, Michigan   313.962.2100

All Joke's Aside features **Comedy at its Best**. The club showcases young nationally known and local comedy talents on Wednesday through Sunday nights. Each "nite" has a theme: there are **Apollo Nites, School Daze Nites** (which offer half-price admission to students with school ID), **Corporate Nites**, and the **Saturday Name Acts Nites**. Call for the calendar of events.
Cover charge ❒ 📱

☆Baker's Keyboard Lounge   20150 Livernois, Detroit, Michigan   313.345.6300

The **World's Oldest Jazz Club** started as a beer-and-sandwich stand when Christopher Baker first opened for business in 1934. In 1939, son Clarence took over and turned his father's place into what was to become a historic musical landmark. Since then, every jazz great from John Coltrane to Thelonius Monk to Earl Klugh has passed through the doors of Baker's Keyboard Lounge.

In May 1996, retired police officer John Colbert and his partner Juanita Jackson became the new owners of the famous establishment. Out went the dressing room for the stars; in came a **Full-Service Kitchen** featuring **Fried Livers and Gizzards, Catfish Dinners, Pork Chops,** and great **Chicken Wings**. Strategically placed mirrors were installed throughout to allow everyone in the club to see the musicians' heads as they play. To the delight of customers old and new, the renowned piano-shaped bar, designed in the Fifties, remained.   The new owners also continued the club's tradition of showcasing great local talent, offering **Live Jazz Saturday through Wednesday Evenings, Blues on Thursdays, and R&B Dance Nights on Fridays**. Most amazing of all is that there is no cover charge most nights to hear great music at Baker's Keyboard Lounge and to see where so many great jazz memories were made.

No Cover charge most nights/ $10 Dinner menu/ ☐ 🍷 🎼

Bert's Marketplace   2727 Russell, Eastern Market, Detroit, Michigan   313.567.2030

Bert's Marketplace has entertained nightcrawling Detroiters since 1969 when it was known as Bert's Black Horse Saloon on Gratiot Avenue. Through the years, Bert's has provided **Great Live Music, Good Soul Food**, and a comfortable environment in which to enjoy it all. The continental menu features "Superb Delights" like **Southern-Fried Catfish, Satchmo's Fried Whiting, The Bird's Fried Chicken Wings, John Coltrane's Corned Beef,** and **Billie Holiday's Turkey Burger**. Local and nationally known acts take center stage most evenings; call for an updated list of entertainers.

Cover charge/ $10–$15 Dinner menu/ ☐ 🍷 🎼

Bo Macs Lounge   281 Gratiot, Downtown, Detroit, Michigan   313.961.5152

Whether it's **Live Jazz on Thursday Evenings** or jumpin' to the jukebox on sleepy Tuesday nights, **There's Always a Party Going On at Bo Macs!** Proprietor and former barber Harry Bolling and his partner James McMurray have been drawing the crowds into their lounge for almost 10 years now. Bolling admits, however, that when he first entertained the notion of opening up a nightclub, he thought it would only take up a little of his free time. A decade later, he and McMurray have no free time but plenty of new and old friends who throng to their nightspot seven nights a week! The club's motto: "Come by, be yourself, relax, and let your hair down!"

Bo Macs caters to a mature crowd and features **Live Vocalists, R&B and Jazz Acts Thursday through Sunday**. Mondays and Tuesdays are meet-and-greet nights at the Lounge, with the jukebox providing the tunes. Of course, there's plenty of soul food (the **Ribs** are good here). A small cover charge applies on the weekends.

Cover charge/ 35+crowd/ ☐ ⛲ 𝄞

☆Flood's Bar & Grill   731 St. Antoine, Downtown, Detroit, Michigan   313.963.1090

No other club in Detroit attracts a more sophisticated group of regulars than Flood's. Proprietor Michael Byrd welcomes a lively professional crowd to his nightspot's spacious art deco-inspired interior. With its large, marble-topped rectangular bar located smack-dab in the center of the room, Flood's is the perfect place to see and be seen. Networking is the buzzword here. **Happy Hour** is *the* time to work the floor, but later in the evening on most nights you've got to kick back and enjoy the **Live Entertainment** ranging from **Jazz to R&B**.

Traditional bar food is nowhere to be found at Flood's. Sure they have **Chicken Wings**, but so good are they that the chef calls them "Soul Style" (the secret's in the seasoning!). And don't miss the **Butterfly Shrimp** or the **Southern-Fried Pork Chops**. But the real reason to come to Flood's is to be a part of a positive social scene that is desperately missing in most cities yet so badly needed and very much in demand everywhere.

Cover charge/ 25+ crowd/ $10–$15 Dinner menu/ ☐ ⛲ 𝄞

The Limit   15535 West Eight Mile, N.W., Detroit, Michigan 313.341.8000

Norman McKenzie got more than he bargained for when he opened The Limit in 1993. "I was a retired policeman, looking for something to do in my spare time," he explains. "I looked into several options and decided on a bar. I thought I would come in, serve a couple of drinks, go home. I didn't expect all this." What McKenzie didn't know was that he was about to open one of the hottest nightclubs in northeast Detroit. (Hey, most club owners should have such problems!) One reason for The Limit's success is that the club caters to a preferred crowd: the 35-and-older set. It also features **Live Music** most nights, **Karaoke** on Mondays, and dancing on Wednesdays, Fridays, and Saturdays. And there's plenty of great soul food to enjoy, from **Fried Catfish**, **Pork Chops**, and **Chicken Wings**, to **Macaroni and Cheese**, **Greens**, and **Candied Yams**. The only thing there's no limit to at The Limit is the good times you'll have!

Cover charge/ 35+ crowd/ $10 Dinner menu/ ☐ ♟ ♫ ♫ V

Caterers

Glenn Williams Catering   2401 Twentieth Street, Detroit, Michigan   313.964.3001

At age 22, Glenn Williams was the first Black executive chef at the esteemed Detroit Club. During his 18 years there, he gained citywide recognition and began building a huge network of clients and business associates. Since striking out on his own he has gained scores of clients, from the mayor's office to large corporations. Glenn Williams Catering has provided service to them all. Although Williams claims that his favorite challenge is to create totally new dishes, he can whip up almost any menu requested. His range of culinary skills spans the globe, from **German**, **Italian**, or **Soul** to **Kosher** (he was trained in a kosher kitchen at age 14). And, as a **Full-Service Caterer**, he can also arrange for tents or valet service, help in selecting a color scheme, whatever needs to be done.

FORT LAUDERDALE & VICINITY

Casual Dining

☆Betty's Restaurant & Catering 601 N.W. 22nd Road, Fort Lauderdale, Florida 954.583.9121

When Betty Taylor jokingly offered to buy the small luncheonette where she worked from her employer in 1980, she really didn't expect him to reply, "Sold!" Two years later, Betty's had outgrown its original location and she moved her business to its current site, where she continues to serve up some of the best soul food in the state of Florida. Yet, with the daily shopping for the restaurant and raising three kids, Taylor still finds time to participate in community activities. She provides meals to feed the homeless, caters lunches for almost a dozen local schools daily, and helps with special events at Mount Bethel Baptist Church. She also does recruitment work for the NAACP, encouraging her patrons to join via a large neon sign hanging in front of her restaurant as a reminder.

Most days you can find Taylor herself in the kitchen, overseeing every meal that goes out of the door. In the dining area, you'll find local politicians, national celebrities, sports figures, and devoted regulars savoring her restaurant's delicious **Southern-Style Cooking**. **Breakfast** doesn't get any better than at Betty's, with your choice of **Chopped Steak with Onions, Smothered Pork Chops, Stewed Snapper**, all served with **Eggs** and **Hot Biscuits**. **Lunch** and **Dinner** selections range from terrific **Fried Chicken, Meat Loaf**, and **Fried Jumbo Shrimp**, to **Stew Beef** and **Smothered Ribs,** with a wide selection of vegetable sides to choose from. Top off your meal with delicious **Hot Cornbread** and plenty of sweet **Homemade Lemonade**, and you'll leave this homey restaurant with just one thought on your mind: "What will I order for breakfast at Betty's tomorrow?"

$10 ❑ ✓ ₵

Cooke's Goose Restaurant & Cocktail Lounge
3750 North State Road 7, Lauderdale Lakes, Florida
954.484.1566

Merton Cooke, proprietor of the Cooke's Goose Restaurant and the nearby Jamaican Herbal & Healing Shop is a real jack-of-all-trades. Prior to coming to Florida in 1991, Cooke owned a number of different businesses in Jamaica. From pawn shop to dry cleaners to restaurants, his expertise was challenged, but his hard work was always rewarded. In search of new opportunities, Cooke eventually moved his family to Fort Lauderdale, where he and his wife opened the Cook's Goose restaurant and lounge. Once again, success followed.

Mr. Cooke prides himself on the fact that his establishment is clean, its food delicious and affordably priced—good reasons, indeed, for anyone to stop by. Cooke's Goose features a large, rustic dining area and a **Full Bar**. Around back is a small **Banquet Room**, great for private parties, equipped with its own bar and **Dance Floor**. Mrs. Cooke is responsible for the good smells coming from the kitchen. You can look forward to her **Authentic Jamaican Specialties** such as **Escoveitch Fish**, **Ackee and Salt Fish**, **Curried Chicken**, and, of course, **Jerk Pork**. A must try is Mr. Cooke's favorite dessert: **Sweet Potato Pudding topped with Rum Cream**.

$10 □ ✓ (〴 🖫🎥

☆Riverwalk Eatery   215 S.W. 2nd Street,
Fort Lauderdale, Florida   954.760.4373

Former model Elizabeth W. Adams started preparing meals for herself when she became tired of eating out. Little did she realize that she had a real hidden talent for cooking. Much to Adams's surprise and delight, friends and colleagues enjoyed her dishes so much that requests for catering started coming in a bit too quickly. So, it was off to culinary school, where she was told by seasoned chefs that formal training would be a waste of her time, there was little left to teach her! Subsequently, she and her husband David moved to Fort Lauderdale, where they opened the Riverwalk Eatery, featuring fine **American Cuisine** with Elizabeth's own creative interpretations flavoring each dish.

Warm and inviting just like its owners, the Riverwalk Eatery doesn't disappoint in atmosphere or cuisine. Upon entering its doors, one cannot help but smile. Bright colors surround you at every angle, giving the room a tropical, "Key West" kind of feeling. Everything on the menu is beautifully presented. From the **Vegetarian's Delight** to the **Chili and Cheese Baked Potato** to the **Riverwalk Super Burger**, no dish will taste like any you have ever had before! (Sorry, no secrets are offered!) The Eatery's **Chili and Cornbread** was hailed as "the best" by nationally known gourmet Chef Tell at the recent "Taste of Fort Lauderdale" event. Indeed, Adams's Cornbread is the most unique I've ever tasted and quite possibly the best in the country. Do yourself a favor, get over there now!

$10–$15 ☐ ✓ 🖢 🖺

Tom Jenkins Bar-B-Q   1236 South Federal Highway, Fort Lauderdale, Florida   954.522.5046

Gary Torrence and Harry Harrell were college roommates who got their start in the barbecue business cooking ribs for their Omega Psi Phi fraternity parties. Once out of school, both went to work for computer giant IBM. Soon disenchanted with corporate life, Gary and Harry started selling barbecue ribs and chicken out of a trailer parked by the side of the road on Federal Highway 1. For five years, folks lined up outside that trailer, the aroma of the ribs their only advertising. When a prime location became available right across the street from their trailer, Gary and Harry began building their dream restaurant from scratch. Their wives pitched in to design and decorate the interior, giving the place a cute, western motif. The result of this hardworking four-some's efforts is a comfortable atmosphere conducive to family dining.

The sauce at Tom Jenkins Bar-B-Q is mild yet tangy and the perfect complement to the smoky, tender **Ribs,** which are marinated in Gary and Harry's own special blend of seasonings and then slow-cooked over a wood grill. The **Chopped Pork** and **Chicken** are a real barbecue-lover's treat, as are the traditional sides of **Collard Greens**, **Macaroni and Cheese**, and **Baked Beans**.
$10/ Slabs of Ribs slightly more/ ☐ ✓ 🖢

☆Tom's Place   7251 North Federal Highway, Boca Raton, Florida   561.997.0920

"We give God the glory" is the motto at Tom's Place. And indeed, the level of professionalism of all who work there, from bus boys to management, is impressive. This place should be a mandatory stop for everyone passing through southern Florida! One of the first things you'll notice is the cleanliness of owner Tom Wright's establishment. Then there are the hundreds of photographs gracing the walls that tell the story of Wright's career in the restaurant business from the very beginning in the Fifties when he worked as a dishwasher. There's the picture of his first place, a shotgun-style shack filled to capacity with hungry patrons and with another 50 or so folks waiting patiently outside. There's also a more recent shot of him mugging for the camera with boxing promoter Don King.

After many hard years of working in every capacity of restaurant duties, Wright opened Tom's Place, Boca Raton's first barbecue restaurant in 1977. Over the years, not only has his restaurant become known as **Boca's Premier Barbecue Spot**, but its reputation for great **Barbecued Ribs, Chicken, Sliced Beef, and Pork** has grown worldwide. The house favorites come topped with a choice of three barbecue sauces—mild and sweet, hot and spicy, or mustard-based—but ask Wright to describe the taste of his famous sauces and his only reply is: "Good, good, good, good!" Tom's also serves an assortment of flavorful homemade sides, including **Mashed Potatoes, Black-Eyed Peas, Corn on the Cob, Collard Greens**, and **Fried Okra**.

$10–$20   □ ✓(🌽🍖

Take-Out Dining

☆**Jerk Machine**
   18352 N.W. 7th Avenue, Miami, Florida
      305.652.9888
   18719 South Dixie Highway, Perrine, Florida
      305.254.9888
   4261 N.W. 12th Street, Lauderhill, Florida
      954.321.8556
   637 South Street Road 7, Hollywood, Florida
      954.962.9992
   8085 Oakland Park Boulevard, Sunrise, Florida
      954.749.8877

What can you say about a couple who catered their own wedding? (After all, they are the best caterers in town!) Desmond and Katherine Malcolm, owners of all five Jerk Machine locations, left Toronto, Canada, in 1989 for southern Florida. Once there, the Malcolms realized that no one was preparing or serving **Good, Quick Jamaican Food** to satisfy the lunchtime crowd. So, with one oven and a second-hand refrigerator, the first Jerk Machine was born. Word spread rapidly that "take-out Jamaican" was available in Fort Lauderdale—hot, authentic, and ready in three to four minutes! Four more units opened soon after, and Jerk Machine was on its way to becoming the Boston Market of Jamaican food with its catchy motto: "We don't joke, we jerk!"

Jerk Machine serves some of the best **Jerk Chicken** you will ever taste—tender and just spicy enough, with extra jerk sauce available for real hotstuff diehards. **Jerk Fish**, **Brown Stew Fish**, **Stew Beef**, **Jerk Pork**, **Oxtails**, and **Curried Goat** are just a sampling of some of the other menu items available, along with **Jamaican Ginger Beer**, **Ting**, and other favorite island drinks. Oh, and by the way, the Malcolms still cater large corporate parties, special events, and, of course, weddings!

$10 ✓₵

Nightclubs

Krystals Restaurant & Lounge   451 North State Road 7, Plantation, Florida   954.792.4111

Krystals Restaurant & Lounge always has something going on: **Live Jazz Mondays, Ladies Night and Comedy on Tuesdays, Exotic Dancers on Thursdays,** and **Dance Music on the Weekends.** This upscale club boast three bars, a large dance floor, a semiprivate VIP room in the back, and a huge **Banquet Room** upstairs. Its **Full-Service Restaurant** offers an extensive menu featuring American–Caribbean cuisine, and the kitchen stays open 'til late, serving up specialties of the house from **Curried Goat** to **Brown Stew Fish** to **Baby Back Ribs.**

Cover charge/ 25+ crowd / $10–$20 Dinner menu/ ☐ ⌾ ⌾

Memory Lane Café   4220 North State Road 7, Lauderdale Lakes, Florida   954.739.5112

Memory Lane Café features Reggae, Soca, R&B, and more on the weekends for Fort Lauderdale's mature adult crowd. Fridays after work, the party starts off right with **Specially Priced Drinks** and a **Buffet. Two Large Bars,** a great **Dance Floor**, and the club's striking hardwood interior accents make Memory Lane a great place to fall into after a long week of work.

Cover charge / 25+ crowd / ☐ 🍶

Peppermint Restaurant & Lounge   3801 West Broward Boulevard, Plantation, Florida   954.327.1400

Roger Freeman, no stranger to the club scene, has brought yet another first-class nightspot to the Fort Lauderdale area. The Peppermint Restaurant & Lounge is a brand-spanking new, beautiful upscale club/restaurant. Its interior is colorful with an authentic tropical Caribbean flair. This club has it all: **After-Work Happy Hours** with **Live Mellow Music, Deejay-Spun Club Music after Midnight, Live Entertainment on Saturdays** (including R&B and jazz), **"Retro" Music Nights**—the list goes on and on. The main room holds up to 400 people and features three bars as well as semiprivate party and VIP lounges. What's more, the **Full-Service Restaurant**, offering an array of southern delights, is open all night!

Cover charge/ $15-$20 Dinner menu/ ☐ 🍶 🎁

HOUSTON

Casual Dining

Drexler's Bar-B-Q   2020 Dowling, Houston, Texas
713.752.0008

The decor at this Houston establishment is "strictly Clyde"—basketball superstar Clyde "The Glide" Drexler, that is. Showcases containing Drexler's autographed shoes and Wheaties boxes featuring his image, sports action posters, and basketball-shaped lamps are everywhere to be seen. And of course, there's also a couple of TV's for watching Drexler and his team play during the season. But while "The Glide" may make personal appearances to this restaurant during special events, he has nothing to do with the great-smelling barbecue coming from the kitchen. That credit goes to James Drexler, Jr.: Clyde's father and the proprietor of Drexler's Bar-B-Q since 1982. James Drexler acquired the restaurant from his brother, who started it in 1966. Altogether, the Drexler family can boast a total of 75 years in the barbecue business, having preserved and passed down great family recipes from one generation to the next.

Drexler's offers a narrow, neat menu of **Barbecued Ribs, Hot Links, Chopped Beef,** and **Chicken** along with **Char-Grilled Burgers** and traditional sides like **Baked Beans, Potato Salad,** and **Fries**. It's a clean, family-oriented place, perfect for "gettin' down" with a heaping plate of spicy barbecue specialties while listening to equally hot zydeco music coming from the jukebox.
$10 ☐ Beer Served

☆Reggae Hut   4814 Almeda Boulevard,
Houston, Texas   713.524.2905

With its funky, handpainted tabletops that pay tribute to the likes of reggae greats Bob Marley and Steel Pulse, the Reggae Hut is a prime example of how far a little hard work and imagination can get you. The brainchild of architect Kevin Bingham, executive chef (and Jamaican native) André Walker, and restauranteur Gary Mosley, this popular Caribbean eatery brings a

Global Diaspora air to the Houston scene. It is run by manager Guy Grigsby, who also lent his creativity to the fabulous interior decor. Together these four have created a dining space where the mood is mellow and the "cookin' is done with a whole lot of soul"!

The Reggae Hut serves "authentic Jamaican food and vibe." Main entrees include **Curried Goat**, **Brown Stew Chicken**, **Red Snapper with Bones**, **Curried Shrimp**, **Oxtails**, **Garlic Crab**, and **Jerk Chicken**. **Cocoa Bread** and **Vegetable Patties** are favorite side dishes. **Fresh Fruit Smoothies**, **Irish Moss**, **Peanut Butter Punch**, and **Jamaican Colas** add to the "home-style island flava." **Poetry readings** are frequent happenings at the Reggae Hut, and local artists are welcomed to display their work for sale or view.

$10 ☐ ✓¢ 🎨

RJ's Rib Joint   2515 Riverside Drive, Houston, Texas
713.521.9601

RJ's Rib Joint looks nothing like its name implies. Hardly a "joint" and located in an upscale residential neighborhood, RJ's is actually a cozy, wood-paneled bistro, complete with Tiffany lamps and baskets of hanging plants. Its **Cocktail Lounge** features comfortable high-back stools, making sitting at the bar almost too pleasurable, and the extensive menu specializes in far more than ribs. Come to RJ's, and along with its signature **Baby Back Ribs**, check out the **Snapper Royale with Shrimp Cream Sauce**, **Flounder Stuffed with Shrimp and Crabmeat**, **Chicken-Fried Steak**, **Rib-Eye Steak**, and **Grilled Shrimp**—just a few of the tempting dishes featured.

$10–$15 ☐ 🍷

Cafeteria/Buffet-Style Dining

Alfreda's Cafeteria   5101 Almeda, Houston, Texas
713.523.6462

Mary Green, proprietor of Alfreda's Cafeteria, has been in the business for over 31 years. Her childhood dream was to own a restaurant, so when the opportunity came along to "take the plunge" and buy one, Green grabbed it, with no prior experience, just a love for cooking! According to Green, she spent the last of her savings, seven thousand dollars, on "something I didn't know a thing about." Six months later, she had netted more than seven times that amount. Needless to say, she never looked back! During the turbulent Eighties, Green opened and closed several other restaurants, yet she always maintained her original location. Today, Alfreda's, named after her daughter, continues to serve "real old-fashioned soul food" and delicious "American home-cooked meals"—just the way you'd expect them to be.

According to Green, the cooks at Alfreda's prepare over a hundred pounds of yams, nearly a hundred bunches of mustard greens, and tons of potatoes daily. House specialties include **Baked Chicken**, **Smothered Steak**, **Greens**, and **Macaroni and Cheese**. You'll also love the **Homemade Biscuits**, **Peach Cobbler**, and Alfreda's famous **Lemon Ice-Box Pie with Vanilla Wafer Crust**. (Better than grandma's? Yes! Thanks, Mary, for taking us back to our childhood!)
$10

Creole's Louisiana Cuisine   2933 Walnut Bend, Houston, Texas   713.785.2340

Louisiana-born Raymond Herbert comes from a family of restauranteurs, so he always had a pretty good idea what he was going to be when he grew up. His parents own the Creole Lunch House in Lafayette, Louisiana, where young Raymond was assigned to every duty that needed to be done. When he headed out on his own for Houston, he knew exactly what type of restaurant he wanted to open: one that serves **Down-Home Creole, South-western Louisiana Cooking** just like mom and dad's! Despite numerous challenges locating a suitable site, Herbert found the perfect spot across the street from several large office complexes filled with scores of hungry lunchtime patrons, and Creole's Louisiana Cuisine was born.

Since its opening in 1995, Creole's has met with rave reviews and brisk business. Entrees change daily, but the house specialty, **Creole's Stuffed Bread** (a tasty sandwich filled with meat, sausage, cheese and jalapeno peppers), **Chicken Fricassee**, and **Red Beans and Sausage** are givens. Other favorites include

Crawfish Fettucine, Catfish Courtboullion, and **Fried Pork Chops**.
$10 ☐ ✓ ₵

D's Delicious Creole Soul Café & Catering
4987 Martin Luther King Jr. Boulevard, Houston, Texas 713.641.1165

Located in a mainly uninteresting strip mall is a tiny café that serves up some very exciting and tasty food. The small dining area at D's has only six tables, but executive chef and owner Duane Davis has infused the place with a light, artistic ambiance, colorful decor, African American prints, and ceiling fans for that southern, front-porch feeling. Is this place great, or what?! The food is served cafeteria-style and it looks, smells, and is fresh and appetizing. **Cajun Baked Fish, Crawfish Etoufee, Down-Home Chitterlings, Creole Gumbo, Bayou Boudin, Dirty Rice,** and **Cajun Cornbread** are just a few of the house offerings.
$10 ✓ ₵

☆Family Café 2712 Blodgett, Houston, Texas
713.520.8444

When Henry Gillum retired from his job at Grocers Supply Company, he was offered the opportunity to open a cafeteria serving hot lunches to the employees. When the company decided to automate its dining facilities, Gillum had to find another location for his lunch business. In 1983, Gillum opened Family Café, featuring **Southern-Style Home Cooking**, cafeteria service, and a spacious, comfortable dining area that can seat up to 250. In 1991, Gillum passed away. His daughter, Mary Baker, carries on the family tradition by continuing to offer Houstonians delicious hot foods, made fresh daily and served family-style.

The menu at the Family Café changes daily, based on the quality and availability of fresh produce and meats. (If the goods are not up to Baker's standards, she won't use them!) **Breakfast** starts at 7am, and selections include **Porkchops, Chapel Hill Beef Sausage, Pancakes,** and **Eggs** prepared any way you like them. The **Lunch/Dinner** cafeteria line typically features **BBQ Beef, Ribs, Liver and Onions, Ham Hocks, Broiled Chicken, Cabbage, Yams, Corn on the Cob,** and **Million Dollar Pie**

(made with cream cheese, pineapple, pecans, and cool whip). Try not to step over people to get to the dessert selection, OK?
$10 ☐ ✓€ 🎁

☆Houston's This Is It   207 Gray, Houston, Texas 713.659.1608

When husband-and-wife team Frank and Matty Jones decided to open a soul food restaurant in the late Fifties, they scoured their Fourth-Ward Houston neighborhood for the perfect location. It wasn't until Matty Jones stepped into the hallway of a house just a few blocks from their home that she smiled and exclaimed, "This is *the* place!! This is it! This is it!" The house subsequently became Houston's This Is It, opening in 1958 and flourishing in that location for the next 22 years. Two moves later, This Is It has gone full circle and is presently located right across the street from the house where the Joneses have lived for the past 50 years! When grandson Craig Joseph took over the family business, his vision was to purchase a lot and erect the perfect building for the restaurant's needs. Although This Is It had a 30-year track record of success, it took four years and eight different lenders before Joseph could secure a loan to realize his dream! He did, though, and the new This Is It is *all that*! It was even featured in the recent movie *Jason's Lyric*.

On any given day, This Is It's buffet line is filled with anxious, hungry folks, patiently waiting their turns and trying to decide which of the three vegetables sides they will select to complement their meals. The dining room is typically packed with folks seated family-style at long tables that stretch the width of the room. Some diners make conversation with the persons sitting next to them. Others keep to themselves, glancing up only to look at the walls of this pleasant establishment, which are covered with photos of famous celebrity diners—including former President George Bush—who may have enjoyed the same meal. The menu changes daily, but rest assured, most days the cafeteria line will feature the restaurant's famous **Baked Chicken, BBQ Rib Ends, Ox Tails, Pork Chops, Chitterlings,** and **Turkey Wings**. There are also lots of sides to choose from. **Breakfast** is served from 6:30 am. This Is It also offers **Catering Services**, with numerous entertainment, corporate, and political clients to its credit.
$10 ☐ ✓€

Mama's Oven   9295 South Main, Houston, Texas 713.661.3656

When Rachel Blake first jogged by the empty storefront that would later become Mama's Oven, she thought to herself: This space would be good for something, but what? The idea of opening a soul food restaurant came to her one day while she was craving some good ol' home-cooking but didn't feel like going out to get it. So, Rachel took a leave of absence from her job, rented the space, hired a cook, bought some tables and chairs, and Mama's Oven was born. Word spread quickly that there was a soul food restaurant in the neighborhood, and business took off! **Located just two blocks away from the Astrodome,** Mama's Oven features **"Old-Fashioned Country Cooking."** **Oxtails, Cornish Hens, Pork Chops, Honey Glazed Ham, Turkey Wings**, and **Meatloaf** are just some of the menu offerings, and **Unlimited Cornbread** comes with your meal. **Breakfast** is served all day long.

$10 ☐ ✓ℂ

Take-Out Dining

☆Frenchy's Chicken   3919 Scott Street, Houston, Texas   713.748.2233

When Percy Creuzot moved to Houston from Louisiana in 1963, he was amazed at the lack of seasoning in the foods he found there. This gave him the idea to go into the food service business. He found a great location one block from the campuses of the University of Houston and Texas Southern University, and on July 3, 1969, opened Frenchy's Po-Boy. Unfortunately, Texans didn't know a thing about oyster Po-Boy sandwiches. But they knew fried chicken, and they soon discovered that the fried chicken at Frenchy's has what other places didn't. It's crispy and flavorful, and seasoned just enough to wake up the tastebuds without setting them on fire. Soon, Frenchy's Po-Boy became Frenchy's Chicken, and Creuzot's take-out became the place for quick, delicious food among the college crowd.

The biggest sellers at Frenchy's are the spicy **Chicken Wings**—so good, you'll be ordering more before you finish licking your fingers from the first batch. **Oyster, Shrimp** and **Hot**

Sausage Po-Boy Sandwiches are still on the menu as well as other Creole specialties like **Gumbo**, **Red Beans**, **Greens**, **Jambalaya**, and **Sweet Potato Pie with Praline Pecan Topping**. It's all *tres bon, n'est pas? Mai oui!*
$10 ✓ ℂ

☆Harlon's Bar-B-Q Houses
11403 Martin Luther King Jr. Boulevard,
Houston, Texas   713.738.2737
6930 Martin Luther King Jr. Boulevard,
Houston, Texas   713.733.5687
Houston Intercontinental Airport, Terminal C
William P. Hobby Airport

They say everything is big in Texas. Harlon Brooks is a big man, with a big, beautiful smile, and a big love for barbecue. He has an even bigger love for his family, his community, and his hard-working staff, all of whom have made the Harlon's Bar-B-Q House chain the success it is today. Brooks started his career by working up the corporate ladder. When he hit the "glass ceiling," he left to take a job as the custodian at his church. It was there that he learned how to prepare excellent barbecue. His grill skills got so good that in 1977 he opened the first Harlon's Bar-B-Q in his own South Houston neighborhood. He opened another location in the same area in 1982, just before the booming Texas economy began to go bust. When it did, his sales dropped by more than half, and, as Harlon recalls, he and his staff "had to *really* learn how to do business." And they did. Offering full-service catering helped turn things around, as did a contract with the Houston Airport authority, which led to the opening of two Harlon's outlets at Houston Intercontinental Airport and one at William P. Hobby Airport. More locations are on the way, but the heart of Harlon's Bar-B-Q remains in South Houston, where one man's big vision continues to provide needed jobs and direction for young people hungry for role models and opportunities. Harlon's business philosophy is simple: "When your pastures are real green, sometimes you think you don't have to plant any more. But we have to keep growing. We have to be in a position so we can give a hand up."

According to the owner, Harlon's barbecue is "prepared with time and patience...on the best pits, with hickory wood...using the same recipes we used over 20 years ago." The sauce, he claims, is "spicy and sweet." The 6930 MLK Boulevard location serves a hot

Soul Food Lunch Buffet seven days a week, featuring all the soul food favorites. And then there's Harlon's famous **Stuffed Baked Potato**, served at all locations, which is a meal in itself, piled high with chopped barbecue and weighing about two pounds!
$10 Slabs of Ribs slightly higher/ ❏ ✓ ℭ

Ice Cream Parlor

☆Hank's Ice Cream   9291 South Main, Houston, Texas 713.665.5103

Hank Wiggins grew up at his grandmother's knee, watching her in the kitchen and learning how to make homemade cakes and ice cream. As a boy, he vowed that he would one day own his own ice cream parlor. Years later, he did just that (with the help of his wife Okemah), and, man, did Hank learn his lessons well! **Located only two blocks from the Astrodome**, Hank's Ice Cream serves **Some of the Best and Most Innovative Frozen Dairy Concoctions** in all of Houston.

Hank's #1 flavor is **Butter Pecan.** What's so innovative about that, you ask? Well, Hank uses whole pecan halves, roasted with a special secret something added to them, and the nuts are folded, not blended, into the mix. Can't you just *taste* the TLC? Other outstanding flavors include **Cinnanna** (a combo of bananas and cinnamon), **Soursop** (a Caribbean-inspired delight), **Irish Cream**, and **Mango**.
$10

Nightclubs

☆Ambiance   5851 Southwest Freeway, Houston, Texas 713.661.6829

In Houston, this is where the party's at! Another Charles Bush production, Ambiance has it all: Up front, a big, splashy, upscale interior offers **Two Large Bars, TV/Video Monitors**, and split-level floors for maximum scoping and posing. On Friday nights, you'll find wall-to-wall people, several birthday parties going on at once, plenty of major networking happening at the bar, and lots of styling and profiling all over the place while **Urban Contemporary**, **R&B**, **Funk**, and **Old-School Music** pumps the crowd. In the back, a **Three-Piece Jazz Combo** entertains those taking a time-out. Nightly events include **Ladies Nights**, **Live Bands**, **Oldies Nights**, etc.

Cover charge/ 25+ crowd/ ☐ ᵞᵉ ᵉᵍᵉ

☆Midtown Live   3400 Montrose, 10th floor   Houston, Texas   713.942.8777

There are many reasons to party at Midtown Live. First, there is the spectacular view of downtown Houston from the sweeping outdoor patio, which features live entertainment. The cast iron street lamps give the patio a romantic, French Quarter air, perfect for stargazing with a new acquaintance! Indoors, **Live Jazz** from some of the city's very best bands or **Pumping Dance Music** moves the crowd. Whether it's for a birthday celebration, an after-work get-together, or simply to wind down from a hard week, Midtown Live is live and the place to do it all!

Cover charge/ 25+ crowd/ ☐ ᵞᵉ 🎵

The Phoenix   64 Woodlake Square, Houston, Texas   713.453.1355

The Phoenix is the **Largest Black-Owned Club in Houston.** With 15,000 square feet of space, it can hold over a thousand people easily. For practical purposes, the club is split in two. The front half has **Two Large Oak Dance Floors**, **Two Bars**, **Six Pool Tables**, **Video Capability**, **Light Shows**, and an **Upstairs VIP Section**. The back half is where the concert stage showcases **Nationally Known and Local Acts**. Great club, great facilities!

Cover charge/ 25+ crowd/ ☐ ᵞᵉ 🎵 ᵉᵍᵉ

KANSAS CITY, MISSOURI & VICINITY

Casual Dining

☆Arthur Bryant's   1727 Brooklyn, Kansas City, Missouri   816.231.1123

Armed with a degree in agriculture from Prairie View A&M in 1931, Calvert, Texas native Arthur Bryant faced a crucial decision: accept a position as a high school agriculture teacher in his home state, or move to Kansas City to join his brother Charlie, who was working in a restaurant and establishing quite a reputation as a barbecue expert. Arthur chose the latter. Over the next 15 years, he too would master the art of barbecue. In 1946, Charlie retired and Arthur took over, adding his own personal touches to the business. His restaurant's reputation for fine barbecue spread across the country. Former presidents Harry S. Truman and Jimmy Carter, big-name celebrities, and grateful locals alike have come from far and wide to experience Arthur's **Award-Winning Barbecue.**

After Arthur Bryant passed away in 1982, the Brooklyn Barbecue Company acquired the leasing rights to his business. The company continues to uphold the traditions established by the Bryant brothers so long ago. Indeed, manager Eddie Echols guarantees that your Arthur Bryant's Restaurant experience will be memorable and delicious. The menu offers, of course, **Ribs—by the slab or pulled**—big, messy **Sandwiches of Sliced Beef, Turkey**, and **Ham**, and all the **Pickles** you want. **Fries** and **Baked Beans** round out the menu.

$10 Slabs of Ribs slightly more / ☐ ✓ ℭ

"The food is delicious and the service outstanding! You owe it to yourself to visit Gates Bar-B-Q!"
Buck O'Neil, Chairman, Negro League Baseball Museum

☆**Gates Bar-B-Q**
>**47th & The Paseo, Kansas City, Missouri**
>**816.923.0900**
>**Linwood & Main, Kansas City, Missouri**
>**816.753.0828**
>**1221 Brooklyn, Kansas City, Missouri**
>**816.483.3880**
>**10440 East 40 Highway, Independence,**
>**Missouri 816.353.5880**
>**10th & State, Kansas City, Kansas 913.621.1134**
>**103rd & State Line Road, Leawood, Kansas**
>**913.383.1752**

"Hi, may I help you?" Anyone who has ever visited Kansas City has undoubtedly eaten at Gates Bar-B-Q and was met with that establishment's signature greeting. Gates is arguably the most famous African American-owned barbecue restaurant in the United States. The story behind its evolution is a relatively simple one: After years of working for the railroad, George Gates and his wife Arzelia decided to try their hands at selling barbecue. In 1946, they opened the first Gates Bar-B-Q at 19th and Vine. Their reputation for excellent barbecue spread across the city, and soon they opened a second location on 12th and Brooklyn. In 1960, George Gates passed away and his son Ollie took over the business, transforming his parents' foundation into the barbecue empire it is today. They say that Ollie Gates used to determine where to open his next location by sitting outside his restaurants and noting the license plates of the customers who pulled up. Well, it must have worked because Gates Bar-B-Q presently has six locations in the Kansas City area and it's still growing!

Now, about that **Award-Winning Barbecue**! Gates's mild barbecue sauce is thick and just sweet enough not to overpower the well-smoked and tender, tender **Ribs**, **Beef Sausage**, **Mutton**, **Chicken**, and **Sliced Beef**, **Ham** or **Turkey—just a few of the** meats the restaurants' able staff work their magic on. **Bar-B-Q Beans** and Gates's **Yummy "Yammer" (Sweet Potato) Pie** are must-have orders to complete the Gates experience. Gates even has its **own Credit Card for Frequent Diners** and for ordering their famous **Bar-B-Q Sauces and Spices by Mail**! And it's a good thing, too. After returning home and going through "Gates Bar-B-Q withdrawal," a bottle of Gates Bar-B-Q Sauce may be the only thing that can save you!

$10 Slabs of Ribs slightly more/ ☐ / Beer served

G's Jamaican Quisine Restaurant and Bar
7940 Troost Avenue, Kansas City, Missouri
816.333.9566

"A taste for the food and a feel for the music." That's how Raquel Ricketts describes the restaurant she and her husband George own and operate. Realizing that Kansas City had many barbecue places but very few Caribbean restaurants, George seized the opportunity to introduce the area to Raquel's cooking. G's Jamaican Quisine has delighted tourists and locals ever since. The objective at G's is to take their customers' memories back to when they may have vacationed in the Caribbean or, if they have never had the pleasure, to give them a taste of what a visit to the islands would be like.

G's Jamaican Quisine is a casual, come-as-you-are kind of place, complete with a **Bar** and a **Pool Room**. On the weekends, the restaurant is host to local deejays, who spin R&B oldies and reggae music till 1:30am. Dinner features Caribbean favorites such as **Jerk Chicken, Curried Chicken and Goat, Cow Feet, Escoveitch Fish**, and **Brown Stew Chicken**. Popular Jamaican drinks like **Irish Moss, Sorrel**, and **Ginger Beer** are also served.

$10–$15 ☐ ✓ € 🍷

Hayward's Pit Bar-B-Que   11051 South Antioch, Overland Park, Kansas   913.451.8080

Since Hayward Spears arrived in Kansas City, he's been obsessed with barbecue. He built a pit in his backyard and worked constantly to develop his own special barbecue technique, quickly earning a reputation as a barbecue master. In 1972, he opened his own restaurant—a large, rustic, family-style place that pays tribute to the days of the Wild, Wild West. Today, it's easy to see why the restaurant's slogan claims, "The name Hayward's is synonymous with barbecue in Kansas City." As Spears notes, over nine tons of barbecued meats are perfectly prepared at his restaurant and served to more than 10,000 regular guests *each week*! The restaurant also features a new **Private Banquet Facility** that can seat up to 140 people and includes a full bar.

Hayward's award-winning menu consists of **Ribs, Burnt Ends, Rib Tips, Sliced Beef, Ham, Pork**, and **Turkey, Smoked Sausage**, and **Chicken**. Pass on the cole slaw; the **Over-Sized Fries** and **Onion Rings** are the way to go!

$10–$20 ☐ ✓ € 🍴

> **"You haven't REALLY experienced breakfast until you have been to Maxine's! Everything is great!"**
> *Randall C. Ferguson, Jr., President,*
> *Board of Directors, Negro Leagues Baseball Museum*

☆Hot Tamale Brown's Cajun Express Restaurant
10 West 39th Street, Kansas City, Missouri 816.561.2020

"★★★★" (*Kansas City Star*), **"Best Lemonade"** (*Kansas City* magazine). That's big praise for a little take-out restaurant located in a former bank building. Festively decorated in Mardi Gras colors and posters, Hot Tamale Brown's unique concept of "semi-fast" Cajun food is the brainchild of its proprietor, Willie Brown. Since the Forties, Brown's Lake Charles, Louisiana family has been known for their **Cajun-Style Tamales**, which differ from Mexican tamales in that they include vegetables with the seasoned meat wrapped in cornmeal dough. With Willie's wife Rosalind preparing the family's recipes, the menu at Hot Tamale Brown's offers the best of Louisiana cooking. **Bourbon Street Hot Tamales, Crawfish Etoufee, Red Beans and Rice, Jambalaya, Chili, File Gumbo, Mint Lemonade**, and **Sweet Cajun Coffee** make up the narrow but tempting menu, but then again, with a selection like that, what else do you need? **Indoor and Outdoor Seating** as well as **Drive-Thru Service** are available.

$10 ☐ 🏍

☆Luther's Finest Bar B Q   8611 Hauser Drive, Lenexa, Kansas 913.438.4238

Luther Tooks began his love affair with barbecue over 20 years ago in Memphis. Working out of his backyard barbecue pit, Luther did quite a bit of barbecue catering, perfecting his unique slow-cooking techniques and special seasonings mix and identifying the right blend of woods to give his barbecue the rich, smoky flavor he is now known for. His corporate job eventually moved him and his family to Kansas City, where his big break came in the form of being laid off (this part we can *all* identify with!). Tooks took that opportunity to make his dream come true, opening Luther's Finest in 1994.

According to Tooks, his restaurant serves only foods he personally likes, using only "top-quality meats and beef, tender as a mother's love." The menu at Luther's Finest features **Ribs, Rib Tips, Beef Brisket** (excellent!), **Sliced Ham, Turkey, and Pork**, and **Barbecued Chicken**. There's also Tooks's own creation, the **Smoked Chef Salad**, and the **Grilled Chicken Breast Salad**. Sides include **Corn on the Cob**, **Baked Beams**, and **Onion Rings**. For dessert, check out the **Apple, Peach, and Blackberry Cobblers**. Good eatin', indeed!

$10–$15 Slabs of Ribs slightly more/ ☐ ✓ ⬧ Beer sold

☆Maxine's Fine Foods   3041 Benton Boulevard, Kansas City, Missouri   816.924.2004

"Maxine's Rest and Retirement Home" reads a sign on the wall of Maxine's Restaurant. Underneath it, a regular patron enjoys the newspaper and his breakfast, looking as if he has no intentions of going anywhere anytime soon. Later, Maxine will ask him to run to the store for her and pick up several dozen eggs, which he will do with pleasure, happy to help. Why? Because as owner Maxine Byrd states, at her restaurant, "We treat people the way I would want to be treated. Like family. When people are feeling down or just need to get out, they come to Maxine's. Leave your problems behind and bring your good feelings here." For over 35 years, Byrd has been a major presence in her community, and nearly everyone in Kansas City, from the Kansas City Chiefs to local politicians to home-town celebrities, has eaten at her restaurant at least a dozen times!

Byrd believes that "personality is the key to success," and it must be true because the restaurant itself is not at all fancy— just a long counter, a few tables, and a jukebox playing soft jazz— but there's plenty of good food and atmosphere. A fiend for photographs, Maxine has captioned pictures of almost every event she has ever participated in and every famous person who has ever dined at her restaurant on proud display. Needless to say, there's very little wall space left!

Breakfast is *the* time to meet and greet here, and Maxine's serves up some hearty combinations to help get your day going: **T-Bone Steak and Eggs**, **Pork Chops and Hot Cakes**, **Polish Sausage and Grits**, and **Bacon and Hash Browns**, to name a few. And don't even think of leaving without tasting some of Maxine's famous **Homemade Biscuits**! In fact, you might want to order a few to go, for when the craving hits later!

$10–$15

Niecie's Restaurant   6902 Prospect, Kansas City, Missouri   816.333.1206

Talk about a family affair! "Big Perry" Ward's wife manages the restaurant that, like the nightclub he runs, bears her name. And believe me, Niecie Ward should be named "Businessperson of the Year" for the tremendous stamina she displays in keeping her home and professional life together. After a long day at the restaurant, she somehow finds the energy to go over to the family's nightclub to spin records until the wee hours of the morning! Niecie's Restaurant serves **Down-Home Food** in a comfortable, luncheonette-style atmosphere.

$10

The Rib Tip House (Formerly Boyd's 'n' Son's Barbecue) 5510 Prospect, Kansas City, Missouri 816.523.0436

Lisa Dozier walked into Boyd's 'n' Son's Barbecue in 1975 hoping to learn all about barbecue from Otis Boyd. Being the old-fashioned kind of guy that he is, Boyd informed her that she couldn't possible prepare barbecue or manage the restaurant because she was "a girl." Well, Dozier showed him! Not only did she learn the secrets of firing up the hickory wood pit and cooking great barbecue, she effectively performed all of the restaurant's day-to-day managerial duties. In 1988, a book titled *Real Barbecue* (published by Harper & Row) awarded Boyd's 'n' Son's its highest rating: "As Good As We've Ever Had!" Well, that's a great honor in a town saturated with great barbecue places. Today, Dozier is the proprietor of Boyd's establishment, which she renamed The Rib Tip House, although Boyd, now retired, still comes in every day to make sure his protege is staying true to his teachings. The Rib Tip House features **Rib Tips**, **Slabs**, **Sliced Beef, Ham or Pork**, **Barbecued Chicken**, and **Burgers**. There are also lots of vegetables and other sides to choose from.

$10 Slabs of Ribs & Combo Dinners slightly more/ ✔ ℭ

Cafeteria/Buffet-Style Dining

☆Madry's Dash of Flavor 26 East 39th Street, Kansas City, Missouri 816.753.3274

Dorothy and James Madry kicked around the idea of opening a restaurant for 20 years before finally doing so in 1993. During that time, they catered numerous events, from weddings to corporate parties, but their dream was to one day own a sit-down eatery with an upscale yet homey feeling to it. Today, that's just what their restaurant offers, with a healthy twist. In response to the "bad rap" soul food has received in recent years for its traditional high-fat and high-salt emphasis, **the food at Madry's is cooked without lard or pork and is low in sodium**. Indeed, Chef Dorothy's preference for bringing out the flavor of foods through expert seasoning is the reason why her son added the title "Dash of Flavor" to the restaurant's name.

Madry's features an **All-You-Can-Eat Buffet for Lunch and Dinner Seven Days a Week**. **Fried Chicken, Turkey and Dressing, Macaroni and Cheese, Fresh Greens, Cabbage, Yams,** the prettiest and most delicious **Homemade Rolls** ever, and **Fresh-Squeezed Lemonade** are just a few of the items on the buffet line. The Sunday buffet offers a few special extras.

$10 ✓C

Papa Lew's Barbecue & Soul Food 1504 Prospect Avenue, Kansas City, Missouri 816.231.2800

Upon entering, Papa Lew's Barbecue & Soul Food offers each and every customer something no other restaurant can: a sincere hug from owner Dorriss Lyman. As Dorriss explains, "If people are having a bad day, at least they know they can go to Papa Lew's for a hug and a big smile." Dorriss and her husband Lewis opened their restaurant 14 years ago with "no money and no experience." Luckily for them, their good down-home cooking and determination have made Lewis's dream of owning his own place a reality. Though Lewis passed away in 1992, Dorriss, her son Marvin, and her very professional staff continue to honor his memory by serving some of the best soul food in town every day.

Papa Lew's is a simple, family-style cafeteria serving **PorkChops**, **Roast Beef**, **Neck Bones**, **Ham Hocks**, **Catfish**, and, of course, **Barbecue Ribs**. There are also endless sides of **Mashed**

Potatoes, **Black-Eyed Peas**, **Macaroni and Cheese**, and **Green Beans**. **Peach Cobbler** and **Banana Pudding**, along with a hug from Dorriss on the way out the door, tops it all off!
$10 Slabs of Ribs slightly more/ ☐

The Peach Tree 6800 Eastwood Trafficway, Kansas City, Missouri 816.923.0099
      Just over a year old, the Peach Tree offers a spacious, peachy, and pleasant dining environment to enjoy its **Daily All-You-Can-Eat Buffet**. Proprietor Vera Willis has included many southern favorites on her restaurant's buffet line to satisfy almost everyone's craving for down-home cooking: **Baked Chicken and Dressing, Beef Neckbones, Meatloaf, Fried Chicken, Okra and Tomatoes, Greens, Mashed Potatoes, Big Mama's Cornbread**, and **Peach Cobbler**, are just a few.
$10 ☐

Take-Out Dining

Jim's Diner 6100 Prospect, Kansas City, Missouri
       816.363.5190
Jim's Fat Burger 6101 Prospect,
       Kansas City, Missouri 816.363.7770
      One evening, Marsha and Jim Williams came across an old photo of Jim's uncle in Louisiana frying a turkey in his back yard. Quite taken with this unique concept, Jim went back to his own kitchen, seasoned a whole turkey, and dropped it into the deep fryer. What came out was the moistest, most delicious gobbler he had ever tasted! Word spread quickly, and soon folks were bringing Jim their turkeys for him to work his magic. The Williams's restaurants received national exposure after Jim recently appeared on TV's "Fox After Breakfast" to demonstrate his frying techniques. Afterwards, orders for fried turkeys started pouring in from as far away as Canada!
      In addition to **Fried Turkeys**, Jim's Diner sells take-out soul food lunches and dinners featuring **Beef Brisket, Neck Bones, Meat Loaf, Smothered Steak, Beef Short Ribs**, and **Catfish**. Across the street, Jim's Fat Burger serves up terrific **Hamburgers**, **Chili**, and **Fries. During holiday seasons, Jim's**

Diner sells complete Turkey Dinners with all the trimmings. Or, bring your own turkey, and Jim and his staff can fry it for you for $.75 per pound. Either way, they do all the work, and you take all the credit!

$10 ☐

Nightclubs

Bodyworks Unlimited   8625 Troost, Kansas City, Missouri   816.363.6910

The Epicurean Lounge's sister club, Bodyworks Unlimited, is large, noisy and too much fun! With the capacity to pack up to 700 people comfortably inside, Bodyworks is the new "see-and-be-seen" spot in K.C.. **Loud, Pumping Hip-Hop, Rap, and Dance Music** keep the 20-something crowd partying all night.

Cover charge/ 21+ crowd/ ☐ ½ 🗑

The Epicurean Lounge   7502 Troost, Kansas City, Missouri   816.333.8383

The Epicurean Lounge is a hot nightspot in Kansas City, large enough to hold up to 300 people, and the perfect place for birthday parties and reunions. It features **Live Jazz on Weekends** in the early evenings and a **Live Deejay Spinning R&B, Top 40s, and Urban Contemporary Sounds** during the week. Plenty of **Good Bar Food** like **Chicken Wings, Catfish**, and **Club Sandwiches** are available.

Cover charge/ 30+ crowd/ $10 bar menu/ ☐ ½ 🗑

Mardi Gras Lounge   19th & Vine, Kansas City, Missouri   816.842.VINE

Located in the historic 19th & Vine district of **Kansas City**, the Mardi Gras Lounge has become a local landmark. This club, which has been around since the Forties, is one of the oldest in the city. On one wall is the huge, handpainted mural, colorfully depicting a lively New Orleans carnival scene, that is the reason behind the club's name. On the other side of the room, in a separate seating area, is a newer, very impressive mural that pays tribute to every jazz great from Charlie Parker to Billie Holliday. During the week, the Mardi Gras Lounge hosts a mature crowd that enjoys grooving to the jukebox and playing electronic darts. On weekends, the club offers **Live Music.**

☆**Niecie's Lounge & Grill   6201 Blue Parkway, Kansas City, Missouri   816.921.5990**

Niecie's Lounge & Grill is *the* Kansas City nightspot! After 6pm on Fridays its parking lot is packed, but the who's who of the city are "in the house" there Friday night and every night. The atmosphere at Niecie's is upscale, lively, and unpretentious. Doors are opened for you by one of the club's courteous valets. Proprietor "Big Perry" Ward welcomes you with a big smile and greeting from behind the bar. He's one busy man, but he treats each and every one of his patrons like a VIP, graciously and with the utmost sincerity. Big Perry collects your party's coats, pulls out your chairs, and even lights cigars or cigarettes for men as well as ladies. **Drinks are Two-for-One until 7pm, and Chicken Wings are a quarter apiece 'til 8pm on Fridays.   A Full Down-Home Dinner Menu** is available from the kitchen, capably run by "Little Perry," Big Perry's son.

No Cover charge/ 25+ crowd/ $10 Dinner menu/

LOS ANGELES & VICINITY

Fine Dining

☆Georgia   7250 Melrose Avenue, Los Angeles, California   213.933.8420

From the moment Georgia, the restaurant, opened in 1993, it was destined to become a mecca for celebrities, models, athletes, and other Who's-Who notables from L.A. and across the country. Under the experienced direction of its creator, Brad Johnson, along with former NBA star Norm Nixon (one of three principle partners) and executive chef Gilroy Bruce, Georgia has emerged as one of L.A.'s most popular restaurants. Screen stars Eddie Murphy and Denzel Washington are among the high-profile personalities with a financial interest in the restaurant. Stevie Wonder and Muhammad Ali have been spotted in its sumptuous dining room, as have Angela Basset, Jamie Foxx, and many others.

Pass through Georgia's wrought iron exterior gates into the large courtyard—which is typically filled with fashionable patrons busily making deals, sharing the latest trade gossip, or simply people-watching—and you'll find the interior to be a lush, lavish combination of southern charm and old Hollywood. The busy dining room is surrounded by seductive lighting that artistically highlights the emerald-green booths, mahogany floors, and oil paintings of golden palm trees lining the walls. And if that isn't tantalizing enough, Georgia offers **Live Music on Thursday and Sunday Nights**.

Chef Bruce suggests you enjoy a **Savannah** (champagne with fresh peach nectar) while deciding on an appetizer from among an array of mouth-watering selections such as **Blue Crab Crabcakes, Creole Fried Oysters** or **Crayfish-and-Crabmeat Strudel**. For an entree, select one of his specialties: **Lobster and Linguini, Grilled Rack of Lamb, Seared Swordfish**, or **Spicy Peppered Broiled Shrimp**. Top off your meal with Georgia's memorable **Warm Peach Cobbler** or **Pecan Pie**, both of which can be served à la mode.

$25+ 📞 ☐ ✓ 🍷 🍴 🍲 🎭 ☕

☆**Hal's Bar & Grill   1349 Abbot Kinney Boulevard, Venice, California   310.396.3105**

Just down the street from Venice Beach is one of the most sophisticated and visually dazzling restaurants in Los Angeles: Hal's Bar & Grill. Proprietor Hal Fredereck's goal was "to cultivate a neighborhood and seduce the people in the area so they will bring their friends from other parts of the city to a fun, joyous place," and that's exactly what he has achieved. Since 1987, his establishment has drawn a chic international crowd of artists, actors, and neighborhood regulars.

Hal's ability to attract just the right crowd mix stems from his days as co-owner of Robert's, the first restaurant on Venice Beach to cater to a culturally diverse clientele, in the mid-Seventies. But the interior of the restaurant that bears his name is in itself inviting. The dining room is richly decorated with black leather booths trimmed in blond wood, and the walls are adorned with an impressive collection of original paintings and sculptures by nationally renowned artists. The private dining room seats 35 comfortably in an intimate setting. Hal's features live jazz on Monday evenings.

According to Fredereck, Hal's Bar & Grill features "**New American Cuisine** with an emphasis on natural, fresh ingredients." The menu changes weekly, but the following is a sampling of what one may expect: **Grilled Half Chicken Basted with Thai Spices** and served with **Hal's Fries** (the best!), **Pan-Roasted Duck in Spicy Passion Fruit Glaze**, **Grilled Ahi Tuna in Vegetable Coulis**, and **Roasted King Salmon on a Bed of Risotto.**

$20+ ☐ ✓ ℭ ⚎ ⛧

> "I love the food at Georgia because they offer a lot
> of things on their menu that my mother used to
> cook for me when I was a kid. It's like having
> a home-cooked meal with 250 people!"
> *Robert Townsend, Filmmaker*

☆**Harold & Belle's Creole Restaurant**
2920 West Jefferson Boulevard, Los Angeles, California
213.735.9023

Harold & Belle's has gained a national reputation as one of the best Creole restaurants outside of New Orleans. It started out as a hamburger joint and bar that co-proprietor Harold LeGaux's father opened for the enjoyment of his friends back in the late Sixties. When Papa LeGaux passed in 1972, his wife held onto the place for a while and eventually handed over control to her son Harold and his wife Denise. Avid restaurant diners themselves, Harold and Denise had little interest in running a bar. Despite protests from the bar crowd, out went the pool table and jukebox. In came a new upscale interior, a larger kitchen, a more sophisticated menu, and **Live Jazz on Weekends**—and Harold & Belle's became one of L.A.'s favorite restaurants.

Harold pulled together his favorite recipes from his Louisiana-born grandmother and aunts. **File** (pronounced "fee-lay") **Gumbo** loaded with shrimp, crab, sausage, chicken, and ham and beautifully presented in a crock pot is the #1 item on the menu, and rightfully so! Very few places outside of New Orleans can truly do justice to gumbo, but after one spoonful, Harold & Belle's will have you longing for a walk on Royal Street. Other delicacies include **Crawfish Etoufee**, **Fish Suzette** (grilled red snapper with crawfish sauce), **Lobster Scampi**, **Fried Frog Legs**, **Fried Oysters**, **New York Steak**, **Grilled Shrimp**, and **Red Beans and Pork Chops**.

$25 + ☐ ✓ ℂ ⛾ 🎼 🍖 ☕

Casual Dining

☆Aunt Kizzy's Back Porch   4325 Glencoe Avenue, Villa Marina Center, Marina Del Rey, California 310.578.1005

Former social workers Adolph and Mary Dulan knew that in order to achieve a more prosperous lifestyle they would have to go into business for themselves. So, in 1982, they opened a place called Hamburger City in Marina Del Rey. The business started off strong but fizzled soon after the 1984 Olympics because many local patrons refused to venture out into the paralyzing traffic jams and crowd chaos caused by that event and simply stayed home. The Dulans were forced into bankruptcy, but they never lost sight of their goals. In 1985, Mary Dulan suggested opening a restaurant that served southern food "just like the kind they served at home." With the log cabin Adolph grew up in near Luther, Oklahoma, as their inspiration, the Dulans opened Aunt Kizzy's Back Porch in 1985. The rest, as they say, is history.

From its cozy log-cabin interior to its friendly staff, from the walls that feature Dulan family photos and memorabilia as well as many famous faces, to Adolph Dulan himself, who regularly goes from table to table, greeting each patron with his dazzling smile—Aunt Kizzy's exudes personality plus. Adolph attributes the restaurant's success to a simple formula: "Good, friendly service, fair prices, and good food in healthy portions."

Aunt Kizzy's menu features the best of the best in **Authentic Down-Home Cuisine**—and all the lemonade you can drink! Dinner choices at Aunt Kizzy's are a "relative" affair, and include **Aunt Johnnie's Fried Chicken, Uncle Wade's Baked Beef Short Ribs, Cousin Willie Mae's Smothered Pork Chops**, and **Sister Zethel's Meatloaf**. There are lots of delicious sides to choose from, like **Fresh Collard Greens** and **Aunt June's Fresh Candied Yams**. Old-time country desserts include **Aunt Kizzy's Sweet Potato Pie** (delicious!), **Sock-it-to-Me Cake** (a knock out!), and **Pineapple Coconut Cake** (hello!). But dieters, don't despair: Aunt Kizzy's will soon be introducing lighter fare among its daily specials.

$10–$15 🍴 ▢ ✓ ☕ ♿

> **"Georgia has a great variety of food, excellently prepared and presented. The atmosphere is comfortable and friendly and the service first-rate."**
> *James Brown, Fox Sports*

Boulevard Café 3710 West Martin Luther King Jr. Boulevard, Los Angeles, California 213.292.7900

Former state legislator Frank Holoman came up with the idea of opening a restaurant when he was refused service at an eatery he used to refer his constituents to! Rather than getting mad, Holoman got even: He located his establishment across the street from that same restaurant and soon captured most of their business! Since 1984, his Boulevard Café has served countless celebrities, politicians, athletes, and loyal locals. The restaurant itself has become a bit of a celebrity as well. Local newscasters reporting on such controversial stories as the L.A. riots, the O.J. Simpson trial, the debate over smoking versus nonsmoking in public areas, and other timely topics frequently use the Boulevard Café as a pulse-point location for opinions from the many concerned citizens who patronize it. The Boulevard Café's interior is modest, unassuming, and best suited for family-style dining.   For larger groups, the **Banquet Room** seats up to 45. Paintings by local artists (many of which are for sale) and photographs of the famous people who have enjoyed their meals at the café take up almost every inch of available wall space.

Ask Holoman what is featured on the Boulevard Café's menu, and he'll tell you his restaurant is known for "whatever people like."   **Beef Short Ribs** (no knife needed, thank you!), **Chicken and Dressing**, **Fried Chicken**, **Red Snapper**, **Fried Catfish**, **Steaks**, **Chitterlings**, and **Gumbo** are just a few of the many down-home offerings from the Boulevard Café's extensive menu.

$10–$15   ❏ ✓ ℂ

> **"Hal's Bar & Grill is simple. Good food + good people."**   *John Faulkner, Photographer*

☆Coley's Kitchen Jamaican Restaurant
4335 Crenshaw Boulevard, Los Angeles, California   213.290.4010

"A taste of Jamaica in the heart of L.A." is how Horace and Beryl Robinson describe the struggling restaurant they took over in 1989.   With Beryl handling the cooking and Horace doing the baking, this hardworking, creative husband-and-wife team have turned Coley's Kitchen into the area's premier Caribbean restaurant.   According to Horace, the secret to their success is elementary: "We use only the finest products and cook healthy." The Robinsons' commitment to quality is reinforced by their attention to customer service. As Horace claims, "When I produce something, it's for myself. Then, when the customer buys it, they will appreciate it because it is the best, done right, with no substitutes or in-betweens." The decor of Coley's Kitchen reflects the tropical setting of the proprietors' home island. Unique works of art depicting scenes and faces from the Caribbean strike a vivid contrast to the pastel pink walls and lace curtains that are so reminiscent of the colorful Jamaican countryside.

Coley's **Jamaican Meat Patties** are considered the best in the city by many critics. The secret, Horace maintains, is in the crust, which has to be flavorful with "just the right blend of spices." Other specialties of the house include **Jerk Chicken, Curried Goat, King Fish Escoveitch, Vegetarian Delight**, and **Brown Stew Fish**. Traditional island beverages—**Sorrel, Irish Moss, Ginger Beer**, and **Sour Sop**—made fresh on the premises, are also available. Enjoy!

$10–$15 ☐ ✓ ℂ

Dulan's Restaurant 4859 Crenshaw Boulevard, Los Angeles, California 213.296.3034

Many people jump into the restaurant business cold-turkey with little or no prior experience. Greg Dulan was fortunate enough to have had 10 years experience running a successful catering concern (Aunt Kizzy's Catering) and learning the restaurant business from a master—two masters, actually: his mom and dad, Mary and Adolph Dulan, owners of Aunt Kizzy's Back Porch in Marina Del Rey. With this wealth of experience and expertise, Greg and his wife Brenda set out to establish a restaurant of their own. Their vision: a genial setting that can accommodate various sizes and types of crowds from the weekend brunch bunch to the movie premier party, class reunion gathering, or bridal shower.

Located in the heart of Los Angeles's African American community but only 15 minutes from downtown, Dulan's is housed in a large Spanish-style hacienda that features a lovely outdoor patio, perfect for dining *al fresco*. **Fried Chicken, Smothered Pork Chops, Meat Loaf, Catfish, Chicken and Sausage Jambalaya, Short Ribs, Collard Greens**, and **Mashed Potatoes** are just a few of the selections awaiting Dulan's patrons. Weekend feasters can enjoy the **Sunday Gospel-and-Jazz "All-You-Can-Eat" Brunch**, which provides a chance to sample all of the restaurant's specialties at once.

$10–$15 ☎ ☐ ✓ ℂ 🍲 ☕

> "**Harold & Belle's is without question the preeminent African American-owned restaurant in Los Angeles. The fresh, tasty, and hearty portions, as well as excellent service, are what fine dining is all about.**"
> *Doug Willis, Accountant/Politician*

Gagnier's of New Orleans   3650 Martin Luther King Jr. Boulevard, Suite 126, Los Angeles, California 213.292.8187

Although Charlena and August Gagnier (pronounced "gone-yah") had no prior restaurant management experience before opening the establishment that bears their name, they had a lot of related skills. August, originally from New Orleans, was a building contractor who specialized in restaurant interiors. Charlena had worked with a caterer and had broad managerial and staffing expertise. In 1989, armed with August's prized collection of family recipes as their foundation, they identified a site in the newly remodeled Crenshaw Plaza located in Baldwin Hills and proceeded to "set up shop."

With its upscale ambiance, authentic cuisine, and professional wait-staff, Gagnier's brings a little bit of New Orleans to L.A.. For dinner patrons, **File Gumbo**, **Jambalaya**, or **Oysters on the Half Shell** start the evening off right. **Jumbo Fried Shrimp**, **Fried Catfish**, **Beef Tenderloin Steaks**, **Fried Scallops**, **Crab Cakes**, and **Gagnier's Special Seafood Platter** are just a few of the choice main course offerings from which to choose. But make sure you save room for **Mama Gloria's Homemade Bread Pudding with Whiskey Sauce**—you'll be glad you did!

$10–$20   ☐ ✓₵ ⛾

☆Jack's Chili Factory   3630 Crenshaw Boulevard, Los Angeles, California   213.296.2930

Jack Olivier has always been a "chili person." Whenever he came across a place that specialized in chili, he would stop in for a taste and take note of all the characteristics or ingredients that brought either delight or disappointment. After many years of tasting and testing, Olivier concluded that a bowl of good chili was hard to find. So, in 1982, with a slew of family chili recipes passed down through the generations and with help from his son, he opened Jack's Chili Factory. The response was so positive, Olivier soon opened two more locations. Today, his chili empire is only one unit strong, but Olivier continues to serve some of the best chili on the West Coast and claims to have regular customers from as far away as Anchorage and Atlanta.

Jack's puts chili over everything!: **Chili Tamales, Chili Hot Dogs, Chili Cheese Burgers, Chili Bean Cheese Fries**, and even **Chili Spaghetti**. Of course, Jack's has **Chili Straight, Beef or Turkey Chili, Chili with Beans or Not**, and plenty of rice, cheese, onions, and sour cream if needed. No matter how you like it, Jack's chili is thick, tasty, filling, and really, really good! The only question is: with so many relying on his chili, how is Mr. Olivier ever going to retire?

$10 ✓ᑕ / Beer served

☆The Jamaican Café   424 Wilshire Boulevard, Santa Monica, California   310.587.2626

What kind of people would leave well-paying jobs to enter a field with a 58% failure rate *and* a host of major financial responsibilities? Aggressive, innovative entrepreneurs like Wanda James and Scott Durrah, the proud new owners of The Jamaican Café, that's who! Durrah recalls that his diverse culinary training began in the kitchen of his grandmother at the age of six. His love affair with food led him to Jamaica where he studied under many of the great chefs there. James's fascination with restaurants began at a tender age. A military "brat," she grew up in Europe, dining out nightly with her soldier–father. James and Durrah's similar life experiences fully prepared them for their biggest challenge to date: resurrecting the four-year-old Jamaican Café and, along with head chef Sonia Telfer, turning the eatery into what *L.A. Weekly* dubbed the "Best Jamaican Restaurant" in Los Angeles in 1996.

The Jamaican Café's extensive menu offers foods prepared to varying degrees of spiciness. The famous jerk dishes, for example, range from hot to "hell hot!"—so order at your own risk! **Jamaican Curried Shrimp Pasta, Curried Goat Roti, Jerk T-Bone Steak, Broiled Lamb with Jamaican Orange Mint Sauce, Smoked Jerk Alaskan King Crab Legs**, and **Escoveitch Snapper** are just a sampling of the many exciting selections awaiting you at this prized Caribbean getaway. You're sure to find something you'll love!

$15–$20 ☐ ✓ᑕ /Beer served

Maurice's Snack 'N Chat   5549 West Pico Boulevard, Los Angeles, California   213.931.3877

At 80 years young, the Snack 'N Chat's proprietor, Ms. Maurice Prince, has done and seen it all. Her restaurant looks more like her family room than a place of business, and every item in the place tells a story of a life well lived. "Happy Birthday" greetings from Los Angelenos dating back 15 years adorn the walls. Countless ribbons and awards and her prized salt- and pepper-shaker collection—some received as gifts and others "picked up here and there"—fight for attention.   These and other mementoes share prized display space with an endless array of photos taken of Ms. Prince on every single one of her vacations and with almost every celebrity known to man (or woman) from the Forties to the present. From Paul Robeson in 1943 to you-name-'em, there's Ms. Maurice standing next to them! As she proudly proclaims, "I've been around show people all of my life. I've worked with them and fed them all!"

The Snack 'N Chat's menu reads like a Broadway playbill, "starring" such renowned players as **CeCe's Meatloaf**, **Home-Fried Chicken**, **Smothered Pork Chops**, **Short Ribs of Beef**, **Liver and Onions**, and **David's Fried Catfish.** All entrees are prepared to order, and special items like **Spoonbread** and **Baked Chicken** require advance notice. The dessert menu features delicious items like **Coconut Cake**, **Banana Pudding**, and **Peach Cobbler à la Mode**, and none of the helpings are "bit parts"! But don't come to the Snack 'N Chat just for the good food—come to meet Ms. Maurice, a true star and living legend.

$10–$15 ☐ 🗝 /Beer & Wine served

☆Mobay   1031 Abbot Kinney Boulevard, Venice, California 310.452.7472

Even if there wasn't customer the first inside Mobay (which would be highly unlikely), there would still be a party going on inside this ultra-chic Caribbean restaurant!   The dining room virtually *explodes* with color and excitement. Hand-painted palm trees, splashes of color on each table and chair, and even life-size wooden "natives" in full festival attire greet you upon arrival. The carnival continues onto the outdoor patio, which borders the lovely sculpture garden designed by Jerry Rowitch. All this and much more is the brainchild of Chef Derek Harrison, whose menu of **"Contemporary Caribbean and California Eclectic Cuisine"** represents the cutting edge in fine ethnic foods.

Jerk Chicken Ravioli, Dungeness Crab in Phylo with Tangerine Sauce, or Salad Mobay with Roasted Goat Cheese and Passion Fruit Vinaigrette are among the savory appetizer selections. For your entree, choose either the Guava Glazed Pork with Chayote and Sweet Potatoes, Spicy Coconut Shrimp, Salmon Roulade with Portobello Mushrooms, Yardbird Curried Chicken with Scallion Roti, or one of several other tempting island dishes. Mobay also features great Tropical Drinks and serves a Champagne Brunch on weekends.

$10–$20 🖼 ☐ ✓ ℭ ⚱ 🏮 ☕

☆Simply Wholesome   4508 West Slauson, Los Angeles, California   213.294.2144

Simply Wholesome is a restaurant...no, it's a grocery store...no, it's a community center! Beyond great food, this establishment offers exercise programs for children and adults, on-site nutritional counseling, Banquet/Meeting Facilities, and live entertainment most evenings. In other words, Simply Wholesome has it all! Recognizing the need for "alternative food" in the predominantly Black Crenshaw area of Los Angeles, Liz and Percell Keeling opened Simply Wholesome in 1981, and the community welcomed them with open arms. Their business grew steadily, so much so that in 1995 they moved to their new, larger location on Slauson.

The menu at Simply Wholesome, while "health-food-oriented," is extensive and will satisfy almost any craving. Sandwiches include Tuna and Avocado, Turkey Burgers, and Lentil Burgers. Then there's the Meatless Melted Cheese and Mushroom White Bean Soup and the Vegetarian Chili. Caribbean favorites "on the healthy tip" range from the Spinach Corn Enchilada to the Vegetarian Lasagna and a dish called Masala's Island Surprise (angel hair pasta, shrimp, and plantain with veggies). What's more, Simply Wholesome offers over 25 different thirst-quencher combinations from Guava Explosion and Apple Banana Fruit Slush to Peach Pizazz. Simply put, with its handsome dining area and well-informed associates to help with any nutritional needs, Simply Wholesome is...simply wonderful!

$10 ☐ ✓ ℭ 🍽

> "Uncle Darrow's is one of my favorites. Whenever my law firm wants to send out for lunch, the first place we contact is Uncle Darrow's. His food is always delicious. It reminds me of my early days in Shreveport, Louisiana."
>
> *Johnnie L. Cochran, Jr., Attorney*

Take-Out Dining

Art's Wings & Things   4213 Crenshaw Boulevard, Los Angeles, California   213.294.9464

You can't miss Art's Wings & Things—just look for the sign with the shapely chicken inviting passers-by to "Let My Wings Do Their Thing to Your Taste Buds." The sign is priceless and so are the healthy wings served at this local landmark since 1991. Despite numerous obstacles, proprietor Art Boone's eatery has emerged as *the* place for tasty, freshly prepared food and **Catering** in the Crenshaw district. The entry way to Art's Wings & Things features an amazing wall-length mural of a grand concert featuring a veritable Who's Who of the music industry, including such notables as Hammer, Whitney Houston, and Tina Turner. Art himself is portrayed playing chess (his passion) with Michael Jackson. Inside, a classic motorcycle graces center stage while rap music blasts away from the speakers. This is a lot of ambience for a wings joint, but, hey, who says hot wings shouldn't have a cool environment?!

Art's Chicken Wings come several ways: **Buffalo Style, Mild, Hot, Sweet-and-Sour, Teriyaki Style,** and **With Mumbo Sauce. Philly Cheese Steak Sandwiches, Fried Vegetables,** and **Burgers** round out this limited but crowd-pleasing menu.

$10 ☐ ✓ ℂ

Mel's Fish Market   4026 West Jefferson Boulevard, Los Angeles, California   213.735.7220

Georgette Powell and her sister Janie Harris, the current proprietors of Mel's Fish Market, are continuing a family tradition that started with their father in 1976. Melvin Powell's vision was to leave something for his children, so in 1982, he opened Mel's Fish Market selling fresh fish and seafood. As the market's popularity grew, Mel's expanded its offerings to include fish dinners and side dishes prepared on-site for take-out. Next came **Full-Service Catering** with a clientele list that included several television and movie studios, and the marketing and selling of Mel's homemade seasonings. Today, Melvin Powell's legacy is embodied in his daughter Georgette's ongoing efforts to inspire young entrepreneurs in and around her community to open their own businesses and strengthen the neighborhood she calls home. Due to her civic-minded nature, Mel's Fish Market is a frequent provider of meals for various local fund-raisers and area events.

Fried Red Snapper, Catfish, Oysters, Whiting, Buffalo, Shrimp, and **Orange Roughy** are just a few of the items on Mel's menu. Sides include **Potato Salad, Macaroni-and-Cheese, Greens, Fries,** and **Cole Slaw,** while favorites like **Peach Cobbler, Sweet Potato Pie, German Chocolate Cake,** and **Sock-it-to-Me Cake** satisfy the sweet tooth.
$10 ☐ ✓ ℂ

☆**Uncle Darrow's Cajun/Creole Eatery** 5301 Venice **Boulevard, Los Angeles, California** 213.938.4293
In 1988, Norwood Clark and his cousins started Uncle Darrow's Cajun Candy Company, specializing in pralines and "Sweet Tater Pies." "Just Keeping America Sweet" was their slogan, and soon large retail department stores came calling to order the company's sweet treats. Next the Clarks set out to test the concept of offering **Authentic "Fast-Food Cajun/Creole Cuisine"** at affordable prices. Their newly acquired food preparation facility provided adequate space for preparing large quantities of Louisiana-style dishes like **File Gumbo** and **Red Beans and Rice** that require slow cooking. Every day, these and other ready-to-eat Cajun/Creole favorites are transported to the Eatery, which is located down the street from Sony Studios, just in time for the busy lunchtime rush.

The menu at Uncle Darrow's also includes **Jumbalaya, Catfish or Shrimp Suppers** (both fried in cornmeal to perfection), and **Turkey, Chicken, or Creole Link Po' Boys.** Desserts include **Homemade Ice Cream, Sweet Tater Pie,** and **Praline Candy.** Oh, and Uncle Darrow's has a **"Try-Before-You-Buy"**

Policy that allows customers a free sample taste of most menu items. After that first try, however, you're sure to come back to buy again and again and again!
$10 ☐ ✓ℂ

Nightclubs

The Comedy Act Theater   3339 West 43rd Street, Los Angeles, California   310.677.4101
The late Robin Harris got his start at The Comedy Act Theater, and you can bet he won't be the last famous comedian to come out of a venue that offers newcomers a chance to upstage themselves. With up to eight different comedians appearing per night (the club is only **Open on Thursday, Friday, and Saturday Nights**), cracking on the audience is par for the course, but that's OK because the Comedy Act serves **Plenty of Munchies** along with the good humor.
Cover charge/ Call for line-up

☆5th Street Dick's Coffee Company   3347-½ West 43rd Place, Los Angeles, California   213.296.3970
At 11:30 on a nice fall evening, a crowd can be found spilling out of 5th Street Dick's, piping hot cups of coffee or tea and slices of carrot cake in hand, to wait for the second jazz set to start. Other folks can be spotted playing chess or bid whist at the club's sidewalk tables. Inside, besides **Coffees, Teas, Cakes,** and an assortment of other goods, 5th Street Dick's serves a very good **Turkey Pot Pie**. Upstairs, it serves **Live Straight-Ahead Jazz** played by local and nationally known acts. It's all part of the very laid-back culture of this re-emerging neighborhood. A very unique scene indeed.
Cover charge/ ☐ 🎶

The Townhouse   6835 La Tijera Boulevard, Los Angeles, California   310.649.0091
September 1, 1988: Two thousand people attend the opening of L.A.'s hottest new upscale nightspot, The Townhouse. And ever

since, proprietor Roosevelt Walker has packed the house with politicians, celebrities, neighborhood regulars, and loyal friends. The Townhouse boasts an **Extensive Wine List, Top-Shelf Liquor, Two Fireplaces, Live Entertainment Seven Nights a Week, Dancing, Monday Sports Nights** (there are **Nine TVs** in the club, so you won't miss a thing), **Banquet Facilities**—and if that's not enough, a **Full-Service Restaurant** featuring an All-American menu. Under Chef Marilyn Cole's direction, the specialties of the house include **Porterhouse Steak, Smothered Chops, Fried Catfish, Blackened Snapper**, and **Alaskan King Crab Legs**. **Cover charge/ 25+ crowd/ $20+ Dinner menu/**
❏ ✓ ☁ ⛾ ⚗

The World Stage   4344 Degnan Boulevard, Los Angeles, California   213.293.2451

The World Stage bills itself as a "performance gallery" dedicated to "seeking light through sound." It's a natural setting for workshops, concerts, jam sessions, readings, and rehearsals requiring a relaxed, intimate venue. The small arena seats only about 45 people—yet the music and the vibes it delivers are so powerful, a larger stage might diminish the intensity of the message. **Cover charge**

MEMPHIS

Casual Dining

The Bar-B-Que Shop   1782 Madison, Near Downtown, Memphis, Tennessee   901.272.1277

For many years, a little place called Brady & Lili's was *the* barbecue spot in Memphis.   Whenever he stopped there for his barbecue, Frank Vernon, a regular customer, used to tease Brady with "Aren't you ready to retire yet? I'm looking to buy." Well, one day Brady answered "Guess what?   I'm ready!" and Vernon took over the operation.   He continued to use the place's old name until 1987 when he changed it to The Bar-B-Que Shop.   Beyond that, consistency is key at Vernon's bistro-like restaurant, which features an extra-long bar lined with photos of famous Memphis natives like Cybill Shephard.   And he continues to prepare everything the way Brady and Lil did 20 years ago: the old-fashioned way!

Pork Boston Butt, **Bar-B-Que Bologna**, **Ribs**, **Beef Brisket**, **Bar-B-Que Chicken**, **Bar-B-Que Spaghetti** (it's a Memphis thing!), **Bar-B-Que Beans**, and **Texas Toast** are a few of this Memphis landmark's specialties.   The Bar-B-Que Shop's famous **"Dancing Pigs" Barb-B-Que Sauce** (yes, there really *are* dancing pigs on the label!) is also available for sale.   It's rich and thick and comes in two varieties: Mild or Hot Hot.

$10 / Slabs of Ribs slightly more/ ☐ Beer only

The Four-Way Grill   998 Mississippi Boulevard, South Memphis, Tennessee   901.775.2351

Since her restaurant was situated at a four-way intersection, Irene Cleaves decided when she opened it in September 1946 that The Four-Way Grill would make an appropriate name.   For almost 50 years, Cleaves worked diligently to turn her modest establishment, located in what was considered the heart of the city's African American community back in the Forties, into what is now a Memphis landmark.   She recently retired, but in March 1997 the restaurant reopened under the direction of her nephew, George Martin, who continues to carry on his aunt's legacy by serving legendary **Home-Style Meals** daily!

$10 ☐

☆Interstate Bar-B-Que Restaurant   2265 South Third Street, South Memphis, Tennessee   901.775.2304

Jim Neely's Interstate Bar-B-Que is arguably the **Most Famous and Finest Barbecue in Memphis**. In 1989, *People* magazine rated it second in a countrywide survey of the top-10 barbecue restaurants. **Pork and Beef Ribs, Chopped or Sliced Pork and Beef, Texas Beef Links, Smoked Turkey Breast, Rib Tips,** and **Bar-B-Que Spaghetti** are just a few of the hearty dishes ready to satisfy anyone's appetite at Interstate Bar-B-Que.
$10 ☐ ✓ ℂ

☆Leach Family Restaurant   694 Madison, Downtown, Memphis, Tennessee   901.521.0867
Melanie's Fine Foods   1070 North Watkins, Memphis, Tennessee   901.278.0751

This is the story of how two restaurants evolved from one woman's faith in God and family. A few years ago, Mrs. Jimmy Leach started baking cakes in order to raise money to repair the roof of her son's church, which collapsed during services one morning. Miraculously, no one was hurt because, just moments before the fall, the minister had asked the congregation to quickly move to the other side of the church. God is good...and so were her sales! Mrs. Leach decided that she could raise even more money if she had the proper space and facilities to prepare not only cakes but home-style meals and other dishes as well. So, with only $800 between them, she and her family opened Melanie's Fine Foods in 1985. Business took off, and soon Melanie's was serving an average of 200 to 300 patrons daily.

To help take some of the pressure off his mom and the rest of the family at Melanie's, Jimmy's son Michael opened the Leach Family Restaurant in downtown Memphis in 1993. Armed with his mother's recipes, Michael has attracted a different type of clientele to this busy location, from business executives to blue-collar workers. On a typical weekday at Leach's, he estimates that his staff prepares at least 85 pounds of **Turkey Necks**, 80 pounds of **Fried Chicken**, and 60 pounds of ground meat for their famous **Meat Loaf**. And you'd better believe they open the doors at Leach's without first making sure that there's enough **Greens** and **Yams** to go around! Other specialties include **Chicken and Dressing**,

Catfish, Buffalo Fish, Ham Hocks, and **BBQ Chicken,** but don't even think of leaving Leach's without a slice of its delicious **Lemon Cake** or a serving of **Banana Pudding.**

$10 ☐ ✓ ℂ

☆**Neely's Bar-B-Que**
>   **670 Jefferson, Near Downtown, Memphis,**
>   **Tennessee   901.521.9798**
>   **5700 Mount Moriah, Memphis, Tennessee**
>   **901.795.4177**

Patrick Neely and his three brothers grew up working for their uncle, Memphis barbecue guru Jim Neely. In 1986, Patrick and brother Tony enrolled in the McDonald's Hamburgers management program and started laying the foundation for what was to become their own fast food mini-empire. Soon after the first restaurant opened, brothers Mark and Gaylan came on board, and Neely's Bar-B-Que quickly secured a reputation for great barbecue, generous portions at a fair price, and top-notch service.

The barbecue at Neely's comes in many forms: **Chopped or Pulled Pork, Sliced Beef,** or **Turkey, Ribs, Rib Tips, Chicken,** and **Sausage.** The sauce, made daily by Tony, is thick, flavorful, and mild. There's also the **Bar-B-Salad** and the **Bar-B-Que Spaghetti Dinner** (their mom's favorite). The **Cole Slaw** is excellent, and a small order of **Fries** at Neely's is not small at all—indeed, it's more than enough.

$10 / Slabs of Ribs slightly more/ ☐ ✓ ℂ **/ Beer served**

Steaks & More Restaurants
>   **67 Madison, Downtown, Memphis, Tennessee**
>   **901.523.2223**
>   **2795 Coleman Road, Memphis, Tennessee**
>   **901.937.8551**

Tony Boyd, proprietor of Steaks & More, loves to tell the story about how his restaurant career began: "I thought I would be a track athlete for the rest of my life," says Tony, "but the vision for Steaks & More came to me in church one night. God revealed to me to open a nonsmoking, nonalcoholic [beverage-serving] restaurant with a Christian atmosphere. The confirmation came when God gave me the vision. He also gave me the name. I wrote the name down in my bible and left it there. When my wife and I started thinking of names, she said, 'What about Boyd's—or Steaks and More?' Well, I jumped up, got out my bible, and there it was: Steaks & More." The rest, as they say, is history.

Steaks & More's downtown location is only open 'till 2pm and features **Breakfast Specials** like the **Pancake on a Stick** (you heard me right!), **6-Ounce Ribeye Steak with Hash Browns**, and **Country Ham with Red-Eye Gravy and Grits**. The downtown lunch crowd goes for the **Steaker's More** (steak and cheese), **Solomon's Grilled Chicken**, and **Simon Peter's Catfish Filet Sandwiches**. The Coleman Road location is a lunch/dinner restaurant that seats 450 people, features **Live Christian Music** most nights, and presents a **Dinner Theater** once a month.

$10/ Dinner at Coleman Road location slightly more

"**Whenever I am really hungry, I go to Crumpy's on Alcy Road for one of their delicious home-style meals. The portions are so huge, I need to put a sideboard under the plate to keep the food from falling off!**" *Nico, Charles Casey Custom Clothiers*

Take-Out Dining

A&R Bar-B-Que   1802 Elvis Presley Boulevard, Memphis, Tennessee   901.774.7444

Everyone in Memphis always looked forward to Anthony Pollard's annual Fourth-of-July barbecues, so it was no surprise when, after 25 years of working for the railroad, Pollard decided to open up A&R Bar-B-Que. In the early years, his daughter Leatrice ran the restaurant while Dad concentrated on bringing in the customers. Like a Pied Piper, Pollard would set up a small pit out front, throw a couple of slabs of ribs on, and then wait for the aroma to work its way around the neighborhood. Today, the lines still form as folks wait to experience the good food and service at A&R Bar-B-Que.

Rib Tips, Slabs of Ribs, Pork and Beef Shoulder, Hot Links, and **Hot Wings** make up the gist of A&R's menu. There are also lots of **Sandwiches** to choose from, like **Smoked Turkey Breast, Chopped Pork, Chopped Beef,** and possibly some of the

best **Hamburgers** you've ever tasted. Grandmother Pollard makes all the **Cakes** and A&R's famous **Fried Pies.**
$10 Slabs of Ribs slightly more/ ✓ C

Cozy Corner Restaurant 745 North Parkway, Memphis, Tennessee 901.527.9158

Like a lot of men, cooking was a hobby for Raymond Robinson, Sr., and he enjoyed barbecuing the most. After turning down a job that would have required him and his family to relocate, Robinson decided it was time to put his other talents to the test. He opened the Cozy Corner in 1977, featuring a slow-cooking, old-fashioned, manned barbecue pit that he built himself. Along with his son, Raymond Jr., Robinson continues at the helm of his restaurant, barbecuing out of that same pit, utilizing a process he claims is "key to putting out a product other barbecue places cannot offer." You see, all of the barbecue at the Cozy Corner is prepared with Robinson's own special dry seasoning mixture and homemade sauce. According to Chef Robinson, Sr.: "If it's cooked right, you don't need the sauce." But you may want just a little on the side for dipping, because it's that good! **Bar-B-Q Ribs, Chicken, Cornish Hens** (excellent!), **Pork Shoulder**, **Turkey**, **Rib Tips**, and **Smoked Sausage** are what's on the menu at the Cozy Corner. Sides include **Cole Slaw, Beans & Bologna**, and **BBQ Spaghetti.**
$10 Slabs of Ribs slightly more

☆Crumpy's Restaurant 1584 Alcy Road, Memphis, Tennessee 901.942.3427
Crumpy's Hot Wings
1381 Elvis Presley Boulevard, Memphis, Tennessee 901.942.3427
1056 East Brooks Road, Memphis, Tennessee 901.345.1503
1724 South White Station, Memphis, Tennessee 901.685.8356
2500 West Goodman Road, Hornlake, Mississippi 601.342.1937
2731 Rangeline Road, Memphis, Tennessee 901.353.3232

Donald Crump is as crazy and funny as his "no-pun-intended" name, and at the rate Crump's going, Donald Trump will have nothing on him after a while! Six take-out restaurants in five years—seven, if you count the catering facilities—is pretty aggressive for a guy who opened his first and still only full-service restaurant on Alcy Road in a location everyone said no restaurant could ever survive! Well, Crump has proved them all wrong, turning all six of his Crumpy's destinations into *the* Memphis hot spots for **Hot Wings**. D. Trump could learn a thing or two from D. Crump!

Crumpy's take-out units serve mostly wings and "things," but you can also order **Burgers** and such. The wings (as in the *whole* wing!) come in five degrees of heat: mild, regular hot, hot, x-hot, and suicide (!). The things are the sides that come with them: **Fries, Carrot and Celery Sticks with Blue Cheese Dressing,** and a **Roll**. And it's *all* good! Crumpy's Restaurant serves up what Crump calls its serious **Hot Plate Dinners—Country-Fried Steak, Meat Loaf, Fried Chicken, Pot Roast, Pork Chops**, and **Turkey and Dressing**—in huge portions for too little money.
$10 ✓ ¢

Pizza on Beale 341 Beale Street, Downtown, Memphis, Tennessee 901.529.1111
Right at the end of the hottest strip in town is the funkiest pizza place in town. Pizza on Beale serves **Pizza by the Slice or Whole, Sandwiches, Burgers,** and the like. But the specialties of the house are the **Frozen Daiquiris**, in a variety of flavors, that this take-out offers at special prices during the early afternoon.
$10

"Now, I've had barbecue from all over the country, and I can honestly say that Neely's is the tastiest I've ever had. Their sauce is thick and rich, and their meats are of the highest quality, reminding me of the down-home barbecue I grew up with in Mississippi." *Caroline Bell, Delta Blues Girl*

Hotels

☆Days Inn Downtown   164 Union Avenue, Downtown, Memphis, Tennessee   901.527.4100

As general manager and the only African American owner of a major hotel chain franchise, Mabra Holeyfield is in a class by himself. Holeyfield was president of the community development corporation that acquired the Days Inn Downtown Memphis in 1979. The hotel opened in 1983 and was later purchased by Holeyfield and his associates as private owners. Since then, he has worked hard to put his own personal mark on the Inn. He created its Memphis Sounds Lounge, he claims, "so visitors and locals could meet" and enjoy great jazz on the weekends. The private suites at his hotel have hosted such notables as the Reverend Jesse Jackson and Vice President Al Gore.

The Days Inn Downtown, located in the heart of Memphis and walking distance to world-famous Beale Street, offers **124 Rooms,** a **Restaurant,** and **Two Ballroom** (one that accommodates up to 300 people, and a smaller one that seats 60).

Nightclubs

B.B. King's Blues Club and Restaurant
143 Beale Street, Downtown, Memphis, Tennessee   901.524.KING

Beale Street would not be complete without B. B. King's Blues Club on the corner, welcoming everyone to the party. When Riley B. King arrived in Memphis at the age of 22 with only his guitar and $2.50 to his name, his singing quickly earned him the name, Riley "Blues Boy" King. He later shortened that moniker to "B. B." and...well, you know the rest!

B. B. King's Blues Club and Restaurant features a **Down-Home Southern Menu** with delicious "Opening Acts" like **Southern-Fried Fingers, Howlin Hot Wings,** and **Quick-Fried Dill Pickles**. "Main Performances" include **Red Beans and Rice, Bar-B-Que Ribs, Delta Fried Catfish, "The King" Steak,** and **Jambalaya Kabobs**. Of course, there's plenty of great **Live Jazz and R&B** music. The thrill is back!

Cover charge/ $10–$20 Dinner menu/ ☐ ✓ ℂ ⑩ 🎶

Memphis Sounds Lounge   164 Union Avenue, Downtown, Memphis, Tennessee   901.527.4100

On Friday evenings, this club—located in the Days Inn Downtown—is packed, filled with the Who's Who of Memphis as well as tourists galore. Why? Because the Memphis Sounds Lounge hosts the **Most Popular After-Work Party in Town**! Local celebs and visitors alike can be found lolling around, enjoying a good argument about politics, football, or whatever the topic of the moment is. Come to the Memphis Sounds to start the weekend off right, make new friends, catch up with old ones, and enjoy the mellow sounds of **Live Jazz**. The **Full-Dinner Restaurant** serves American cuisine as well as standard bar fare.

Cover charge on weekends/ Mature crowd/ $10–$15 Dinner menu/ ☐ ✓ ℂ ℉

☆This Is It!   167 Beale Street, Downtown, Memphis, Tennessee   901.527.8200

Some of the best **Live Jazz** is falling out of the front door of This Is It!, the newest addition to Beale Street's legendary block. Opened May 1996, the building that houses this club stood closed for 16 years. It took This Is It!'s proprietor Gene Fowler to bring it back to life, and, boy, did he ever! The interior of the club is colorful, with almost a Caribbean feel to it.   The full kitchen serves up an American menu of **Catfish**, **Butterfly Chicken Breasts**, **Filet Mignon**, a large selection of **Side Dishes**, and, last but not least, the **Cobbler of the Day**, which is best accompanied by the restaurant's fine **Espresso** or **Cappucino**. The **Chicken Wings** at this club are the best and hottest on the strip, with a heat intensity ranging from mild to Watch Out!

The only thing hotter than the wings at This Is It! is the jazz. Top local jazz and blues artists like Monday's Child, featuring the seductive vocals of Austin Bradley, hold court Tuesday through Sunday nights. Between sets, select a favorite jazz CD from a list of over a hundred sounds that Fowler, who also serves as house deejay, will gladly play. Is this place great, or what?!

Cover charge on weekends/ $10–$20 Dinner menu / ☐ ℉ 🎼

☆Willie Mitchell's Rhythm & Blues Club
326 Beale Street, Memphis, Tennessee   901.523.7444

Beale Street truly comes alive on the weekends when Willie Mitchell's Rhythm & Blues Club throws open its doors and lets all that good **Live Down-Home R&B** music spill out. Owned by and named after the famous musician and producer, Willie Mitchell's is *the* place to go in Memphis for great music, good **Home-Style Food**, and **Dancing** the night away!
Cover charge/ $10–$15 Dinner menu/ ☐ 🍽 🎶

Catering

Sanders Catering   2600 Elvis Presley Boulevard, Memphis, Tennessee   901.774.8735

Odell Sanders, president of Sanders Catering, believes that "you are only as good as your last job." That's why he is so passionate about providing great service as well as good food for every affair he is hired to cater. With over 25 years in food service, Sanders has used his wealth of experience to establish a business that not only provides **Full-Service Catering and Event Planning** but offers clients a wide variety of cuisines from which to choose. **Whether it's American, French, southern, or kosher, Sanders can tailor a menu to fit your needs!** His firm has serviced large corporate affairs such as the huge Thanksgiving dinner the Nike Corporation recently hosted in Memphis—for a mere 3,000 persons!—to small, intimate gatherings in private homes. Sanders's **On-Site Banquet Facility** can accommodate up to 300, but use of other halls can be arranged for larger affairs.

MIAMI

Fine Dining

☆Norma's on the Beach   646 Lincoln Road, Miami Beach, Florida   305.532.2809

When the *Miami New Times* hailed Norma's on the Beach as the **"Best Caribbean Restaurant"** in 1997, it offered the following claim: "When it comes to Caribbean cuisine in Miami, there's Norma's and there's everyone else." Although Norma's is nowhere near the beach, as its name implies, the food and decor will leave you so satisfied that by the time your meal is over, you'll swear you feel the sting of saltwater air on your face! Norma's is owned by Delius Shirley, son of Norma Shirley, famed Jamaican restaurant owner and the restaurant's namesake, and executive chef Cindy Hutson. Together they bring a festive and creative menu to Miami's newly crowded and trendy Lincoln Road.

Norma's beautifully presented **French Caribbean Cuisine** shoots down the myth that all island food is heavy, thick, and over-spiced. **Conch and Callaloo Fritters, Phyllo Encrusted Shrimp**, or the restaurant's famous **Rasta Salad** (red and yellow bell peppers, hearts of palm, and artichoke hearts) are excellent selections to start your meal. **Jerk Pork Tenderloin, Seared Jerk Tuna, Bahamian Black Grouper,** and **Escovitched Yellowtail Snapper** are just some of the tempting entree offerings. It seems, though, that Norma's truly decadent **Appleton Golden Rum Cake,** savored with a cup of **Jamaican Blue Mountain Coffee,** receives the most praises from critics, tourists, and native Floridians alike. Does it get any better than this?

$20+ ☎ ❑ ✓ (⛾

☆Savannah   431–33 Washington Avenue, Miami Beach, Florida   305.604.8040

Savannah, the newest entry to the South Beach scene, puts all the other local restaurants in its class to shame. And that class would be first-class, all the way. Let's talk decor. Interior designer Alex Locadia waved his magic wand and graced Savannah with a setting that combines old-world Hollywood with modern-day Miami. A sophisticated, neutral-color palette of sage and wheat play off the creamy walls of the dining room. Hand-set red stones trace the length of the main room. And then, the hippest crowd on the strip can be found sashaying between the glass-topped bar in the main front room and the caramel-colored chaise lounges in the back. As breathtaking as this restaurant is, however, owner Peter Thomas guarantees that Savannah will not only be a feast for the eyes but will indeed satisfy the most discriminating palate.

With this restaurant, Executive Chef Marvin Woods introduces the Miami area to **South Carolina "Low-Country" Cuisine**, a type of cooking found in the southeastern coastal regions of that state. His goal, he claims, is to elevate the simple, rice-based dishes of that area by presenting them in an upscale manner, in much the same way other provincial cuisines like Country French have been raised to the level of haute cuisine. The results: nothing short of genius! Take, for example, Savannah's signature appetizer: its **Hushpuppies**. Believe me, these crusty, succulent morsels are no kin to the kind served at those fast-food fish places. They're made with whole Shrimp and Oysters, folded into a seasoned corn meal batter and lightly fried. Main courses are no less spectacular and include such delights as **Bourbon-Soaked Pork Chop Smothered with Sweet Onion–Apple Glaze, Slow-Roasted Barbeque Duck**, and **Corn-Dusted Snapper**.

$20+ 🕾 ☐ 🍴 📷

Casual Dining

☆Bahamian Connection Restaurant   4490 N.W. 2nd Avenue, Near Downtown, Miami, Florida 305.576.6999

Why fly all the way to Nassau when South Florida has it all? The sun, the sand, the sea...and when you want authentic island food, simply head over to the Bahamian Connection Restaurant—*the* place to go for Caribbean food in Miami. Upon entering this small, no-frills neighborhood spot, you'll be instantly transported to the islands by the aromas from the kitchen and the chatter from the regulars. With Chef Ann working her magic with her special recipes from Exuma in the Bahamas, manager Philip Ingraham treats his patrons to all the foods he enjoyed during his childhood. Since his father, "Big Link," started the business 14 years ago, the two have entertained their customers from all over the state with their charm and wit. Meeting Philip and his dad are two very good reasons to visit the Bahamian Connection. The #1 reason, however, is the food.

Breakfast is the main event at the Bahamian Connection, with **Boiled Fish** as the specialty of the house. Swimming in lemon, onion, and pepper, this dish is what puts this restaurant on the map. The **Stewed Fish** is just as fine. And both are served with what a devoted regular calls "**the best Johnny Cake in Miami**."
Of course, there are traditional fares for breakfast, but why bother? The fish doesn't get any fresher, and besides, Philip claims, boiled fish is very low in calories! At lunchtime, **Fried or Steamed Conch**, **Steamed Fish**, and **Ox Tails** are among the favorites.
$10 ✓€

☆**Jackson's Soul Food   950 N.W. 3rd Avenue, Downtown, Miami, Florida   305.377.6710**
Continuing in their parents' tradition, Shirlene and Dwight Jackson opened Jackson's Soul Food in Miami's historic Overtown section three years ago. Formerly with the Miami Police Department, Shirlene claims that opening a restaurant was the farthest thing from her mind. However, when the right location became available, she immediately recognized a great business opportunity. With family and friends pitching in and a little gray paint, she turned a run-down storefront into *the* **Soul Food Breakfast** spot in downtown Miami. Jackson's is located in the 'hood, so don't expect a fancy interior. You will, however, find a clean and friendly atmosphere, good service, and great biscuits!
Shirlene starts her preparations for each day in the wee hours of the morning because Jackson's starts serving breakfast at 5:45am. **Fried or Smothered Chicken Wings**, **Liver and Onions**, or **Pork Chops** with **Eggs**, **Grits**, and **Homemade Biscuits** are among the typical offerings. The **Steamed Catfish** is another local breakfast favorite, flaky and well-seasoned, with bell peppers and onions. **No place in Miami Beach can offer a finer breakfast at a better price**, and is it ever worth getting up for!
$10 ✓€

☆**Tangerine's Restaurant & Jazz Cabaret
      10760 Biscayne Boulevard, Miami Shores,
      Florida   305.892.8006**
Located in the fashionable neighborhood of Miami Shores, Tangerine's is just as sunny and warm inside as its name implies. The walls and floors of this handsome, European-style restaurant

glow in the colors of terra cotta.   The chairs are trimmed in assorted mid-tone colors that accent the hand-painted tabletops. The main room features a low, brick wall separating the dining area from the large, exposed kitchen.

Tangerine's ambience is reason enough to seek out this new restaurant.   Indeed, the large square bar in the center of the dining room is usually bustling with young professionals. But come for the food and the jazz! Whatever your mood, Tangerine's menu has it a covered. Chef Herbert Coleman works his magic in this busy kitchen, providing real cross-section of dishes and delicacies from **Southern and Caribbean Specialties** as well as **Italian, Steak, and Seafood Entrees**. Get started with tasty **Conch Fritters** or **Florida Grouper Curried Fingers**.   Move on to Tangerine's **Jambalaya, Jamaican Chicken, Seafood Scampi** (offering shrimp, scallops, fish, calamari, lobster meat, mussels, and clams!) or the **12-Ounce New York Strip Steak**. Weekends, **Live Jazz** combos entertain throughout the night.

$15–$20 ☎ ☐ ♉ ♫♪ ✿

☆**Tap Tap   819 - 5th Street, Miami Beach, Florida 305.672.2898**

Tap Tap is an **Authentic Haitian Café** disguised as an elaborate gallery showcasing the finest in Caribbean art.   Or is it the other way around? In any event, the festive decor promises to thrill your visual senses as the menu tantalizes your tastebuds. **Live Music** is featured on weekends.

$15–$20 ☐ ♉ ♫♪

"Tangerine's Restaurant & Jazz Cabaret is a great place to take clients for a tasty and tasteful business meeting." *Norbert Seals, The Ptolemy Group*

Cafeteria/Buffet-Style Dining

☆**People's Bar-B-Que   360 N.W. 8th Street, Downtown, Miami, Florida 305.373.8080**

On an 80-degree afternoon in Miami, George Lewis, Sr., enjoys sitting outdoors, greeting customers as they enter his family-owned barbecue restaurant and drug store. A handsome man at 96 years young, Lewis is Florida's oldest living pharmacist. When he opened People's Drug Store in 1925, he also became the state's first Black pharmacist. His son, George Jr., however, while also a pharmacist like his dad, realized the need for good barbecue in Miami. So, in 1961 he opened People's Bar-B-Que right next door to the drug store, serving (you guessed it!) barbecue. Other soul food selections were later added to the menu. As the younger Lewis's business grew, the need for more space became apparent. A new, larger location was secured just across the street, but moving into it proved a difficult task. After facing too many construction problems to mention, yards of bureaucratic red tape, Hurricane Andrew, and countless other obstacles, People's Bar-B-Que finally moved to its new home in fall 1996. Alas, the completion of the new site was bittersweet: George Lewis, Jr., passed away before he saw his dream fulfilled. Today, his wife Gloria and their four children keep the People's Bar-B-Que tradition alive, offering **Soul Food at a Terrific Price**.

In addition to great **Bar-B-Que Chicken** and **Ribs**, People's buffet line serves up **Meat Loaf**, **Beef Stew**, **Fried Fish**, **Pork Chops**, and **Baked Ham** as well as a large assortment of side dishes. On Sundays, Mrs. Lewis makes on average about nine pans of **Banana Pudding** for the dinner crowd, but within two-and-half hours, she claims, the pans are empty! So, you've been advised. Doors open at 4pm; be there or miss out!

$10 ✓ℭ

Nightclubs

Studio 183 2860 N.W. 183rd Street, Miami, Florida
305.621.7295

Studio 183 is a **Huge Complex** showcasing a variety of entertainment under one roof. Under the professional management of Zeek Hodge, this Miami hot spot attracts a global clientele. Headliners from Sinbad to Bobby Womack as well as talented local artists have performed on its main stage. Among other features of the Studio 183 complex is the **Jazz Room Lounge**, open nightly for cocktails and offering **Live Jazz on Weekends**. Then there's the club, **Miami Nights,** where the party people come to dance hard. Catering to a 21-and-older crowd, Miami Nights has **Two Pool Tables, Two Bars**, and room for up to 750 people. Studio 183 also houses a **Full-Service Restaurant**. The entire venue can hold up to 2,000 people and is **Available for Banquets or Concerts**.

Cover charge/ 21+ crowd / ☐ ⛄ 🎼 🎧

NEW ORLEANS

Fine Dining

☆Dooky Chase's   2301 Orleans Avenue, Downtown, New Orleans, Louisiana   504.821.0600

Few New Orleans restaurants have gained the national recognition and appreciation that Dooky Chase's has. In 1941, Edgar "Dooky" Chase, Sr., and his wife Emily opened a sandwich shop and bar that eventually expanded to a small restaurant. When Leah Chase, current proprietor and head chef of Dooky Chase's, married Edgar Jr., she too started working in the family business, bringing with her all that she had learned from her early culinary training in the French Quarter. Little by little, Ms. Leah introduced new ways to prepare and serve food that have turned Dooky Chase's into **New Orleans's Premiere Restaurant for Authentic Creole Cuisine**. She has also been the guiding hand behind the artistic setting created in the restaurant's main dining room, with its original works by famous African American artists, its fine table settings, and rich mauve decor. And all this in the same spot the founders' humble sandwich shop occupied over 50 years ago!

The reasons behind the success and longevity of this New Orleans culinary landmark? Quite simple: Leah Chase, ever the gracious hostess, has rules she likes to live by. "Since slavery days," she reflects, referring to the African American experience, "all we had to look forward to was a good meal. Our goal at Dooky Chase's is to provide our customer with a delicious meal and serve it elegantly, in the manner in which we deserve to be treated." Thank you, Ms. Leah!

Dooky Chase's offers a **Complete Dinner Menu, à la Carte Dining**, and a **Lunch Buffet Monday through Friday**. Entrees include **Crawfish Etoufee, Shrimp Clemenceau** (shrimp sautéed in garlic butter and mixed with vegetables), **Veal Grillades, Fried Oysters**, and **Stuffed Lobster**. And let's not forget **Creole Gumbo** and **Mamere's Crab Soup** for starters!

$20+ ☎ ☐ ✔ ℂ 🍷 📷

☆ **Olivier's Restaurant   204 Decatur Street, French Quarter, New Orleans, Louisiana   540.525.7734**
Armand Olivier, Sr., founder of Olivier's Restaurant, **One of the Loveliest Dining Spots in the French Quarter**, comes from a long line of fine Creole cooks—five generations, to be exact! He acknowledges his great-grandmother, Mama Jeanne Gaudet Doublet, for passing down many of the recipes served at his restaurant today. When Olivier's was located in the Gentilly area, Armand's wife Cheryl enjoyed not only preparing the food but serving it as well. Now his son, Chef Armand, is in charge of the kitchen at the French Quarter location, with its inviting, Old World charm and rich decor. And the younger Olivier is widely known for his constant experimenting with different spices as well as his delicious updating of classic family recipes for his patrons' pleasure.
A trip to New Orleans is not complete with out a plate of Olivier's famous oysters, and the restaurant offers them two ways: **Oysters Rockefeller** and **Pecan Breaded Oysters.** Other specialties of the house include **Creole Rabbit**, **Poulet au Fromage**, **Taster's Platter** (fried seafood), **Pork Medallions**, and **Beef Bourguignonne**. And then there's the **Gumbo Sampler**, which allows you to try three versions of Louisiana Gumbo. An upstairs dining area, which seats 60, is available for private parties.
$20+ ☎ ❑ ✓ 🍷 🎁

Casual Dining

☆**Barrow's Catfish Restaurant   2714 Mistletoe Street, New Orleans, Louisiana   504.486.1749**
"If U park in front of the gate, make sure U buy some fish" reads the sign outside of Billy Barrow's Catfish Restaurant. And that's the only reason to go to this restaurant because **Fried Catfish is pretty much all Barrow's serves**. However, when the restaurant first opened in 1943, Barrow's served a full menu. That was when William Barrow, Sr., and his wife opened a restaurant and bar on the first floor of a two-story house and moved their family into the level above. When Mrs. Barrow took ill a few years later, the menu was reduced to only **Fried Catfish** and **Potato Salad** because that was all Mr. Barrow knew how to prepare.

Current proprietor William ("Billy") Barrow, Jr., recalls that he was only 14 years old when his father taught him the secrets of frying fish. To make sure that the oil was just right, Billy would stick his finger into the grease to see if it was hot enough! Well, he doesn't do that anymore, but he learned his father's secrets well enough to earn the reputation of serving the **Freshest and Crispiest Catfish in All New Orleans!** Ask any native of New Orleans, and they'll tell you: Barrow's catfish "is so good, it tastes like candy"!
$10–$15 ☐

☆Bennachin   133 North Carrollton, New Orleans, Louisiana   504.486.1313

Alyse Njenge, a native of Cameroon, attended the University of New Orleans, where she met Fanta Tambajang, who hails from The Gambia. Both women loved to cook, so in 1992, they decided to open a restaurant together. Voilà—Bennachin was born! The name means "one pot," as in the many African dishes this restaurant specializes in that are prepared in one pot, like **Jambalaya**. Bennachin's reputation for terrific African cuisine earned it a much-coveted spot at the annual New Orleans Jazz Festival; in turn, the exposure helped establish Bennachin as a favorite local eatery. Folks at the Jazz Fest stand in long lines to sample Njenga's and Tambajan's **Spicy Spinach** (the best!) as well as many other African delights.

Bennachin's customers are treated to a **Tantalizing Blend of African Cuisines**, served in a casual, "down-home" setting garnished with African artifacts and paintings. The names of the dishes served at Bennachin may be foreign, but the tastes are very, very familiar: spicy, saucy, and delightful. Favorites include **Kembel–Ioppa** (sautéed lamb strips and bell pepper with ginger), **Bomok–Chobi** (baked stuffed trout), **Bennachin** (beef jambalaya served with sautéed spinach), and **Janga** (sautéed shrimp and veggies served with cous–cous). The prices are right, too. **Daily Lunch Specials** typically run under $5 for a generous portion. So be adventurous and try something new next time you're in the N'awlins. After all, how many oyster Po-Boys can one person eat?
$10–$15 ☐ ✓Ⅽ ⛾

> "Outside, it looks like a dump. But inside,
> Two Sisters serves the best down-home cooking
> New Orleans has to offer!"
> *Leo Alexander, Broadcast Television News Reporter*

Café Benet Restaurant   3925 Washington Avenue, New Orleans, Louisiana   504.822.1376

Why would a banker leave a prestigious yet demanding job for an even more hectic one as a restaurant owner? To follow a dream, of course! And that's exactly what Kevin Bennette did. In 1989, with no prior experience, he and his wife took over a small luncheonette, gave it an old-fashioned blue-and-white interior, added a **Banquet Facility** upstairs and—Ta-Da!—Café Benet was born! No more banker's hours for him, Kevin's days now start before 6am, as daybreak finds him up and at work in his restaurant, getting ready for the early breakfast crowd. He's there for the lunch rush, too, serving everyone from blue-collar workers to business executives. Dinner at Café Benet is another matter: it's served only on Fridays and Saturdays.

Po-Boys and **Deli Sandwiches** are the specialties at Café Benet, and they come in many varieties: **Liver**, **Hot Sausage**, **Catfish**, **Pork Chop**, and **Roast Beef.** The lunch favorites are its **Macaroni and Cheese** and **Red Beans and Rice**, both of which are great with Café Benet's **Fried Chicken**, **Hot Sausage**, **Pork Chops**, or **Panee Meat** entrees, served every day of the week. You can't leave New Orleans without a good plate of this restaurant's red beans, so don't even try!

$10 ❑ ✓❢ ⛟

Café New Orleans   3827 Frenchmen Street, Gentilly, New Orleans, Louisiana   504.943.0570

Tucked away in a small pocket across from Dillard University is a lovely little neighborhood place with a creative Creole menu. Chef Sherman Johnson, proprietor of Café New Orleans, started his restaurant career washing dishes. He quickly moved up the ranks to sous chef, later serving as executive chef at several area hotels and restaurants. When the opportunity to acquire the Café New Orleans from its former owner came up,

Johnson jumped at the chance. With a fresh coat of paint and several beautifully framed works of African American art adorning the walls, Johnson's café was ready to serve the New Orleans dining public "soul food with a touch of class."

Get started at the Café New Orleans with **Stuffed Mushrooms**, or how about a nice bowl of **File Gumbo**? Entrees include **Crawfish Etoufee**, **Shrimp Scampi**, **Stuffed Bell Peppers**, **Steak and Shrimp**, **Catfish LaComb** (sautéed catfish topped with crawfish tails and herb sauce) and **Pasta Frenchmen** (sautéed onion, garlic, and tricolored peppers with chicken breast over pasta). **Lunch Specials** are very reasonable and feature the same delicious fare.

$10–$15 ❑ ✓ ℂ

Dunbar's Fine Foods   4927 Freret Street, Uptown, New Orleans, Louisiana   504.899.0734

Celestine Dunbar began her career in food service when she opened a small sandwich shop inside a dress shop. When the dress shop owner became ill, Dunbar took over and grew both businesses until she could no longer manage by herself. So, she closed the dress shop in 1990, and moved the food business to its present Uptown location, where she opened Dunbar's Fine Foods.

A modest, smallish restaurant specializing in **Creole/ Soul Food**, Dunbar's is a family-owned business. Daughter Peggy is the restaurant's manager, daughter Lisa works there too, and her son-in-law serves as the head chef. Mrs. Dunbar attributes her restaurant's success to the simple formula for the treatment she and her children give to each customer: "Loving care, like you would give your mother. And food prepared fresh, like at home."

Traditional New Orleans dishes like **Gumbo**, **Red Beans and Rice**, **Fried Chicken**, and **Cornbread** are just a few of the items featured at Dunbar's; the menu changes daily.

$10 ✓ ℂ

East African Harvest Vegetarian   1643 Gentilly Boulevard, Gentilly, New Orleans, Louisiana   540.943.0787

Right next to the fair grounds in the Gentilly section of New Orleans is a small, casual place featuring a unique meatless menu "in the tradition of up-country East Africa." A vegetarian for over 25 years, proprietor R. C. Johnson spent quite a bit of time in that part of the world. While there, she learned how to use the various spices, herbs, and vegetables available to the local folk. Upon returning to New Orleans, and tired of salads and baked potatoes being her only options when dining out, Johnson decided that what the city needed was a good vegetarian restaurant. Taking family recipes as well as dishes she discovered in Africa and converting them to fit her needs, she open East African Harvest Vegetarian in 1991.

Balance is a key philosophy in vegetarian culture; therefore, Johnson insists that her menu selections always combine something cooked with something raw. For Example, the **Burger 'n' Bun Combo** (a vegetable burger dressed with eggless mayo, lettuce, tomato, and alfalfa sprouts) is one of her restaurant's best sellers. **Daily Specials** consist of **Vegetarian Salisbury Steak, Spinach Lasagna with Vegetable Cheese and Crushed Olives.** Be sure to try the **Drop Biscuits**, and for dessert, check out the **Sorbet, Bread Pudding**, and **Sweet Potato Pie.** Items can also be cooked to order to accommodate different types of vegetarian needs.

$10 ☐ ✓ℂ

> "One of my favorite restaurants is Zachary's on Oak Street. Though relatively new to the New Orleans scene, Zachary's is owned by the legendary Baquet family, which began Eddie's Restaurant in New Orleans' Seventh Ward. Eddie Baquet trained his sons well in the Creole cuisine tradition, and the food is spicy and plentiful. Zachary's has a great variety of Soul and Creole cooking, and is great for lunch and dinner." *Antoine M. Garibaldi, Ph.D., Provost and Chief Academic Officer, Howard University*

☆Eddie's Restaurant   5700 Lake Forest Boulevard, New Orleans, Louisiana   504.246.0437

The Baquets, one of New Orleans's oldest restaurant families, have continuously served delicious food in their community for over 50 years. It all started when Ada Baquet Gross and her husband Paul opened Paul Gross' Chicken Coop in 1940. Eddie Baquet, Sr.,

Ms. Ada's nephew, joined the staff of the Coop five years later. In 1966, he left to open his own place, Eddie's Restaurant on Law Street. Eddie's son Wayne loved the business and joined him in running it for a while, but he twice walked away from it to pursue other ventures, later returning to help make Eddie's one of New Orleans's most famous Creole restaurants.   Today, Wayne has moved the restaurant from it's Seventh Ward location to a casual, contemporary setting in the Lake Forest Mall. But he still serves the same delicious Creole cuisine prepared by his great-aunt so many years ago.

To take part in the true dining experience that is New Orleans, one must consume certain foods—all of which can be enjoyed at Eddie's.   **Po-Boy Sandwiches** make lunchtime a heavenly meal, and you can't go wrong with Eddie's **Oyster**, **Catfish**, **Shrimp** or **Hot Sausage Po-Boys**, all "dressed," of course.   For dinner, start with **File Gumbo** or **Oyster-Stuffed Bread**. **Red Beans and Rice**, **Paneed Veal**, **Stuffed Shrimp in Seafood Sauce**, and **Trout Baquet** (broiled trout with lump crab meat) are just a few of the many favorites served daily. And Eddie's wife Myrtle's **Bread Pudding in Rum Butter Sauce** is still a must-have item on the menu. The restaurant's **Sunday Gospel Brunch** gives patrons a chance to try many of the dishes served at Eddie's as well as a chance to start the week off right.

$10–$15 □ ✓ ₵ 🍴 🍲 ☕

> **"I grew up on Dooky Chase's dinners. They're a family tradition!"** *Fran McManus, Native of New Orleans*

Jayde's
> **2523 Perdido, Downtown, New Orleans,**
> **Louisiana 504.822.6814**
> **7204 Hayne Boulevard, New Orleans, Louisiana**
> **504.245.1235**

Russell Kelly is doing exactly what he had planned on doing since he was 12 years old. That was when he proclaimed to his mother that one day he was going to build her a restaurant where she could prepare for others the delicious meals he had enjoyed all his life. With the help of family and friends, Kelly transformed a former crackhouse into an upscale soul food restaurant. He named it Jayde's after his lovely young daughter, who happens to be autistic.

Jayde's award-winning menu starts with **Fried Chicken Livers and Gizzards, Gumbo of the Day, Sautéed Coventry Sausages,** or **Hog's Head Cheese.** House specialties include the **Seafood Platter, 12-Ounce Smoked Barbecue Pork Chop, Catfish Dijon, Beans (Red, White, Navy,** or **Limas) with Smoked Ham Hocks,** and **Stewed Turkey Necks and Wings.** Everything comes with large squares of sweet **Cornbread. Sunday Brunch** and **Live Jazz** at Jayde's make the weekend right flavorful.

$10–$15 ☐ ✓ ℂ 🍴 🖼

Montrel's Creole Café 4116 Marigny, Gentilly, New Orleans, Louisiana 504.288.6374

Tanya Montrel and her husband found the perfect location for their Creole restaurant in 1993. Only problem was that it used to be an office building, complete with a garage. With help from family and friends, they transformed the run-down old building into a cozy neighborhood restaurant. Four small offices became the dining room. The bar area was carved out of the garage space, its walls adorned with a lovely mural of a French Quarter courtyard. Another dining area, perfect for private affairs and for **Live Jazz on Friday Nights**, was added upstairs.

Montrel's provides an enjoyable dining experience with friendly service and **Good Creole Food.** Of course, there's **Seafood Gumbo** on the menu for starters (meals don't start in New Orleans without a bowl of gumbo!). Other favorites include **Red Beans and Rice, Shrimp Creole, Fettucini Montrel** (shrimp and crawfish over pasta), **Stuffed Crabs, Scampi Marigny,** and the **Fried Seafood Platter.** Need a perfect ending for a great meal? Try Montrel's **Brownie à la Mode** or their **Bread Pudding.**

$10–$15 ☐ ✓ ℂ 🍴 🖼

☆Palmer's Jamaican Restaurant   135 North Carrollton Avenue, New Orleans, Louisiana   504.482.3658

With a rating of "three red beans" (very good) from the *New Orleans Times–Picayune*, Palmer's Jamaican Restaurant is considered one of the best in a city flooded with great eateries. A simple place, Palmer's did not get its high rating for its decor. No, it's all about the food here, perfectly seasoned and plenty of it! Chef/proprietor Cecil Palmer attended cooking school in Jamaica, working his way up to chef status at a local resort. In 1973, he moved to New Orleans and, after working in several hotels, opened his own place in 1990.

Let's get this out of the way now: Palmer's has the **Best Curried Chicken Patties**—period! The crust is flaky and light, and the filling is the perfect combination of chicken, onions, vegetables, and spices. While they're guaranteed not to burn your tongue, your eyes will water, with pleasure! Other Palmer's must-tries are the **Shrimp Joanne** (sautéed shrimp on a slice of eggplant), **Melange de Rebecca** (shrimp and chicken sautéed with vegetables in a chardonnay cream sauce), **Curried Goat,** and **Jamaican Chicken**. Top off your meal with a cup of **Blue Mountain Coffee**. A **Lunch Buffet** is served daily.

$10–$15 ☐ ✓ℂ ⵜ

"I always look forward to traveling to New Orleans for great food, especially when I dine at The Praline Connection!" *David Dixon, Vice President & Director, Boston EquiServe*

☆The Praline Connection
542 Frenchmen Street, French Quarter, New Orleans, Louisiana   504.943.3934
Terminal B, New Orleans International Airport (Candy Only)
☆ The Praline Connection Gospel & Blues Hall
901–07 South Peters Street, Downtown, New Orleans, Louisiana 540.523.3973

Four months after The Praline Connection on Frenchmen Street opened in 1990, Gene Bourg, food critic at the *New Orleans*

Times–Picayune, had only a few words to say about the food served there: "This is how it should be, and there's nothing more to be said about it." Well, there you have it! From the beginning, The Praline Connection's proprietors Curtis Moore and Cecil Kaigler have been two very busy men. With their signature black fedoras and white aprons, they have catered events nationwide, from posh affairs in California's Napa Valley to funky sets in Manhattan. They've also hosted private parties in their new Gospel & Blues Hall for diverse clients ranging from The Rolling Stones and George Clinton to the National Urban League and the National Association of Black MBAs.

Moore describes the menu at The Praline Connection as "down-home cooking that no one wants to prepare anymore." The restaurants' **Gospel Sunday Brunch** is the best way to sample it all. **Live Inspirational Music** and an extensive buffet will satisfy both hungers. Pass on the breakfast bar and head straight for the **File Gumbo, Red Beans and Rice, Fried Chicken, Stuffed Bell Peppers with Crab Meat, BBQ Ribs, Sliced Beef, Fried Catfish, Greens**, and **Pasta** on the buffet. Don't forget the desserts: **Bread Pudding with Praline Sauce** and, of course, fresh **Pralines**. And if that's not enough to get you there, enjoy a drink at the long cherry wood bar once owned by the infamous Al Capone (yes, the gangster!).

$15–$20 / Sunday Live Gospel Brunch $20+/

❐ ✔ ℂ ⑂ ♫ ⑂🎁 ☕

Rita's Olde French Quarter Restaurant
945 Rue Chartres Street, New Orleans,
Louisiana 504.525.7543

Rita Davis always wanted a restaurant in the French Quarter where she could cook both Creole and Cajun meals "with a soulful flair" for adventurous out-of-towners and locals alike. So, with her husband of 40 years, Elwood Davis, she opened Rita's Olde French Quarter Restaurant in 1989, serving dishes that are a combination of these two distinct cooking styles and Rita's own unique blend of time-tested family recipes.

Located just three blocks from Jackson Square, Rita's is a cozy, casual family restaurant with a friendly wait staff and an extensive menu. One of her most popular menu selections is the **"Taste of New Orleans."** It's an **All-Inclusive Meal** that starts with **Gumbo**, then (get ready!) offers up **Red Beans and Rice**, **Jambalaya**, **BBQ Ribs**, **Crawfish Pie**, **Shrimp Creole**, **Louisiana Yams**, and other **Vegetables,** and ends (whew!) with **Rita's Bread Pudding**, a delicious dessert made from a recipe that has been in her family for generations. Better walk around the French Market twice to work that meal off because you'll want to come back tomorrow for more!

$20 ☐ ⛟

☆Two Sisters Restaurant   223 North Derbigny Street, Downtown, New Orleans, Louisiana   540.524.0056

Two Sisters Restaurant sits on the outskirts of the French Quarter, and it's well worth crossing North Claiborne to get there. When you walk into this small, homey restaurant, the unbelievable aroma from the kitchen is the first thing that hits you. Then you notice all the photos of local police officers and public officials who have enjoyed their meals at Two Sisters.   Third, you gasp at the huge amount of piping hot food that is piled high on the plates being served to everyone else's table but yours because you haven't ordered yet! Hey, Two Sisters is the *Real Deal* Creole /Soul Food **Restaurant in New Orleans**!   That's because Doris Finister, proprietor, and her three daughters strive to make sure that each patron is well fed and totally satisfied.

Specials change daily, but you can be sure the following will be there to greet you: for appetizers, there's **Stewed Shrimp with Okra** (they sell approximately 15 to 20 pounds of it a day, claims Finister).   Among the entrees: **Stewed Turkey Wings**, **Jambalaya**, **Fried Chicken**, **Fried Fish**, and **Chitterlings**. On the side, try the **Butter Beans**, and if you have room for dessert, it's **Peach Cobbler** all the way!

$10

☆Zachary's Creole Cuisine   8400 Oak Street, Uptown, New Orleans, Louisiana   540.865.1559

Wayne Baquet, Sr., always dreamed of owning a fine-dining establishment. His family's rich culinary history, his many years of success running Eddie's Restaurant in the Seventh Ward, and numerous other ventures prepared him for such a challenge.

He renovated an old cottage in the now trendy, uptown Carrollton neighborhood, transforming it into the bright, charming restaurant he christened Zachary's, after his grandson. With Zachary's father, Wayne Jr., overseeing the day-to-day operations, the restaurant boasts two dining rooms, a businesspersons' bar and lounge, and a menu that incorporates Creole family recipes with new imaginative dishes.

Lunchtime at this very popular restaurant finds local politicians and executives talking shop over a plate of **Red Beans and Hot Sausage**. On any given evening, a birthday party or bridal rehearsal dinner is typically being enjoyed in the back dining room. **Crawfish Pie** and **Shrimp Remoulade** are two Creole standards given worthy treatment as appetizers at Zachary's. Also noteworthy include entrees such as **Trout Geri** (broiled trout with light crawfish dressing), **Veal Zachary** (breaded baby veal topped with seafood au gratin), and the **Shrimp and Oyster Plate.** Also recommended are the **Veal Chops**, served with an onion glaze, and the **Eggplant Casserole. Chocolate Ecstasy Cake** is the dessert of choice.

$15–$20 ▢ ✓ ℂ 🍷 🎁

Cafeteria/Buffet-Style Dining

☆The Tourist Trap   91 French Market Place, French Quarter, New Orleans, Louisiana   504.588.1588

Well, the location of this restaurant couldn't be any better. After perusing through the French Market looking for antiques and African American memorabilia, you're almost certain to find the best bargains at a location across the street from it, right on the edge of the French Quarter. That place? A new restaurant called, appropriately enough, The Tourist Trap. This colorful cafeteria is perfect for tourists and locals alike who are short on time but want a good, filling meal.

Greg Walker, proprietor of The Tourist Trap, felt the name was perfect because of the restaurant's great location. The interior is very New Orleans, with a fabulous cherrywood bar, Spanish tile floors, and colorful hand-painted tables. The Trap opens at 6am, serving a hearty breakfast of morning favorites like **Pork Chops**, **Liver and Onions**, and **Chopped Steak and Eggs**. Noontime shoppers line up for its **Baked** or **Barbecued Chicken**,

Smothered Chops, **Glazed Ham**, and **Baked Fish**. There are also tons of sides to choose from, and, of course, it wouldn't be New Orleans or The Tourist Trap without **Bread Pudding** for dessert! $10 ✓ ℂ

> "Since I moved to New Orleans in 1995, I have enjoyed so many terrific restaurants, I could never single any one of them out as my favorite. I have eaten at most of the restaurants featured in this guide and while many of them may be found far off the beaten path, they are all outstanding!"
> *Richard Pennington, Chief of Police*
> *New Orleans Police Department*

Sweet Shop

☆**Loretta's New Orleans Authentic Pralines**
1100 North Peters, Stall 17, French Market,
French Quarter, New Orleans, Louisiana
540.529.6170

Sixteen years ago, Loretta Harrison took a big chance: she quit her job at Louisiana State University Medical Library to make and sell pralines! See, ever since her mother taught her and her 11 brothers and sisters the art of making pralines (God bless her mother!), Harrison had dreamed of owning a candy shop. Her first sale was to a cafeteria where she dropped off 60 pralines, all of which were sold in just two days! Today, you can watch Harrison and her staff actually making the melt-in-your-mouth confectionery delights in her cheery candy shop in the French Market the same way her mother and grandmother did many years ago. Harrison gives God the credits for all the opportunities and successes that have come her way over the years. "Acknowledge Him and He will direct thy path," she affirms with almost praline-sweet conviction. Great words to live by! In addition to the **Creamiest Pralines in New Orleans**, Loretta's also sells **Sweet Potato Cookies**, **Muffins**, **Praline Sauces**, **Assorted Fudges**, and **Gourmet Coffees**, all of which can be ordered by phone and delivered directly to your home.

Nightclubs

Club Whispers   8700 Lake Forest Boulevard, New Orleans, Louisiana 504.245.1059

The biggest dance party in this party town can be found at Club Whispers, where the deejays play enough **Hip-Hop, R&B, Old-School,** and **Rap** to keep everyone groovin' all night long. The **Large Dance Floor** is perfect for the college crowd that flocks to this club weekly.

Cover charge/ 21+ crowd/ ☐ 🍴 🗲🍷

☆The New Showcase Lounge   1915 North Broad, New Orleans, Louisiana 504.945.5612

When they first learned that the old Showcase Lounge was available for sale in 1993, brothers Robert and Julius Kimbrough didn't think the funky neighborhood bar was quite the spot they were looking for. It did, however, have promise. So, the two pharmacists took a chance and turned the old nightspot into a world-class jazz club. Starting out by offering **Live Jazz on Sunday Nights** only, the New Showcase became so popular that the Kimbroughs were soon able to host local bands five nights out of the week. Now, area jazz musicians like bass player Walter Payton and his Snapbean Band, vocalist Betty Shirley, and the James Rivers Movement have a regular place to come and jam.

Since its opening, the New Showcase Lounge has received national recognition. National Public Radio did a live broadcast from the club on New Year's Eve in 1996. It even has its own web page on the Internet! And if that's not enough, the locals swear that the Showcase Lounge serves the **Best Hot Tamales in New Orleans**.

Cover charge/ Bar food / ☐ 🍴 🎵

Pampy's Restaurant & Bar   2005 North Broad, Gentilly, New Orleans, Louisiana 504.949.7970

Pampy's is a neighborhood bar in the truest sense of the word. Located down the street from the racetrack, it plays host to a broad range of clientele, from surgeons to blue-collar workers. But it's not about class at this modest, nothing bar—it's all about the music! On weekends, Pampy's features **Some of the Best Live Music Anywhere in the New Orleans area**. Just push back the chairs for impromptu **Dancing** and you've got a party, New Orleans-style! Hey, Labat!

Cover charge/ □ ♟ ♫ ✉

Prime Example   1909 North Broad, Gentilly, New Orleans, Louisiana   504.947.0763

This upscale dance and supper club rocks on the weekends when the deejay comes in to spin everything from **Hip Hop, R&B,** and **Oldies** to **Soft Rap**. The interior is much slicker than that of its neighbors, and the crowd is a little younger and hipper. The dinner menu features a broad selection of New Orleans favorites, everything from **Gumbo** and **Po-Boy Sandwiches** to **Rib-Eye Steak**. **Live Music** is featured on select nights, so call for a calendar of events.

Cover charge/ 21+ crowd/ □ ♟ ♫ ✉

Caterers

Bertha Pichon Catering   3861 Virgil Boulevard, New Orleans, Louisiana   504.288.6015

Party planner, consultant, and caterer describes the many duties Bertha Pichon performs as **One of New Orleans's Premier Caterers**. Pichon started her catering career in the Fifties as a server with a renowned African American firm that specialized in working for the city's elite. This meant that she worked on numerous jobs within the Jewish community. It was then that Pichon decided to become a **Kosher Caterer**. After seven years of training in kosher kitchens and homes, Pichon's big break came in 1963 when an orthodox rabbi asked her to prepare a luncheon at Beth Israel Synagogue. With that event, Pichon became known as *the* kosher caterer in New Orleans. Thirty-plus years later, she still prepares for kosher events, but her first love remains Creole cuisine. Her firm has catered affairs for the late Mayor Dutch Morial and Congresswoman Lindsey Boggs, and she had the honor of serving former President Gerald Ford upon his visit to Dillard University. **Fresh Marinated Vegetables, Grillades and Grits, Oysters**

and Artichokes, and **Blackened Pepper Filet** are a few of Pichon Catering's specialty dishes. But for owner Bertha Pichon, "Everything is special, because I make it that way!"

Courtney's Deli and Catering 2916 Orleans Avenue, New Orleans, Louisiana 540.482.7387

Chef James Battiste started his restaurant career as a dishwasher at the tender age of 13. He worked his way up to night cook at the famous Chez Helene Restaurant and learned Creole cooking from the master, Chef Austin Leslie. When Battiste was offered the opportunity to take over Courtney's Deli, a little pink-and-blue take-out place that looks like a snowball stand, he didn't have enough money to close the deal. Eventually, with a little help from his family and credit from his suppliers, he immediately went into the lunch-stand business selling **Po-Boys**, **Red Beans and Rice**, and **Seafood**. The lunches weren't paying the bills, but the catering jobs that started coming in did. Today, Chef Battiste offers **Full-Service Catering**, featuring what he considers "the **Best Fried Chicken in the World**"—his own—and specializing in **New Orleans Soul/Creole Cuisine**. Although he loves catering, Chef Battiste claims he ultimately seeks to open a fine-dining establishment where he can serve Creole cooking the way it should be served: with real southern hospitality and great service. We can't wait!

The Gumbo Man New Orleans East, Louisiana 504.242.2501

Rudy Pierce started his catering career by hosting suppers at his home. Well, it just so happens that a guest one evening was a member of the 1987 New Orleans Jazz Festival's food committee. One taste of Pierce's gumbo and Rudy instantly gained a coveted spot at the festival that year selling his specialty to hungry tourists and natives. And that's how Pierce came to be known as "The Gumbo Man." The attention, customers, and catering jobs gained from this exposure enabled him to stop working at the Jazz Fest in 1993 and concentrate on catering. In addition to **Gumbo**, Pierce specializes in **Creole Cuisine**, everything from **Seafood** dishes to **Mirliton Casserole**, a unique and delicious side dish made with chayote squash stuffed with shrimp.

"The New Showcase Lounge is the kind of place that people would want to go to when visiting New Orleans. It may be just a neighborhood bar, but the multicultural mix of supportive local patrons and adventurous tourists gives this spot all the ambience that it needs. Of course, it doesn't hurt that they offer world-class jazz along with some of the best down-home blues night after night! Only in New Orleans!"

Ann Jackson, lover of jazz, good food, and New Orleans

NEW YORK CITY

Fine Dining

☆**Bambou   243 East 14ᵗʰ Street, Downtown,
New York, New York   212.358.0012**
Class and sophistication have descended on East 14ᵗʰ Street in the form of a restaurant named Bambou. The quiet elegance that surrounds this establishment and the desire to keep their haven private and special prevents proprietors Jean–Claude Samuel, Noel Mignott, and Daphne Mahoney from hanging out a neon sign to announce their location to the world. Their discreetness has in no way resulted in a lack of customers, however. Numerous celebrities and connoisseurs have found their way to Bambou.

Bambou gives New York a unique gift: an upscale Caribbean restaurant with excellent wait service, beautiful decor, and panache. Samuel's impeccable eye has transformed the modest space into a paradise lost. Upon entering, relax in the handsome Reefer Bar, with its gorgeous copper and high-gloss bamboo appointments surrounded by lush tropical plants. Revel in the main dining room, which is divided by heavy silk and linen draperies and dotted with exotic floral arrangements, fine art pieces, white ceiling fans, and island-green accents. One half expects to peer through the room's ivory-colored pane-glass windows and see the beckoning turquoise waters and white sands of Jamaica!

Categorized as **"Caribbean Fusion" Cuisine**, the food at Bambou is colorful as well as inventive. The perfect meal starts with **Soup Aubergines Saveur Coconut** (eggplant soup), **Crab Cake with Avocado Butter**, or **Pumpkin Ravioli with Callaloo Coulis**. **Grilled Jerk Breast of Chicken, Arawak Spice Shell Steak** with **Plantain Medallions**, and a dazzling **Dorade Royale** with **Patate and Ginger** are just a few of the entree offerings. Top the evening off with a **Warm Chocolate Souffle Cake** and a cup of **Blue Mountain Coffee**. Ah, the delightful decadence of it all!
$20+ ☎ ☐ ✔ ℂ 🍴

"I love Café Beulah! Wonderful food, soft environment, honest prices, and that cool, calm elegance."   *James C. Buford, Fashion Designer*

☆B. Smith's Restaurant   7771 Eighth Avenue, Midtown, New York, New York   212.582.3108

In the thick of the theater district is B. Smith's Restaurant, a precious rose on a street filled with many thorns. It took a visionary like former Wilhelmina model Barbara Smith and her partners at Ark Restaurants to recognize an opportunity to help change the caked-on make-up of Eighth Avenue. Smith brings sophistication and a sense of personal style to the restaurant's decor. Its spacious dining room is anchored on one wall by a stunning metallic mural, and this glisteny copper-colored scheme is continued throughout the restaurant. The by-now famous silver bar at B. Smith's is usually filled with the best-looking professional crowd in town. This bar scene is even more exciting to those on the street looking through the restaurant's huge picture window. Upstairs, the open-air rooftop café showcases Big-Name Jazz Talents on Weekends.

B. Smith's offers an "International Eclectic" Menu, with food most of us are familiar with but that have been re-interpreted for our dining pleasure. **Fried Oysters with Wasabi Soy Sauce, Low-Country Crab-and-Corn Chowder**, and **Grilled Long Island Duck Breast with Watercress, Endive, and Raspberry Vinaigrette** are great evening starters. **Spiced Scampi on a Mango Glace with Fried Plantains, Grilled Flank Steak in Jamaican Jerk Spice with Garlic Mashed Potatoes**, and **Maine Lobster Raviolis** are just a sampling of the extensive entree offerings at B. Smith's. To complete a memorable dining experience, try the **Sweet Potato Pecan Pie with Pecan Caramel Sauce**.

$20+ ☎ ☐ ✓₡ 🍷 🎼 🕍 🎭 ☕

☆Café Beulah   39 East 19th Street, Downtown, New York, New York   212.777.9700

The leap from acclaimed opera singer to proprietor of the hottest restaurant on the island was not that far for Alexander Smalls. Not only do all great opera singers cook (that oral fixation, you know!), but Smalls claims he comes from "a family of dedicated eaters," who start planning for their next meal as soon as they finish eating the last one. (Sound familiar?) Smalls brings together all the charm, history, and "culinary discipline" he encountered growing up in Charleston, Beaufort, and the Gullah Islands of South Carolina to Manhattan in the shape of Café

Beulah. With its sunny yellow walls and vintage photos of days gone by, he contends that his restaurant is "an arena for the celebration of southern revival cooking."

Smalls classifies the cuisine at Café Beulah as "**Reinvented Traditional Low-Country Fare**" that combines all of the cooking influences of his home locale's African, European, and Native American heritages. In short, Café Beulah presents a rare culinary experience! Entrees include **Farm-raised Southern Fried Catfish with Spicy Shrimp Remoulade and Emerald Rice, Free-Range Fried Chicken with Peach Cranberry Relish**, and **Alexander's Gumbo Plate** (the restaurant's most sought after and expensive dish). You simply cannot leave without a slice of the **Banana Pudding Pie**—absolute heaven! Oh, and the **Sunday Brunch** at Café Beulah's?—it's a new New York tradition!

$20+ ☎ ❑ ✓ ℂ ⦷ ☕

"**Jezebel's is so hot, its like listening to a live jazz performance. With it's spicy food and beautiful decor, Jezebel's is a place I look forward to when visiting New York.**"
Shirley Horn, Legendary Jazz Vocalist / Pianist

☆**Jezebel's   630 Ninth Avenue, Midtown, New York, New York   212.582.1045**

Jezebel's is by far one of Manhattan's premier dining experiences. Since 1983, proprietor Alberta Wright has delighted her guests with her restaurant's upscale, genteel setting and **Sophisticated Down-Home Cuisine**. The small brass nameplate next to the non-descript exterior door gives no indication of what is in store. Upon entering the dining room, you are immediately transported to a world of fantasy and seduction. Handwoven shawls hang from the ceiling, old-fashioned porch swings sway by themselves to the delight of patrons, a lively player piano generates melodies late into the evening, and heavy velvet drapes shield diners from the hustle and bustle of Ninth Avenue.

And the food at Jezebel's! The basket of **Sweet Potato Muffins and Hot Biscuits** brought to each table disappears quickly. **Honey-Glazed Fried Chicken, Cornmeal-Coated**

Catfish, **Smothered Pork Chops**, and **Jumbo Shrimp Scampi** are just a few of the classic menu items Wright brings to her patrons. If you have any room left for dessert, save it for the **Bread Pudding with Bourbon Sauce**!

$20+   ☎ ❑ ✓ (♀ 𝄞

The Sugar Bar   254 West 72nd Street, Upper West Side, New York, New York, 212.579.0222

Opened June 1997. Recording artist Nick Ashford and Valerie Simpson's newest entree to the New York restaurant scene. The Sugar Bar is filled with African artifacts hand-picked by Ashford himself and serving the finest in **International Haute Cuisine.**

$20+   ☎ ❑ ♀

> **"In the cozy and seductive environment of Soul Café, one can dine on hearty food, then retreat to a friendly bar scene."**   *Nicolette Mesiah, Senior Territory Manager,Cosmetics*

Casual Dining

☆**Dayo   103 Greenwich Avenue, Greenwich Village, New York, New York   212.924.3161**

Dayo puts a fun, funky spin on Caribbean life. Coconut-head bongo drum players and Goya-can-covered palm trees boogie to a reggae beat. Larger-than-life, banana-peel bikini-clad figures seem to dance to the rhythms. Metallic gold and copper walls, decked out with striking tribal masks, reflect the warmth of the islands. This is Dayo: New York's first animated restaurant!

Dayo specializes in **"New World Cuisine,"** a combination of Caribbean and southern American favorites. Start your evening off right with a cocktail, either a **Margarita Royal** (made with Grand Marnier, Contreau, and Cuervo Gold) or a **Negril Killer** (made with overproof rum). For appetizers, the Sampler Special combines **Conch Fritters, BBQ Ribs, Catfish Fingers, Sweet Potato Chips, and Shirley Strips** (chicken fingers). Entrees range from classic dishes to "try something new." As a main course, how about a **Jerk Chicken**

Burrito, **Walnut Crusted Catfish** (my brother licked his plate of this dish clean!), **Vegetarian Island** (assorted vegetables), **Coconut Shrimp**, and **Dixie-Fried Chicken** served with **Candied Yams** and a mountain of **Greens**? On Sundays, Dayo's **All-You-Can-Eat Brunch** is notorious with the after-church crowd!

$15–$20 📞 ☐ ✓🍷 🍴 ☕

Emily's Restaurant   1325 Fifth Avenue, Harlem, New York, New York   212.996.1212

Leon Ellis, owner of Emily's on the corner of 111th Street and Fifth Avenue, remembers when his restaurant's entire neighborhood was nothing but a shell. He helped rebuild the area from scratch in hopes that one day all of New York would come to see its progress. There's still a lot to be done, but what progress Ellis and his community have made! From one of Emily's front window seats, you can enjoy a virtual parade of proud residents going by, and the extra-long bar is a great meeting place during Happy Hour. In the evenings, the soft decor and lovely fresh flower settings in the restaurant's dining area bring out its romantic side.

Emily's is an inviting, contemporary place with a down-home menu and extensive international wine list. It has gained quite a reputation for its **Breakfast**, of which the **Southern-Fried Chicken and Waffles** is a must-have. Dinner offers a diverse, continental menu that includes **Authentic Jamaican Jerk Chicken, Emily's Famous BBQ Baby Back Ribs**, and **Jumbo Shrimp**. **Live Jazz** is featured **Thursdays** and **Saturdays**, and **Sunday Brunch** should not be missed!

$10–$20 ☐ ✓🍷 🍴 ☕

☆Island Spice   402 West 44th Street, Theater District,   New York, New York   212.765.1737
☆Negril   362 West 23rd Street, Chelsea, New York,   New York   212.807.6411

If you can't make it to Jamaica this year, don't worry, Mon, be happy! Marva Layne, proprietor of both the Island Spice and Negril restaurants, has brought the islands to New York! Layne started out in Queens with a pastry shop she financed with credit cards. (She swears that she made the best tuna fish sandwiches in the borough!) From there, it was off to Manhattan and the heart of the theater district, where she opened Island Spice, which serves delicious Jamaican cuisine in an intimate setting at excellent prices—a rare treat, especially in this prestigious, high-rent locale. Layne's follow-up venture, Negril, caters to the funkier, downtown crowd that's ready to "lime" the night away! Its vibrant decor, tropical beach scenery, colorful aquarium, and whirling ceiling fans take you away to the islands!

Have either restaurant's main man behind the bar whip you up one of their famous **Pina Coladas or Kahlua Shakes** (the best in the city!) while you ease into the flavor of the crowd. The menu of both will present a pleasant problem: What, out of all these great dishes, to order? For starters, try the **Codfish** Fritters with Avocado Salsa, then go straight for the **Jerk Chicken** (it's not your normal jerk fare!), **Ginger Lime Chicken**, **Shrimp Negril**, **Oxtails and Beans**, or the **Whole Red Snapper**. You can't go wrong with any of these entrees or with either restaurant, Mon!

$15–$20 ☎ ❒ ✓ ◖ ⛾

☆Laurita's Café Soul 311 Church Street, Tribeca, New York, New York 212.941.0202

When you want to get away from the stuffed shirts of midtown Manhattan, Laurita's is your oasis! The proprietor of Laurita's Café Soul has designed her namesake restaurant to soothe and seduce. Deep purple velvet curtains and warm violet neon lights beckon patrons to "enter at your own risk." Huge gold-framed mirrors hang everywhere. Funky downtowners, dressed as only downtown New Yorkers can, fill the long marble-and-wood bar.

While diving into the basket of **Sweet Potato Corn Bread**, linger over a menu that alone is worth the trip. The **Friday Night Chittlin Nite Special, Step Back Rudy's Smothered Pork Chops,** and **Sweet Daddy's Barbecued Baby Back Ribs** are just a sampling of what's in store for your dining excitement. Sides include **Sweet Jimmy's Candied Apple Yams** and **Cora Mamma's Black-Eyed Peas**—you get two with your meal, but will probably want more! And don't forget to save room for **Laurita's Slap My Face Peach Cobbler**. Ouch!

$20+ ❒ ✓ ◖ ⛾

> "For one month I could not go a day without eating at Soul Fixin's. A bunch of good-looking brothers who can cook...everyone should get there!"
>
> *Beverly Peele, Super Model*

Londel's 2620 Frederick Douglass Boulevard, Harlem, New York, New York 212.234.6114

Londel Davis is very proud of his Harlem neighborhood. His plan in developing the upscale restaurant that bears his name was to entice people to return uptown and "to promote Harlem in a positive light with all of the history and respect it is due." He wanted to create a place where neighborhood residents as well as others could come, relax, enjoy, and feel safe. And that is exactly what he has done. With its exposed brick walls, burgundy chairs, and neat white tablecloths, Londel's exudes casual elegance. The walls of the side dining room showcase the talent of artist Bryan Collier, whose oil paintings project moving images of the Black family's joys and struggles.

Davis is the perfect host, and he looks the part. Tall in stature, his sincere smile is framed by a salt-and-pepper beard. And good service is mandatory at Londel's. As Davis says, "without customers, there would be no me." The menu reflects his personal style by specializing in what he calls **"New York-Style Cooking"**—a Mix of Cajun, Southern, **and International Cuisines**. Entrees include **Pan-Seared Red Snapper with Lobster Sauce, Louisiana Blackened Catfish, Chicken and Belgian Waffles, Steak Diane,** and **Filet Mignon with Tarragon Sauce.**

$15–$20 ☐ ✓ ⓒ ♩ ♫

☆Motown Café 104 West 57th Street, Midtown, New York, New York 212.581.9543

With theme restaurants located everywhere you turn on 57th Street, only the Motown Café truly satisfies everyone's craving for food, music, and fun. This is the brainchild of Traci Jordan, partner, senior vice president, and creative director of Motown Café, L.L.C.. Hailing from the Motor City, Jordan always dreamed of working for the third most recognizable label in recording history. "Motown is the soundtrack for an entire generation," she claims, "so it was inevitable that the Motown Café would have such a broad appeal."

Upon entering the Motown Café, look upward to see the world's largest record (a "45," of course!) spinning from the ceiling. Check out the gold albums and sequined costumes of Motown's renowned recording artists, and gaze at the bronze statues of your favorite Motown stars. While you consider your selection from the restaurant's extensive menu featuring **Regional American Cuisine**, travel down **R&B's Memory Lane** as the "Motown Moments" shimmy across the stage to belt out a favorite tune. And musical memories, constantly reminding patrons of days gone by but never forgotten, are what make dining at the Motown Café pure pleasure! This is one place where your Mom won't be able to say, "No singing at the table!" Too late, Mom, you can't even help yourself!

$20+ ☐ ✓ ℂ 🍴 📷 ☕

Mr. Leo's Southern Cuisine   17 West 27th Street, Midtown, NewYork, New York   212.532.6673

Pale pink and ivory spotlights softly bounce off of cream-colored banquettes in the main dining room of a place considered by many to be the **Granddaddy of Soul Food Restaurants**. A family-owned business established in 1983, Mr. Leo's Southern Cuisine is the brainchild of Leo Collins, the first restauranteur to bring quality soul food served in an upscale setting to the midtown Manhattan area. In a town where restaurants open and close in a heartbeat, Mr. Leo's has survived years of successful as well as turbulent times.

Liz Coakley, Collins's sister and now proprietor of Mr. Leo's, attributes the restaurant's longevity to the strength her family brings to its day-to-day operations. But let's not forget to credit the great food and drink at Mr. Leo's! An extensive selection of cocktails and liquors is available for you to enjoy while your meal is being prepared. To whet your appetite, try a bowl of **Cream of Collard Greens Soup**. Select your entree from a menu that includes **Red Snapper and Clams, Bar-B-Que Fish, Pigs' Feet Platter** and **Champagne (the only way to eat them!), Georgia Honey-Dipped Golden Brown Southern-Fried Chicken, and Mom's Smothered T-Bone Steak**. Wrap up your evening with a slice of **Mr. Leo's Banana Pie**. Yummy! **Live Jazz Most Thursday Nights**.

$20+ ☐ ✓ ℂ 🍴 ☕

☆The Pink Tea Cup   42 Grove Street, Greenwich Village, New York, New York   212.807.6755

What other soul food restaurant can claim to be a resident of Greenwich Village for the past 40 years? The Pink Tea Cup is so much a part of the Village that it's a stop on the neighborhood's famous walking tour! Original owner Charles Raye named the restaurant after his sister-in-law Pinky, a passionate china collector. Serita Ford, the current proprietor and Raye's niece, took over when her uncle went on vacation and opted not to return. Left in her very capable hands, however, the Pink Tea Cup continues to be the most famous soul food restaurant in Manhattan. Obviously, consistency is the secret to the Pink Tea Cup's longevity—two of Ford's cooks have been with her since 1969!

When you go to the Pink Tea Cup, leave your diet behind! Large portions of the following are in order: **Smothered Pork Chops, Bar-B-Que Beef, and Frog Legs Sautéed in Wine Sauce** are just a few items to select from. The restaurant's **Breakfast of Fried Chicken with Apple Fritters** is a not-to-be-missed experience! **$10–$20**

☆The Savannah Club   2420 Broadway, Upper West Side, New York, New York   212.496.1066

On a sunny summer's day, the Savannah Club's outdoor patio is one of a New Yorker's favorite places to order a Catfish Po-Boy, sip a glass of champagne, and watch the city go by. Frank Horn, Savannah Club designer and one of its proprietors, came up with the idea for creating a restaurant that would exude a very lush and lovely southern ambiance—and he has succeeded beautifully. Indeed, the graceful wicker chairs, large tropical plants, and front porch-type seating of the Savannah Club are so southern, all that's missing is a porch swing and a mint julep to complete the mood! The restaurant's busy bar scene is very Upper West Side, however, and sprinkled with models, celebrities, and a host of other "beautiful people."

The Savannah Club specializes in (what else?) **Traditional Southern Cuisine**.   Appetizers of **Sweet Potato Fries**, the restaurant's famous **Fat and Juicy Hot Wings, Crispy Fried Boneless Pigs' Feet** (yes, child!), and **Chicken Livers Sautéed with Mushrooms** put diners in the mood for what's to come. And that can include entrees such as **Mama's Fried Chicken** with **Gravy, Griddled Fried Hamsteak, BBQ Shrimp with Dirty**

Rice, and **Baked Whitefish with Sweet Potato Pecan Hash**. And what southern restaurant would be complete without **Bananas Foster and Dark Chocolate Pie** for dessert?

$20+ ☐ ✓ € ♈ 🐾 ☕

☆**The Shark Bar   307 Amsterdam Avenue, Upper West Side, New York, New York   212.874.8500**
☆**Mekka   14 Avenue A, East Village, New York, New York   212.475.8500**

shark: n. Being of a smooth character. Possessing a suave demeanor. Having a classic flavor; see The Shark Bar. If this establishment started off in 1990 to be the **Ultimate in Cool Restaurants**, then it has succeeded, because it continues to hold that title seven years later. The Shark Bar is well known for attracting the hippest crowd in the city. It's not unusual to see a celebrity or two eating there on any given night, possibly dining behind a curtain of burgundy velvet in one of the restaurant's semiprivate booths.

The creamy parchment walls at The Shark Bar show off an impressive collection of black-and-white photos by famous Harlem Renaissance photographers like James Van Der Zee. The food is also reminiscent of good old-fashioned meals. Try not to eat all of the **Sweet Potato Muffins, corny Corn Bread**, and fluffy **White Biscuits** brought to the table prior to your meal; they are meant to be shared! Besides, you want to save room for either the **Louisiana Crab Cakes** or **Grilled Oysters** appetizers, and for a plate of **Pan-Blackened Catfish, Shrimp Etouffe, Honey-Dipped Fried Chicken, St. Louis Backyard Barbecued Ribs, or Mike's Pork Chops**. **Sunday Brunch** is legendary. Oh, and try not to stare at the rap star sitting at the table next to yours licking his fingers. After all, he is only human!

Mekka, The Shark Bar's younger sister restaurant, is located on ultra-trendy Avenue A in the East Village and attracts a younger, funkier, "hip-hop" crowd. The food is comparable but the ambience and the greens offer more sass than The Shark Bar's. Whichever restaurant you choose, however, you're "in the mix."

$20 ☎ ☐ ✓ € ♈ ☕

☆**Soul Café   444 West 42nd Street, Midtown,
New York, New York   212.244.7685**
"**The Rebirth of Cool Dining**" is how proprietor Michael
Vann describes his ambitious and wildly successful new soul food
restaurant, Soul Café. With pride, Vann uses the term "soul food,"
shunned by many because of the negative stigma attached to it from
the slavery-era past, as a simple and accurate definition of his
restaurant's cuisine. In his view, soul food is about "that cultural and
spiritual essence—the nature—of being Black." "The concept of fashion,
seduction, warmth, texture, soulful atmosphere, and understated
elegance," he adds, "is what Soul Café is about." Enough said!
   With partner Malik Yoba and investors Roberta Flack and
Natalie Cole, Vann has brought panache and pride back to 42nd
Street. Sculpted metal masks, etched with the African symbols for
healing and harmony, provide a dramatic complement to the
restaurant's sensual lighting. Nut-brown, tie-dyed, crushed velvet
banquettes line the walls of the Soul Café's main dining area—the
site of the best people-watching seats!
   According to Vann, the menu at Soul Café represents "a
vertical integration of foods, **Vegetarian, Caribbean, African,
Southern American.**" Appetizers include delicious **Crisp Chicken
Wings with Tangerine Barbecue Sauce and Baked African
Vegetable Samosa with Spicy Carrot Jam**. **African-Style
Yam Dumplings** (filled with vegetables), **Louisiana-Style
Seafood Gumbo, Roasted Whole Red Snapper Cuban-Style,
Carolina Smothered Pork Chops**, and **Grilled Jamaican Jerk
Chicken** are just a few of the soulful entree selections. P.S.: Soul
Café hosts Live Music on Select Evenings and One of the Liveliest
Bar Scenes in Town—a virtual "meet market"!
$20+ ☎ ▢ ✓ ℂ ⑪ ☕

> "**I must say that the times I have been to Bambou,
> I've found that the food is always appetizing,
> flavorful, and quite syncopated!**" *Valence Williams
> Vice President, Investments / Stuart Coleman*

☆**Sweet Ophelia's   430 Broome Street, Soho,
New York, New York   212.343.8000**
   Scarlet red walls, shutters, and drapes surround the
sensuous dining area of Sweet Ophelia's. Spotlights pierce the

sultry darkness of the room. Up front, the bar plays host to the chic downtown crowd.   The extensive wine list and well-thought-out menu offer lots of "Stuff" from which to select from as you groove to the excellent selection of music played by the house deejay. Apparently, Alexander Smalls, proprietor of Café Beulah's as well as Sweet Ophelia's, has waved his magic wand even further downtown to show the folks in Soho what real good food tastes like!

The menu at Sweet Ophelia's offers a sassy blend of **Southern and Low-Country Cuisines**—all your favorites, but with a little oomph added! Sweat the "Small Stuff" by ordering a **Basket of Hushpuppies or Catfish Spring Rolls with Dill Tartar Sauce** as an appetizer. The "Big Stuff" starts with **Hominy Grits** and **Greens** with **possibly Cornish Hens** as the side meat selection! A choice of even "More Stuff" leads to **Fried Chicken Livers Laying, Raging BBQ Ribs, Screaming Fried Shrimp, Ophelia's Creamy Sweet Potato Ravioli, and Collard Greens and Ham**. There's no reason to stop now, so go ahead and order that **Banana Pudding or Black Cherry Amaretto Cheesecake with Cherries** on the Side! I told you it would be worth the trip!

$20+ ☎ ▢ ✓ ໂ ⫙ ☕

☆Sylvia's Restaurant   328 Lenox Avenue, Harlem, New York, New York   212.996.0660

In 1954, Sylvia Woods came to New York and started working as a waitress in a restaurant that she later bought in 1962. Her mother, the late Mrs. Julia Pressley, to whom Woods gives all of the credit for her successes, "mortgaged the farm" to lend her the money she needed to buy the restaurant. By 1979, Gael Greene, food critic for New York magazine, had dubbed Sylvia Woods "the Queen of Soul Food." This started a stampede by downtown customers who normally wouldn't be caught dead north of 96th Street to Sylvia's Restaurant in "big, bad Harlem." The rest, as they say, is history. With the help of husband Herbert, son Van, and 3 other children, 15 grandchildren, and 2 great-grand children, Sylvia's is a true family business. It is also **arguably the Most Famous Soul Food Restaurant in the United States**. And Woods's Catering company, Sylvia's Also, is located in a larger facility next door. Not bad for a product of Harlem. Not bad at all!

The interior at Sylvia's is down-home and simple, with several semiprivate dining rooms. But whether you sit at the counter or in the restaurant's Tropical Room, it's all about food at

Sylvia's! Breakfast gets off to a soulful start with **Southern-Fried Chicken and Eggs** or **Pork Chops and Grits**. **Daily Lunch** and **Dinner Specials** include **Stewed Chicken and Dumplings**, **Sylvia's World-Famous Talked About Bar-B-Que Ribs**, **Turkey Wings with that Down-Home Dressing**, and **Pork Chitterlings**. The **Jazz Brunch** on Saturdays and **Gospel Brunch** on Sundays will give you two more reasons to look forward to the weekend!
$10–$15 □ ✓Ɛ 🍴 📷 ☕

> "The Shark Bar's brunch is the only place to be on a Sunday afternoon in New York. Fried chicken and peach cobbler, what else could be better?"
> *Francine K. Cowan, Operational Manager, FAO Schwarz*

Cafeteria/Buffet-Style Dining

☆**Daphne's Caribbean Express   233 East 14th Street, Downtown, New York, New York   212.228.8971**
You know when you want something really good for lunch, but you're not sure what, and you're sick of turkey on rye and pizza...plus, you're on a budget? Who you gonna call? Daphne's Caribbean Express, that's who! Fresh, delicious, and quick, Daphne's is the creation of proprietor Daphne Mahoney. No stranger to the business, Mahoney closed her other popular Jamaican café, Daphne's Hibiscus, to make room for her new upscale venture, Bambou. Luckily for the lunch crowd, she located this new take-out restaurant just a few doors away, to continue bringing all the exotic spices **and flavors of Authentic Caribbean Cuisine** to folks in the big city. **Curried Chicken, Oxtail, Stew Beef, Jerk Chicken, Cod Fish and Callaloo**, and **Stuffed Roti** are the favorites at Daphne's. And on Thursdays and Fridays, she adds a little **Soul Food** to the menu, along with **Vegetarian** and **Daily Specials**.
$10 ✓Ɛ

☆Little Jezebel's Plantation   529 Columbus Avenue, Upper West Side, New York, New York   212.579.4952

Meanwhile, on Manhattan's Upper West Side, Alberta Wright's newest jewel, Little Jezebel's Plantation, stands—a perfect escape from the congestion of Columbus Avenue. The atmosphere this restaurant seeks to create is reminiscent of long, lazy summer days spent sitting on grandma's porch down South. White tile walls, exotic plants, and antique china cabinets displaying delicate tableware provide a tranquil setting for fine dining. The menu mirrors that at Jezebel's, but at a fraction of the price.

Charleston She-Crab Soup; Hot and Spicy Shrimp; Swamp Fox Southern Fried Chicken; Baked Ham with Orange, Raisin, and Red Wine Sauce; and Baked Beef Short Ribs are just a few of the scrumptious offering at Little Jezebel's. There's also **Brunch and Tea** and desserts like **Southern Pecan Rum Cake and Coconut-Flecked Sweet Potato Pie,** served with delicious **Hawaiian Lion Coffee.** Oh dear, Miz Eva, what trouble have we gotten ourselves into now?!

$15–$20 ❏ ✓C

Soul Fixin's   371 West 34th Street, Midtown, New York, New York   212.736.1345

Keith Berry and his brother Eric started a take-out business out of their apartment, fixing lunches for companies in the Upper West Side area. Their big break came when they were hired to cater a huge corporate event for a firm that had ordered one of their luncheons. At that point, the brothers began looking for a larger location, relying on their belief in the power of prayer to literally open doors for them and lead them to their new site. Today, with the help of their other two brothers, Kevin and Jon, Keith and Eric's Soul Fixin's is a much-sought-out dining spot in Midtown. Indeed, the first thing you notice upon entering the red-and-white storefront of the brothers' restaurant is a wall covered with dollar bills signed by well-wishers. Their **Catering** concern continues to thrive as well, with a client list that includes filmmaker Spike Lee and singer Tony Braxton. This place is **Cheap and Cheerful** with great service, attitude, and, of course, serious down-home food! Check out Chef Raymond in the back, working his magic on the **Barbecue Chicken, Fried Whiting, Smothered Chicken,** and **Meat Loaf.** And don't miss Mom's **Potato Salad** or the **Sweet Potato Pie!**

$10 ✓C

T.J.'s Southern Gourmet   92 Chambers Street, Financial District, New York, New York   212.406.3442

"I'm too blessed to be stressed!" reads the sign at T.J.'s. (We should all have such a sign in our homes and workplaces!) And the owner of this place knows a thing or two about both. She opened her restaurant in 1992, right next to City Hall, on a street lined with eateries offering every type of food known to man and servicing a clientele ranging from stockbrokers to on-location movie crews. So, how does one restaurant stand out in a sea of eateries?: Serve it fast, serve it good, and serve it at a fair price. T.J.'s does! Its **Pork Chop, Fried Chicken, Meat Loaf and Fried Fish Sandwiches** are all priced under $4, and served in nothing flat. Sides of serious **Potato Salad, Fresh Collard Greens, Yams,** and **Sweet Cornbread** are big hits with the Wall Street crowd. The **Peach Cobbler** itself is worth a subway ride downtown! **$10** ✔ ℂ

"Sylvia's is the most authentic soul food restaurant in New York—the atmosphere, the helpful staff, and the best sweet potato pie ever! Even better than my cousin Jamie's, and hers is good!"
Blonnie Thomas, Professional Shopper

Take-Out Dining

Moncks Corner   644 Ninth Avenue, Midtown, New York, New York   212.397.1117

If you know Manhattan, you know that Ninth Avenue outside of this small storefront take-out spot is...well...grungy! Inside, Moncks Corner is an explosion of colorful walls and beautiful posters celebrating African American heritage. It's not your everyday take-out joint, nor does it serve your everyday take-out fare. **Honey Chicken, Carolina Shrimp Creole, Baked Ham, Fried Whiting,** and **Oxtail Stew** are just a few of the delicious hot meals available, accompanied by generous sides of **Collard Greens, Red Beans and Rice, Potato Salad, and Yams**. Why not let Moncks Corner do the home-cooking for you, and you can take the credit?
$10

Nightclubs

☆Birdland   315 West 44th Street, Midtown, New York, New York   212.581.3080

The old Birdland nightclub uptown was a great neighborhood spot with terrific music, food, and people. It was upscale, friendly, and there was always someone there to talk to. It will be missed. But the new Birdland's proprietors' attention to details guarantees a pleasurable dining and musical experience. **Live Music** is featured at the club **Seven Nights a Week**. Nationally known acts such as the Count Basie Orchestra are on the calendar for 1997. The acoustics are fabulous, the sound system crystal clear. Even the tables have been perfectly arranged so no one will have a obstructed view of the large center stage. But with all these new additions, there's still something missing. Oh yeah...the neighborhood regulars—those friendly, familiar faces that brought the real magic to the old Birdland—*where are they*?

The new Birdland's U-shaped black lacquer bar offers lots of appetizers, and the club's dinner menu concentrates on **Real Southern Cuisine**. Specialties include **Seafood Gumbo, Bourbon-Glazed Tuna, Pan-Roasted Salmon,** and **BBQ Shrimp**.
Cover charge with 2-drink minimum/ Dinner menu $20

The Cotton Club   656 West 125th Street, Harlem, New York, New York   212.663.7980

In 1923, former heavyweight boxer Jack Johnson was forced to sell his failed Club De Lux to gangster Owney Madden, who reopened the establishment under the name The Cotton Club. Even though the segregated club hosted Whites only, it launched the careers of some of the most talented and well-loved Black entertainers of our time. Names such as Cab Calloway, Duke Ellington, Lena Horne, and Bill "Bojangles" Robinson drew a gangster and celebrity clientele that included Dutch Shultz, Bing Cosby, and Cole Porter. The Cotton Club thrived at its Harlem location until the mid-Thirties, when the owners attempted to relocate it to midtown Manhattan. That venture failed in 1940 and the club stayed shut for the next 38 years, when The Cotton Club returned to Harlem and re-opened under the direction of current owner John Beatty.

The new Cotton Club offers a bistro-style interior (capacity up to 200; ideal for corporate and private functions), bi-level seating, and the **Best in Live Entertainment**. Saturdays and Sundays feature a **Live Gospel Brunch and Dinner Show**, and a delicious **Southern-Style Buffet**.
Cover charge/ Gospel Brunch $25+/ ☎ ❒ ✓ ₵ 🍴 🎼 🎁 ☕

☆Perk's Fine Cuisine   553 Manhattan Avenue, Harlem, New York, New York   212.666.8500

Perk's is know by New York City insiders for many things, but mostly it is associated with **Great Live Music** and the **Busiest** and **Prettiest Pink Bar in Harlem**. With its modern maplewood and shiny brass accents, Perk's bar area is the see-and-be-seen spot uptown. This is the heart of the club, and it plays host to a terrific-looking mature crowd nightly. Downstairs, dinner and jazz is served up hot and plenty! **Big-Name and Local Entertainers** heat up the night while the kitchen provides delicious continental dishes like **Lobster Bisque, Sirloin Steak, Shrimp Linguine**, and **Crab Cakes**. The bar menu is just as satisfying, with **Cayenne Ribbon Onion Rings and Chili Grilled Shrimp with Green Beans and Oyster Sauce** among the favorites of the club's regulars.
Cover charge/ Mature crowd/ Dinner menu $20
☎ ❒ 🍴 🎼 🎁

Showman's Lounge   2321 Eighth Avenue, Harlem, New York, New York   212.864.8941

Established in 1940, the Showman's Lounge is the oldest nightclub in Harlem and still going strong. It's not unusual to see tour buses parked outside the club and German or Japanese tourists inside enjoying the great music and mingling with the neighborhood regulars. Mona Lopez, manager of Showman's since 1979, attributes the club's longevity to its superb, friendly staff and comfortable surroundings. Al Howard, proprietor, is a retired cop who was credited with saving Dr. Martin Luther King, Jr.'s life in 1958 after he was stabbed by a woman on 125th Street. The two have a chemistry that keeps the club alive and the patrons coming back for more, again and again. **Live Music** is featured Tuesdays through Saturday Nights. The club's **Full-Service Kitchen offers Grilled Salmon, Jumbo Shrimp, Short Ribs of Beef,** and **Fried Catfish**, and its **Extensive Wine and Champagne List** helps keep the party going all night long!

No Cover charge / 2-drink minimum/ Mature crowd/ $20 Dinner menu / ☐ 🍷 🎵

Caterers

La Toque   1690 East New York Avenue, Brooklyn, New York   718.922.4770

Master chef Geddes Journet spent 25 years in France, perfecting his haute cuisine techniques. He studied at the famous Cordon Bleu in Burgundy and owned and operated a restaurant, the Relais de la Belle Ecluse, in Bollene, Provence. Since returning home to American soil, Journet has coupled his European expertise with recipes drawn from his Creole heritage and, with his partners, has established a **First-Class, Full-Service Catering Facility**. La Toque ("The Chef's Hat") also houses a **Culinary School**, which educates both chefs and staff in "The Art of the Table," covering everything from budget planning to proper table setting. La Toque **specializes in French Creole and Middle Eastern Halal Cuisine**, catering everything from small affairs to large corporate functions. Its festive offerings, from a creative array of Hors d'oeuvres to **Jambalaya, Stuffed Fowl,** and luscious **Creme Brulée,** guarantee that your event will be a memorable one.

PHILADELPHIA & VICINITY

Fine Dining

☆**Melange Café   1601 Chapel Avenue, Cherry Hill, New Jersey   609.663.7339**

The youngest of 10 children, Joseph J. Brown, chef and owner of the Melange Café, learned to cook for himself at an early age. Little did he know that his youthful cooking was the start of a life-long love affair with food! After 20 years as a professional chef in other fine-dining establishments, Brown decided it was time to venture out on his own.   His dream was to open a sophisticated, upscale establish-ment where diners could be comfortable and he could be proud. With only chain restaurants as his competition in this sleepy suburban setting, he launched the Melange Café, featuring what he calls **"New American Cuisine, with a Louisiana and Italian Influence."**

Melange Café provides a real fine-dining experience. Start with the **Fried Oysters**, and move on to the excellent **Pan-Smoked Tomato Crab Bisque**. Next, try to decide between the **Chicken Maque Choux with Scallops**, **Pasta Pescatore**, **Roast Rack of Lamb**, or the **Bayou Filet Mignon with Sea Scallops and Shrimp in Brandy Cream**. With food and a menu like this, Chef Brown has no problem enticing customers to leave Philly and come to his restaurant!

$20+ 🕿 ⬜ ✓ 🥂 ⛾

☆**Zanzibar Blue   200 South Broad, Downtown, Philadelphia, Pennsylvania   215.732.5200**

Located at the corner of Broad and Walnut in Philadelphia's exclusive Bellevue Hotel, Zanzibar Blue has arrived and joined ranks with the big boys.   Robert and Benjamin Bynum recently moved their wildly successful restaurant and jazz club from its sleepy South 11th Street location to this bright-lights and high-rent district only a stone's-throw away from the most exclusive shops and restaurants in downtown Philly. But Zanzibar Blue not only can compete with every restaurant on the row, it offers something none of the others can: **World-Class Jazz, Seven Nights a Week.** From local jazz greats to nationally known artists featured in the club's "Evolution of Jazz" series, Zanzibar Blue brings the very best to a very appreciative city.

Zanzibar Blue's menu features a **International Selection of Dishes**, beautifully presented and certain to satisfy the most discriminating palate. The evening may start with a choice of **Roasted Tomato Lobster Bisque, Dungeness Crab Empanada, Coconut Chicken Tempura,** or **Andouille Sausage Bruschetta.** Take your time deciding between **Asian Barbequed Yellowfin Tuna, Tangerine Szechuan Duck, Moroccan Oven-Roasted Chicken,** or **Sirloin Steak Au Poivre.** After you've ordered, sit back, relax and enjoy the music, the sophisticated crowd, and the handsome surroundings that is Zanzibar Blue. Also open for **Sunday Brunch.**

$25+ ☐ ✓ (♈ ♫ ♨ ☕ V

Casual Dining

Champagne   21 East Chelten Avenue, Germantown, Philadelphia, Pennsylvania   215.849.7366

Chef George Stovall's life-long career in the restaurant business has taught him a lot: "Do most things well, deliver fresh, delicious food, and offer a variety of entertainment that the customer wants." He has shared these truths with his restaurant's other cooks (there are at least seven in the kitchen at any one time). He has also shared with them recipes he has perfected over some 30-odd years. The result of all this experience and direction is Champagne: an upscale supper club specializing in **the Best in Seafood Dining and Entertainment.**

Night-time activities at Champagne include **Karaoke** (for the talented and brave), **Live R&B Bands**, and **Dancing to Oldies, R&B, and Reggae**, depending on what night you decide to join the fun. **Mussels, Fresh Fish and Shrimp, Combination Platters of Butterfly Shrimp and Beef Kabobs,** and Broiled Salmon with Sautéed Cajun Shrimp are just a few selections from Champagne's extensive menu. Of course, there's an **Impressive Champagne Menu**, hence the name. Also featured are several healthy, hearty **Salads and Pastas**—popular late-night fare perfect for those midnight cravings. And you can easily indulge those cravings at

Champagne since the kitchen doesn't close 'til 2am! The upstairs **Banquet Room** can accommodate large parties of 200 or more.

$20+ ☐ ✓ ₵ ⅊ 🎵 🐚

"Moody's On The Pike has the best and the biggest fish platter in Philly and they always give service with a smile!" *Lowanda Scott, Philadelphian*

Charley's Open Pit Barbecue & Seafood Restaurant
5917 North Broad, North Philadelphia, Pennsylvania 215.549.7550

"We have the Best Chitterlings in Philly! And the best Beef Short Ribs in Gravy, Pork Ribs in Smoky BBQ Sauce, and Potato Salad with a Kick!" Charles (Charley) Pollock, proprietor of Charley's Open Pit, believes in tooting his own horn, but he also has over 15 years of success to back up his claims. Since his first job as a cook in his native North Carolina, Pollock recalls that he has always enjoyed experimenting with recipes and mixing spices for maximum flavor to minimize the use of salt.

Pollock's restaurant may be small and modest, but one whiff of the tempting aromas coming from its kitchen and you'll remember exactly why you came. **Short Ribs, Chitterlings, New York Strip Steak, Collard Greens, and that serious Potato Salad (thick and spicy)** are his most popular dishes, and they're all made with "good, fresh spices and all-natural ingredients." Portions are huge, so bring your appetite!
$10 Slabs of Ribs slightly more

☆Diane & Tom's Café   26 West Maplewood Mall,
Germantown, Philadelphia, Pennsylvania 215.842.1996

Diane Barnette and her husband Tom started out in the restaurant business with a small foodstand on Chelten Avenue that became so popular they could no longer serve their customers in the manner they felt they deserved. Their current establishment, located in the historic Maplewood Mall, may be small and quaint (only five tables), but the Barnettes consider themselves blessed to have found it. They opened Diane & Tom's Café in February 1995 to rave reviews, and it was quickly voted the **#1 Eatery in the Germantown Area!**

"Where home-cooking is only a mouthful away," claims the slogan at Diane & Tom's. Yeah, but do you know anyone who can prepare **Shrimp Alfredo over Fettuccine** or **Chicken Stir-Fry** like theirs at home?! Actually, this café offers a rather sophisticated menu specializing in **Pastas, Vegetarian Dishes, Stir-Fries, and Gourmet Salads.** Their top-rated and most popular dish since their foodstand days, the **Jumbo Shrimp and Chicken Breast Combo Stir-Fry**, is still on the menu. And before you leave, don't forget to personally meet and thank Diane and Tom, who believe God's blessings brings them the absolute best customers. Oh, get a slice of their scrumptious **Seven-Layer Pound Cake** to go! Diane & Tom's is **Open for Breakfast** but **Closes at Midday** to prepare for their **Early Dinner Service**. Dinner reservations are suggested.

$10–$15 ✓ ₵

☆Moody's On The Pike   6834 Limekiln Pike, Philadelphia, Pennsylvania   215.924.7077

Continuing in the great tradition that was Tolins Inn, Walter Moody, proprietor of Moody's On The Pike, feels that it is an privilege and honor to run a restaurant. That's why, he says, he serves only the finest meats and the freshest seafood and strives so hard to create a pleasant, appealing atmosphere for dining out. Now approaching its sixth year of operation, Moody's On The Pike is Philadelphia's premier spot not only for good food but also for meetings, after-work cocktails, and large private affairs.

Moody's menu consists of **Traditional American Cuisine: Lobster Tail, Fried Shrimp, Porterhouse Steaks, Stuffed Flounder, Veal Parmesan, Crab Cakes, and Fried Chicken** (fried the old-fashioned way, in cast-iron skillets). His signature **Sweet Potato Pies** are also sold whole for take-out in the same glass dish they're baked in, but Moody doesn't have to worry about replacing the dishes. The pies are so good, his patrons always return them for refills!

$20+ ☐ ✓ ₵ 🍷

☆Warmdaddy's   4–6 South Front Street, Philadelphia, Pennsylvania   215.627.2500

Warmdaddy's is like no other blues joint you've ever been to. Sure, it features **Real Down-Home Blues** and local and nationally known artists, but this club is no cramped, dark, and smoky den like most nightclubs. The deep cranberry walls illuminated with soft lighting provide a richly textured back-ground for the vivid works of art hanging all around the dining area. The setting is perfect for a small family gathering, an intimate date, or an evening of just plain fun with the gang. Serious blues lovers will find tables up close and personal to the stage ideally suited to their tastes. The bar area makes it easy to make new friends. There's even a parallel counter for you to put your southern brew down while standing or dancing. Brought to you by Robert and Benjamin Bynum, the young, visionary brothers who put the jazz back into Philadelphia with their other place, Zanzibar Blue, this much-needed good-time house is a definite hit!

In a recent Warmdaddy's newsletter, the Bynums offered the following comments on the "soul food–southern food" debate: "Soul food is food that is soulfully cooked. It's richly flavored food rich in tradition. Southern food, by comparison, is a broader array of foods and styles. It includes soul food, but it is much more." So which cuisine does Warmdaddy's serve? Both! Warmdaddy's **Down-Home Menu** has it all and more. Begin with **Uncle Smoke's Oyster Salad with Buttermilk Dressing, Crazy Clara's Fish Fingers,** or **Fried Grits Cakes with Crawfish Etouffe**. For the big plate, you can't go wrong with Warmdaddy's **Down-Home Smothered Chicken and Waffles, Big Moose's Fried Chicken** and **Baby Back Ribs Combo, Back Woods Fried Cornmeal Catfish,** or **Vegetable Jambalaya**. And for goodness sake, save room for the ever-so-seriously-delicious **Bread Pudding with Bourbon Sauce.** Aw right now!

Music Charge/ $20 ☎ ☐ ✓ ℭ ⅋ 🎼

> ## "At Warmdaddy's, the music and the red beans and rice are on the money!"
> *Harrison Baker, National Account Manager*

> **"This is definitely the place to satisfy your taste!**
> **Because if it isn't Dwight's, its not ribs!"**
> *Rae Williams, Renaissance Woman*

Take-Out Dining

Delilah's
> **Reading Terminal Market, 12 & Arch Street,**
> **Philadelphia, Pennsylvania 215.574.0929**
> **30th Street Amtrak Station, 30th & Market**
> **Philadelphia, Pennsylvana 215.243.2440**
> **Terminal B, Philadelphia International Airport**
> **Terminal E, Philadelphia International Airport**

Since 1984, Delilah Winder has developed a multi-concept food franchise that includes two downtown restaurants serving home-style cooking and two "Eat-and-Fly" units serving sandwiches and ice cream from their airport locations. Not bad for a woman whose simple joy of cooking has turned her into a savvy and successful entrepreneur! Her secrets?: Stay small and remain in control. Provide fresh, quality food. Prepare all dishes from scratch. Not bad, not bad at all!

What's that that smells so good? At Delilah's Reading Terminal location, the aroma of her **Southern-Fried Chicken, Chopped Chicken Barbecue, Virginia Country Ham, Smothered Turkey Chops**, or **Cajun Fried Catfish**, served with sides like **Collard Greens** and **Macaroni and Cheese**, leads busy commuters, hungry travelers with time on their hands, and other patrons straight to her counter to find out. Delilah has created a cozy, dining-room environment right in the middle of the station's bustling food emporium. Black art posters and plum wallpaper give her place the look of an old-fashioned parlor. Seating is limited to only about 20 people, but that's OK because most of Delilah's patrons take their plates of southern comfort back to their offices or homes to enjoy.

$10 ✓C

☆Dwight's Southern Bar-B-Q 4345 Lancaster Avenue, Philadelphia, Pennsylvania 215.879.2497

John and Rosanna Nelson opened the first Dwight's location (named after their son) in 1965. Three years later, they moved to their present site where, with the help of their five children, their business has become something of a local legend. Eleanor Nelson, the proprietor of Dwight's since 1986 when she bought the business from her parents, recalls that her compensation for her early years of service to the take-out was "car fare and a sense of pride." Today, Eleanor proudly carries on the family tradition of serving food that is prepared with the highest-quality ingredients and lots of love.

Service is take-out only, but you probably won't make it to your car without sneaking a bite from your order! **It's all about barbecue at Dwight's: Long Ribs and Short, Chopped Beef, Pork,** and **Chicken,** cooked over a pit built by Eleanor's father and based on the principles of earth cooking. Sides of **Broccoli and Cabbage, Macaroni and Cheese**, and **Corn on the Cob** round out the menu.
$10–$15 Slabs of Ribs slightly more / ✓ C

☆Mama Rosa Restaurant & Catering
3838 North Broad Street, North Philadelphia, Pennsylvania 215.225.2177

Voted "Best Ribs in Philly" by *Philadelphia* magazine four years in a row, the Mama Rosa Restaurant certainly lives up to its praise. There really is a Mama Rosa, and she and her late husband Walter "Doc" Ritter started out in the food service business over 30 years ago. Their daughter Rosemarie became involved when her dad asked her to draw up a proposal for the restaurant's involvement in the city's Meals on Wheels program in the mid-Seventies. The Mama Rosa Restaurant received the contract, and Rosemarie began her new career: working alongside her mother and Mama Rosa's chef and event coordinator Dionne Ritter–Bright.

Rosemarie is committed to seeing that Mama Rosa's provides **Home-Style Food** and serves it proudly. As she contends, "Some people make fun of what is considered 'soul food,' as if it isn't real cuisine. It is food from our ancestors. Its flavors are borrowed from by every other major group, never giving any credit to us." Thank goodness we have Mama Rosa's to remind us what an accomplishment **Fried Chicken** and **Perfect Ribs** (no sauce needed, thank you) are. Other specialties include **Baked Chicken**, **Pigs' Feet**, **Turkey Wings**, **Fried Flounder**, and **Smothered Chicken**. Don't leave without trying one or more of Mama Rosa's excellent side dishes like the **Potato Salad**, **Macaroni and Cheese**, or **the Best Yams with Apples and Raisins**—they're delicacies on their own.
$10–$15 Slabs of Ribs slightly more / ☐ ✓ C

"Diane and Tom's Restaurant offers a delicious blend of home cookin' with a Philadelphia flair. Their portions will surely satisfy a hearty appetite for breakfast, lunch, or dinner. You really do get your money's worth." *Gary Shepherd, Afternoon Drive-Time Radio Personality, 105.3 WDAS–FM*

Bakery

☆**Denise's Delicacies 2916 North 22nd Street, Philadelphia, Pennsylvania 215.225.5425**
Denise Gause always preferring baking over cooking, so her first clients were friends and relatives who were familiar with her first love. When her business grew too big for her home and she finally got tired of wiping flour off her furniture, Denise's father helped her to relocate to a small bakery in North Philly. Thus, what started as a hobby is now a thriving business that includes wholesale distribution to several local restaurants and caterers.
Denise's #1 seller is her unbelievably delicious **Cream Cheese Pound Cake**. Sales of this item alone are enough to put her on the map. She estimates that her company bakes approximately 4,000 pounds of it a week! Other delicacies coming from her ovens include **Sweet Potato Cheesecake**, and her company also specializes in **Wedding Cakes** and fancy **Birthday Cakes**—all of which are made from scratch on the premises. Denise's Delicacies **Will Ship Pound Cakes** anywhere, so do yourself a favor...call now!

Nightclubs

Philadelphia is filled with lots of lively neighborhood taverns and lounges that regularly feature live entertainment, including big-name acts, on the weekends. Here is a short listing of a few places frequented by the locals and worth exploring. Note that most offer many amenities, however, it's always best to call first for times and schedules of events as well as specific menu information.

Checker Club 2125 Ridge Avenue, Philadelphia, Pennsylvania 215.978.8736

Johnny Ace Lounge   1801 North 27th Street,
Philadelphia, Pennsylvania   215.769.0545

La Mirage   2123 West Hunting Park Avenue,
Philadelphia, Pennsylvania   215.229.3684

Prince's Total Experience   1410–12 West Hunting Park
Avenue, Philadelphia, Pennsylvania   215.324.7562

☆Rivage   4300 Kelly Drive, Philadelphia,
Pennsylvania   215.849.2003

Slim Coopers   6402 Stenton Avenue, Philadelphia,
Pennsylvania   215.224.0509

Caterers

**Sadie's Country & Gourmet Kitchen   Philadelphia,
Pennsylvania   215.849.3927**
     In 1981, Sadie Torrance, owner and operator of Sadie's
Country & Gourmet Kitchen, walked away from her catering
service when business got slow and failed to meet her
expectations. Fortunately for us, she has made another go of it.
Business has been steady, thanks to referrals and a terrific client
base that includes local church groups and city government officials.
     Using what she refers to as her "God-given" talents,
Torrance specializes in all types of cuisine, but she's best known
for her incredible Crab Cakes. Her bakery products include the
best Pies, Pound Cake, and a wonderful dessert called Sweet
Potato Crunch, which comes with a delicious pecan topping. Truly
a Full-Service Caterer, Torrance prides herself in being flexible
and professional. Her motto: "Catering to your every need is our
only business." 'Nuff said!

SAN FRANCISCO/OAKLAND & VICINITY

SAN FRANCISCO

Casual Dining

Jewels 922 Presidio Avenue, San Francisco, California 415.563.JEWL

Going to Jewels is like going to a relative's house for Sunday dinner. First, the restaurant specializes in **Home-Style Cooking**. Then, its walls are covered with old photographs of family and friends from days gone by, and the intimate dining areas, with their neat little tables, offer all sorts of nic–nacs. Everything about this place conveys the homey, neighborhood feeling that proprietor Larry Nichols wanted his restaurant to have.

With such a small kitchen, it's amazing the size of the portions coming out of there! **Smothered Pork Chops** (with huge fried onions on top), **Chicken-Fried Steak, Red Snapper, Fried Catfish,** and **Large Prawns** are featured on the menu, and they're served with thick slices of **Cornbread** to sop up the gravy. Jewels is **Only Open for Breakfast** and **Lunch** from Thursday through Sunday, but it's open for **Dinner on Friday Nights,** so call first to make sure the food is ready for you. Just like home!

$10 -$15 ❒ ⏍

Leon's Bar-B-Que 1911 Fillmore Street, San Francisco, California 415.922.2436

With its black-and-white tile floors, red cushion seats, and nostalgic soda fountain counter, Leon's Bar-B-Que takes you back to the Fifties. Located on trendy Fillmore Street, Leon's interior is designed to resemble the old-fashioned railroad dining cars of yesteryear. And it's just the right kind of fun, casual family setting to get down with a plate of ribs! Leon McHenry started his career in food service in 1963 when he took over operation of the café at the Seal Rock Inn. While there, he perfected his barbecue techniques. In

1973, he struck out on his own, opening the first Leon's Bar-B-Que. He moved his restaurant to the Fillmore area in 1977, and the rest, as they say, is history.

As Leon proclaims: "If you have been around as long as I have, your food has got to be good!" (Amen!) Leon's serves **Pork and Beef Ribs, Hot Links, Chicken, Boneless Pork, Bar-B-Que Beef, Chili**, and **Cajun-Style Jambalaya**. There are **Combo** and **Sampler Plates** for those who can't make up their minds, and lots of sides to choose from. Leon's also sells his barbecue sauce, seasonings, and hot links from his shop; these items are also available for sale at local supermarkets.

$10–$15 Slabs of Ribs slightly more/ ☐ ✓ ₵ / Beer & Wine served

☆Powell's Place   511 Hayes Street, San Francisco, California   415.863.1404

Located on a funky little block on the infamous Hayes Street, Powell's Place (established 1972) offers Soul Food with Lots of Sass. Its owner, Emmit Powell, is an accomplished gospel singer who, inspired by a soul food restaurant he visited in Chicago, decided he wanted to get into the business. No cook himself, Powell hired some great chefs to work in his restaurant, and, among other credits, they have gained city-wide recognition and numerous awards for the delicious **Fried Chicken** served at Powell's Place.

Powell's Place offers family dining in an upbeat, eclectic setting. Each wall is a different color, the chairs are purposely mismatched, there are lots of photos and paintings all around, and it all seems to work. When the owner is away touring Europe or the U.S. with his group, the Emmit Powell Gospel Elites, brother Mel manages the restaurant and makes sure everyone is happy. Aside from Powell's famous **Fried Chicken**, the menu offers **Smothered Pork Chops, Liver and Onions, Fried Pork Chops, Bar-B-Que Pork** and **Meat Loaf** to tantalize the tastebuds, along with plenty of sides. But save room for the beautiful **Homemade Pies**, made by Emmit's godmother and proudly displayed in the restaurant's dessert case. Having a hard time trying to decide which one to order—**Banana, Lemon, Coconut, Peach, or Sweet Potato**? Ah, what the heck, get a slice of each!

$10–$15 ☐ ✓ ₵

Take-Out Dining

☆Big Nate's Barbeque 1665 Folsom Street, San Francisco, California 415.861.4242

You can't miss Big Nate's Barbeque: just follow your nose to the large canary-yellow building and you're there! Voted one of the top-50 basketball players of all time, Nate Thurmond has left his days of glory behind and now concentrates on delivering the best-quality barbecue to your home or office. Nate's first restaurant, called The Beginning, was a tribute to his grandmother, who taught him the art of soul food cooking. Big Nate's Barbeque is his second venture, and it's based on the premise that barbecue is one of the few foods that delivers well and still tastes good at room temperature. (Pass the phone! I'll take barbecued ribs over pizza any day!)

Big Nate's features **Pork Ribs, Memphis Pork Butt, Beef Brisket, Links,** and **Chicken**, all cooked in traditional wood-and-brick ovens. Sides include **Nate's Mean Greens, Country Beans, Potato Salad**, and **Corn Muffins**. The **Baked Potato** is stuffed with Memphis-style pork, green onions, and barbeque sauce.

$10–$15 Slabs of Ribs slightly more / ☐ ✔𝄢 / Beer & Wine

Brother's in Law Bar-B-Que
705 Divisadero Street, San Francisco, California 415.931.RIBS
2666 Geneva Avenue, San Francisco, California 415.467.9335

These two restaurants may not be much to look at on the outside, and the insides are no better, but the barbecue they fix is good and tasty! And it's cooked the old-fashioned way: slowly, with lots of attention. The spicy aromas coming out of Brother's in Law's can stop street traffic, teasing your senses until you come in and order. But according to Eugene Ponds, Sr., proprietor, the specialty of the house is Catering. So, from tailgate parties to group corporate luncheons, if you want barbecue, Brother's in Law Bar-B-Q has got you covered!

The menu at Brother's in Law's is short but sweet: **Pork Ribs, Links, Beef Brisket, and Bird** (that's short for chicken). Orders can be half or whole, and combos can include up to four meats, served with sides like **Greens, Bar-B-Que Baked Beans,** and **Cornbread** to finish off the meal.

$10–$15 Slabs of Ribs slightly more/ ☐ ✔𝄢

OAKLAND

Fine Dining

☆TJ's Gingerbread House   741 Fifth Street, Downtown, Oakland, California   510.444.7373

From a distance, this restaurant is a wonder to behold. Up close, it's breathtaking: a larger-than-life gingerbread house, straight out of a fairy tale, right down to its dancing gingerbread men and red-and-white candy cane poles. Inside, you'll be immediately tempted by the foyer **Candy/Bakery Shop** with its Gingercakes, Pralines, Rag Dolls, and Sassy Corn Bread. But be careful, you don't want to spoil your appetite! There's so much good food and more in store for you at TJ's!

The dining-area gazebo opens onto a lovely rose garden, in which sits a smaller replica of the restaurant. The attention to detail of this model is amazing. Rag dolls peek through lace-covered windows. Lavender bows and pink hearts grace the tree limbs. Lovebirds fly high in the skies above. Proprietor T.J. Robinson views this setting as the place where all her customers' food fantasies come true! Indeed, the only thing that surpasses the decor at TJ's Gingerbread House is the Exceptional Edibles.

Originally from Louisiana, Robinson takes great pride in her restaurant's **Cajun–Creole Cuisine**. Highly recommended: everything on the menu! Highlights include **Louisiana Fancy Fine Gumbo, Smoked Prime Rib, Whiskey Stuffed Lobster, Pheasant Bon Temps** (bathed in coconut milk), and **Red Snapper Stuffed with Crab.** Save room for the **Hot Bread Pudding with Brandy Sauce** or the **Pecan Pie.** At TJ's, every calorie is well worth it!

$20+ ☎ ❑ ✓ ₵ ⛄ 🎁

> **"TJ's Gingerbread House has *the* best gumbo and jambalaya in the Bay Area!"** *Anthony Smith, Defensive End, Oakland Raiders*

Casual Dining

Asmara Restaurant   5020 Telegraph Avenue, North Oakland, California   510.547.5100

Specializing in Eritrean and Ethiopian Cuisine served in a lovely dining room filled with exotic artifacts collected from the two countries, Asmara is a feast for the eyes as well as the palate! Beautiful paintings depicting everyday life in the Horn of Africa decorate the walls. Bamboo screens section off the main room into semiprivate dining areas. Traditional woven cloth and straw rugs drape from the ceiling. For over 10 years, Asmara has catered to Oakland's diverse culinary appetites. Specials include **Gored Gored** (cubes of tenderloin tips served rare in a spicy butter dip), **Ye-Beg Alicha** (cubes of lamb stewed with curry), **Tebsi** (pan-roasted strips of beef simmered in onion), and **Ye-Gomen Alicha** (mustard greens simmered in Asmara's special spices). Fresh natural fruit drinks and a strong cup of Ethiopian coffee top off a delicious meal.

$10 ☐ ✓ ℂ ⅞

Caribbean Spice Restaurant   1920 San Pablo Avenue, Berkeley, California   510.843.3035

Chef Clifford Brown's culinary quest has taken him from his hometown of Kingston, Jamaica, to Miami and the cruise ship circuit, and to Barcelona for the 1992 Olympics. Eventually, he ended up in Berkeley, where he fell in love with the town and opened up his own little restaurant in 1994, serving a clientele that ranges from college kids to their parents.

The decor at Caribbean Spice pays homage to the owner's island roots. Flags of Caribbean nations serve as tablecloths, and posters of reggae icons are everywhere. Local artists' work, much of it available for sale, also adorn the walls. The menu features Caribbean delicacies such as **Oxtails**, **Jamaican Jerk Chicken, Curried Beef, Lambada-Fried Fish with Sexy Rice** (dare you ask?), **Crazy Goat**, and **Escoveitch Fish Ghana-Style**. A **Deejay** and **Dancing** liven up things on the weekends, and **Tuesdays** are **Salsa Nights**. There's also **Live Music Twice a Month**. Are you ready to "lime and wine"?

$10–$15 ☐ ✓ ℂ ⅞

Emma's Cajun Fish & Poultry 3112 Market Street, Oakland, California 510.547.2864

Just look for the line of folks standing outside the door of a small free-standing house on Market Street and you'll know when you've found Emma's. It's just a little place, but since 1989, this restaurant has gained a reputation for frying up some of the best and freshest fish in all of Oakland. According to owner Emma Chappell: "It's the batter that makes it so good." Of course, Chappell wouldn't divulge her batter secrets, but luckily, she opened Emma's so she could share her recipes through her food.

Everything at Emma's is fried and cooked to order. **Oysters, Catfish, Red Snapper, Perch, Buffalo, Whiting**, and **English Sole** are among the seafood offerings. **Fried Chicken, Macaroni Salad, Fries,** and beautiful large **Cakes, Pies, and Cheesecakes** round out the menu.
$10

☆Everett & Jones

2676 Fruitvale Avenue, Oakland, California
  510.533.0900
296 A Street, Hayward, California 510.581.3222
1955 San Pablo, Berkeley, California
  510.548.8261
3415 Telegraph Avenue, Oakland, California
  510.601.9377
8740 East 14ᵗʰ Street, Oakland, California
  510.638.6400
7083 Village Parkway, Dublin, California
  510.803.8568

Talk about a Cinderella story! With nine children to feed, family matriarch Dorothy Ellington, founder of Everett & Jones, was barely able to provide for her brood by working as a maid. Then she got a job at a restaurant, which led to the opportunity to open her own place. After a short partnership with another barbecue house, Ellington opened her first Everett & Jones restaurant (at 92nd & East 14th) in 1973, and she has met with one success after another ever since. To this day, she continues to "pack 'em in" with the promise of **Award-Winning Barbecue**, cooked to perfection daily, at all six locations. As Lamont Payton, one of Ellington's grand-children who works for the family business, proclaims, "At Everett & Jones, we smoke the meats so pretty, they have a pink glow!"

The Everett & Jones restaurants offer a neat, narrow menu of **Pork Ribs, Beef Brisket, Chicken, and Beef Links**, with three sauces to choose from: mild, medium, or Watch Out! The portions are hefty, the meat is fresh, and the taste is like none to be had anywhere else in northern California.

$10 Slabs of Ribs slightly more / ✓ C

Lady "G" African International Cuisine
1739 Broadway, Downtown, Oakland, California
510.832.0280

Located in the center of town is the Lady "G," a pleasant restaurant celebrating the differences as well as the similarities in West African and American soul food. Lady "G" (for Gloria) is the gracious hostess and proprietor of this establishment where, she claims, you'll find "no chefs, just plenty of good cooks and good vibes that create a great atmosphere...just a simple place where strangers become family!" Sounds like a date to me!

Lady "G" believes in offering a lot of food for very little money. The **All-You-Can-Eat Breakfast, Lunch, and Dinner Buffets** are big hits with Lady "G" patrons and feature a variety of **West African and Soul Food Dishes**. West African á la carte specials include **Yor Ke Gari** (Ghanaian black-eyed peas served with fried plantains), **Beef, Chicken, or Fish** served with **Omo–Tuo** (mashed rice), and **Baa Flor Or Kontomere** (spinach stew with chicken).

$10 □ ✓ C 🍴 / Beer & Wine served

☆Le Belle Caribbean   3278 Adeline Street, Oakland, California   510.652.4668

The revelry never stops at Le Belle Caribbean, where the glittery ambiance and colorful menu fight for attention—and both should get all the recognition they deserve! Proprietor Annabelle Goodridge has decorated her restaurant with festive, authentic costumes from the carnival parades of her native Trinidad and Tobago. Huge, fully skirted pink, blue, and gold lamée butterfly wings drape the entrance to the dining room. Gold-dipped coconut branches and lofty palm trees complete the scenario, transforming

Goodridge's stateside eatery into an celebration of Caribbean food and culture.

The menu at Le Belle Caribbean offers the best of the islands, with emphasis on Trinidadian cuisine. Highly recommended entrees are the **Curried Goat with Herb Butter Rice** ("This dish will make yuh do de reggae soca!" claims Goodridge), **Creole Pineapple Chicken with Flamingo Rice**, and **Flaming Fish with Vegetable Rice** ("Imagine you are in [Trinidad's famed] Skinner Park..."). **Exotic Drinks** served in funky glasses and **Steel Bands** on Saturday Nights add to the merriment.

$10–$15 ☐ ✓ ₵ 🍴 🎼

☆Lois The Pie Queen 851 - 60th Street, North Oakland, California 510.658.5616

For the past 45 or so years, this friendly, neighborhood spot has faithfully served the citizens of Oakland delicious, hearty meals. With its homey lunch counter and black-and-white checkerboard tablecloths, it boasts an old-fashioned soda fountain atmosphere. The name pays tribute to founder Lois (The Pie Queen) Davis and her expertise in the dessert division. Movie posters and photos of Davis with scores of celebrities who have come to dine at her restaurant and pictures of family members fondly decorate the walls. An especially prized photograph is the one of The Pie Queen and her son and current proprietor Chris Davis.

OK, the biggest decision of the day for Lois The Pie Queen diners is this: what to order for Breakfast? Why? Because there are tons of choices! How about the **Reggie Jackson Special** (two pork chops, eggs, and grits), **Rib-Eye Steak with Eggs, Mixed-Fruit Waffle with Whipped Cream, Salmon Croquettes**, or **Fried Chicken with Hash Browns**? **Early Dinner** selections (Lois's closes at 2pm on weekdays, 3pm on Saturdays, and 4pm on Sundays) include **Baked Ham, Smothered Porkchops,** and **Meat Loaf**. But it's obviously the desserts that reign here. Choose from **Lemon Ice Box Pie, French Apple, and Sweet Potato** by the slice with your meal, and take home a **Potato, Pecan, Chocolate Silk**, or **Mixed Berry Whole Pie** for later. See anything you like?

$10–$15 ✓ ₵ 🎁

> "Everything on Everett & Jones's menu is delicious; however, my favorite is the barbecue chicken. So tender and juicy, the meat just falls off the bone!"
>
> *Darrell Pitts, Stock Broker*

☆Red Sea Restaurant & Bar 5200 Claremont Avenue, Oakland, California 510.655.3757

Why do patrons regularly come to Tadesse Teklemichael's nationally acclaimed Red Sea Restaurant from San Francisco and points beyond? According to Teklemichael, "Not only do they come for the great food, they come to see me!" Indeed, this enterprising businessman's dynamic personality is reflected in both his restaurant's cuisine and its authentic decor, which depicts scenes from daily life in his native Eritrea. Voted four times the "World's Best African Restaurant" by San Francisco Focus magazine in conjunction with American Express, Teklemichael is quick to share the secrets of his success. "My wife is a great cook," he attests proudly. "When I told her I wanted to open a restaurant, she said 'OK, I'll teach you how to cook!'" She's obviously no fool, and apparently Teklemichael learned well! Many of the award-winning dishes at the Red Sea Restaurant are his own creations. (See, you can teach an old husband new tricks!)

Red Sea offers an extensive menu of **Poultry, Lamb, Seafood, Vegan Vegetarian**, and **Pasta Dishes**. House specialties include **Kilwa Dorho** (chicken sautéed in spices), **Kitfo** (spicy chopped beef with spiced butter), **Sebhi Shrimp** (shrimp sautéed in spicy red pepper sauce, and **Atakilt Alitcha** (a mixture of vegetables sautéed with garlic and ginger root).

$15-$20 ☐ ✓ ℂ ⅊

Soul Brothers Kitchen 5239 Telegraph Avenue, Oakland, California 510.655.9367

Rip Wilson left the Bay Area for five years to get his culinary training from some of the greatest chefs in New Orleans, but prior to that he earned his living as a building contractor. That is, until he came across a little Greek restaurant for sale on Telegraph Avenue. Thinking he was going to get rich in four months time by turning it into a soul food restaurant, Wilson borrowed $3,000 to get started. "I'd like to starved to death!" he remembers with a chuckle, reflecting on those lean early days. Somehow, whether it was due to the good food or to its owner's outgoing personality, Soul Brothers Kitchen survived and prospered. And it's a good thing Wilson knew how to handle a saw as well as a saucepan because a nasty fire nearly destroyed his restaurant a few years ago, requiring a full interior renovation, including expansion of the kitchen. Today, Wilson proudly shows off his newly refurbished establishment as he reflects on the long road he has traveled to get to this point.

Soul Brothers Kitchen features **Cajun Specialties** such as **Jambalaya, Catfish Creole, and Crawfish Etoufee. Fried Chicken, Smothered Steak, Fried Oysters, and Stuffed Red Snapper are** a few other delicious entrees available on its Lunch and Dinner menus. If you can't wait 'til then, **Breakfast Starts at 8am** with **Salmon Croquettes, New York Strip, or Shrimp with Eggs**. Now that's the way to start a day!
$10–$15

Your Black Muslim Bakery
      5832 San Pablo Avenue, Oakland, California
          510.658.7080
      365 17th Street Oakland, California
          510.839.1313
      7200 Bancroft Avenue, Oakland, California
          510.568.6024
      1474 University Avenue, Berkeley, California
          510.644.3043
      160 Eddy Street, San Francisco, California
          415.929.7082

"As-salaam alaikum" ("peace be unto you") is the greeting you'll hear from the friendly, dedicated staff when you enter any Your Black Muslim Bakery location. Thirty-year veteran entrepreneur Dr. Yusuf Bey's dream of providing a healthier alternative to the high-fat, empty-calorie diet many African Americans consume took shape back in the day when this idea was not very popular. But he persevered with the conviction that Your Black Muslim Bakery is "dedicated to motivating our people to strive for ownership in our community and cultivating physical, mental, and spiritual health among our people." Today, Bey's food service empire has grown to 10 bakeries, booths in the Oakland Coliseum and at the city's airport, and a health food store. In addition, Your Black Muslim Bakery sponsors a local child care center, a drug rehabilitation program, and a shelter for the homeless.

Your Black Muslim Bakery outlets offer **All-Natural, Egg-Free Baked Goods**, a variety of **Natural Whole Wheat Breads**, including **Parker House Rolls and Sweet Rolls**. **Delicious Cobblers, Carrot Cakes, and their famous Bean Pies** are very popular. **Fish and Tofu Burgers** are best-sellers among the lunch crowd, as are the Spiced Pound Cake and the Cookies (oatmeal, carob chip, and chocolate chip).

$10

Nightclubs

☆Geoffrey's Inner Circle   410 - 14th Street, Oakland, California   510.839.4644

Geoffrey's Inner Circle is located in an historic townhouse that was for 80 years a private, all-male club. Today, stylish decor, first-class cuisine, and a sophisticated crowd makes Geoffrey's the place to be in Oakland. But according to owner Geoffrey Pete, his establishment offers the Bay Area more than just another nightclub. To Pete, Geoffrey's is a "an extension of the [Oakland] community," a neighborhood meeting place whose high standards he hopes will "make our people proud." **Jazz, Reggae, Comedy**, and **Dancing** are featured at Geoffrey's in the evenings, and the **Dinner Menu** offers such favorites as **Honey-Glazed Chicken, Shrimp Creole,** and **Fettucine Alfredo**. There's also a **Gospel Brunch** on Sundays. Oh, and be sure to check out a copy of The Inner Circle, the monthly newsletter Pete publishes to keep patrons updated on current club events and activities.

Cover charge/ 25+ crowd / $20 dinner menu/ ❏ ✔ ℭ ♟ 🎁

Jimmie's Entertainment Complex   1731 San Pablo Avenue, Oakland, California   510.268.8445

Jimmie Ward has all his bases covered. On Thursday nights, his club features **Exotic Male Dancers** (have mercy!) to unleash any inhibitions the all-female audience might have when they walk in the door. In the main dance room, party people can jam to Old-School, R&B, Funk, and Top-40s Music. **Nationally**

Known Acts like the Chi-Lites and the Dramatics as well as local talent have performed at Jimmie's. The upstairs balcony, located over the Dance Floor, is large enough for private parties. And up front, there's a **Restaurant** that serves full meals, with daily specials ranging from **Smothered Steak** to **Chitterlings**, along with **Fried Chicken** and **Fried Catfish** every night. How about that?
Cover charge/ 25+ crowd / $10 Dinner menu /

☐ ✓ⓒ Ⓨ ♫ 🎁

Tyrone's On Broadway   201 Broadway, Oakland, California   510.893.6000

One block away from Jack London Square is Tyrone's On Broadway, a nightclub featuring **Live Local Jazz and Blues Bands, Karaoke**, a **Top-40s Deejay**, and **Dancing**. Open until 2am, Tyrone's caters to an over-40 crowd looking for a place to meet and greet others in a pleasant, friendly atmosphere. The club also offers a **Full Dinner Menu** ranging from appetizers and sandwiches to entrees and nightly specials. **Shrimp Scampi, Chicken Cordon Bleu, Teriyaki Stir Fry,** and **Lasagna** are a few of the featured dishes. Call for a calendar of events.
Cover charge / 40+ crowd/ $10–$15 Dinner menu/

☐ Ⓨ ♫ 🎁

ST. LOUIS & VICINITY

Casual Dining

Del Monico's Diner   4909 Delmar, St. Louis, Missouri 314.361.0973

Eva Bobo, proprietor of Del Monico's Diner, laughs when she recalls her early years in the food-service business. "Well, I tell ya, it was such a hard start....I'm telling you the truth! But, I always wanted a restaurant. I worked 12 years for Woolworth's. I figured if I could work that hard for someone else, I could work for myself!" So, with very little, she opened Del Monico's, where she's been cooking and serving "real food" since 1968. Today, Ms. Bobo's daughter, Dorothy Dunn, manages the restaurant, and her grandson Chef Ray prepares the delicious food that continues to draw customers from all over the city to this casual, down-home eatery. But the main reason the visit Del Monico's is to meet Ms. Bobo, a true personality and genuinely lovely lady. If you're lucky, maybe she'll let you sit a spell and help her snap some beans!

When asked what the specialty of the house is, Ms. Bobo replies, "Everyone tells me it's all good!" For Breakfast, Del Monico's serves everything from **Fried Green Tomatoes** to **Salmon Croquettes**, but Lunch is the main meal of the day. Entrees include **Baked Chicken, Ham Hocks, Smothered Pork Chops, Prime Rib,** and **Roast Beef**. **Greens, Squash, Mashed Potatoes**, and lots of other veggies are available as side dishes.
$10–$15 ✓ ₵

☆Smoke Masters Bar-B-Que & Fish House
3723 Gravois, St. Louis, Missouri   314.773.5030

Located less than 10 minutes from downtown St. Louis, Smoke Masters Bar-B-Que & Fish House is the culmination of its two owners' many years of experience in cooking and restaurant management. And although Joe Bayne and Curt Bostic can really fry up some fish, they are known for their **Pulled Pork**. The secret? According to Bayne, "We slow smoke the shoulder portion for about 12 hours or so, then pull the meat from the bone. We add an extra special seasoning, our delicious barbecue sauce, a tease of cole slaw and present it on a soft bun." Wow, talk about things that make you say "mmmmmm"!

Serious **Ribs, Rib Tips, Pork Steak, Pulled Pork, Chicken, Beef Brisket** and **Snoots** (or pig snouts—it's a St. Louis thang!) make up the barbecue portion of the Smoke Masters menu. Fish dishes include **Catfish Nuggets, Jack Salmon,** and **Filet O' Fish. Seasoned Steak Fries, Baked Beans, Candied Yams, Corn on the Cob,** and **Blackberry Cobbler** are great complements to the fish or barbecue dinners.

$10 Slabs of Ribs slightly more / ✓ ℂ

> **"Voyager South is a great place to meet and greet, and the daily specials are full of flavor and variety."**
> *Wayne Harvey, Attorney*

☆Voyager South Restaurant & Bar   4301 Manchester, St. Louis, Missouri   314.535.2266

James Banks, the outgoing "captain" of the Voyager South Restaurant & Bar, claims he never really wanted to be a chef, but thank goodness for us a strong sea breeze blew him in that direction! After several years in the service and 15 years working for the St. Louis Playboy Club, Banks figured it was time to set out on his own. So, in 1975, he opened his first Voyager restaurant, so named because Banks believes life and business are "a trip." After 15 successful years at the helm of that venture, which he closed after a few business deals went sour, he opened the Voyager South. Aye, Captain, keep running that tight ship!

One look at the decor of the Voyager South and you'll know this restaurant is owned by a man. A long, gorgeous bar frames the forest green dining room, which is paneled in deep mahogany with brass accents. An antique clock reminds patrons of the time flying by. Over a hundred baseball caps, most given to Banks as gifts from friends, hang from the ceiling.

Come to this restaurant when you're ready to do some major eating because the owner loves to cook! According to Banks, Voyager South serves **"American-Style Cooking,** Fresh and Plentiful." **Fried Chicken,** fabulous **Short Ribs of Beef, Buffalo Fish, Catfish, Cornbread Dressing, Mean Greens,** and huge **Burgers** are just a few of the bountiful menu selections. And be sure to check out Banks's **Homemade Sweet & Sour and Caesar Salad Dressings** with your pre-dinner greenery. Voyager South presents **Live Blues** or **Comedy Acts** or a **Deejay Playing R&B Favorites Every Night of the Week**. The large, handsome **Banquet Room** upstairs is ideal for private parties.

$10–$15 ☐ ✓ 🍷 🎁

Cafeteria/Buffet-Style Dining

☆**Crown Cafeteria   2618 Martin Luther King Jr. Drive, St. Louis, Missouri   314.535.0590**

   The oldest African American-owned restaurant in St. Louis (circa 1947) is the Crown Cafeteria.   Conveniently located near downtown, the Crown serves **Home-Style Cooking** "like mama prepared down South."   Or at least that's how proprietor Ernest Halbert, describes the cuisine at his venerable establishment. Halbert believes the key to running a successful restaurant is "providing fresh, wholesome food and treating customers right." As he says, "If it isn't right, it won't come out"—of the kitchen, that is! Plus, he continues, "If you are not satisfied with your service, don't tell someone else. Tell me!"   Still, Halbert must be doing something right at Crown Cafeteria, because he will soon be going on his third decade of managing it.   And just recently he added on a new dining area, handsomely decorated with rose-colored chairs and matching framed posters celebrating African American art.

   Breakfast, Lunch, and **Dinner** at Crown are served cafeteria-style, but the food is first-class. **Tender Roast Pork, Duck**, **Chitterlings** (according to Halbert, the #1-selling entree), **Turkey Wings, Pigs' Feet**, and **Chicken and Dumplings** are just a few of many choices at the buffet. And Crown makes an excellent **Cornbread Dressing** and, according to Halbert, "**the best Sweet Potatoes in St. Louis**." It also offers **Catering** and a large upstairs **Banquet/Meeting Room** available for private parties.

$10 ✓ 🎁

Take-Out Dining

☆Reynolds' Barbecue   6409 Natural Bridge, Pine Lawn, Missouri   314.385.3100

James Reynolds knows his barbecue is good! Not because practically every local food critic says so, but because people come from all over the St. Louis area to sit at the counter of his modest diner—while they're waiting for their food, of course! It all began in 1956, when Reynolds's father Noah built a smokehouse behind the family house in North Wilkesboro, North Carolina. There, he taught his son the secrets of preparing perfect barbecue. James learned well, and when he moved to St. Louis, he brought his daddy's recipes along. Soon, he was dazzling the folks in his new community with North Carolina-style hickory-smoked ribs and rich, homemade sauce. Today, James's son Mitch continues the family tradition. He has helped grow the business by adding **Delivery Service** and **Family-Pack Specials**, and, of course, by keeping those secret recipes secret. After all, not everyone is privy to such important information!

Pork Ribs, Beef Brisket, Chopped Pork (serious business!), excellent **Rib Tips,** perfect **Barbecue Chicken Wings, Snoots,** and **Hot Links** make up the menu. Spicy **Cole Slaw, Tangy Baked Beans,** and **Fresh Lemonade** complement the barbecue. It's a narrow menu, but what else do you need with barbecue this good but a pile of napkins and some room?!
$10   Slabs of Ribs, Family Packs slightly more/ ❑ ✓ ℭ

☆Richard's Ribs   10727 Big Bend, Kirkwood, Missouri   314.966.1015

One of Richard Hollins's first catering jobs involved barbecuing for a corporate picnic. Only problem was that he knew nothing about barbecue! So, with the help of a close friend who schooled him in Barbecue 101, Hollins learned how to select, season, and smoke meats for the grill. He also learned how to make delicious sauce—rich, thick, and perfectly seasoned. He was such a good student that he picked up the contract for that catering job every year after that! Hollins's catering business grew so steadily, he decided to set up shop and realize his dream of "a white-tablecloths barbecue place." Today, that place may be small, but the food coming out of its kitchen packs a BIG taste. And Richard's Ribs may be a little far out, about 20 minutes from downtown, but that doesn't stop fans from all over the area from seeking Hollins's cooking out.

Main attractions at Richard's Ribs include **Pulled Brisket** (divine!), **Baby Back Ribs, Pork Steak, Barbecue Chicken, Jack Salmon, Catfish Nuggets,** and **Wings**. But it would be a crime to leave without some of Hollins's heavenly **Homemade Peach Cobbler** or a slice of his wife's **Sweet Potato Pie** (the best!)—perfect for that long ride back to town!

$10 Slabs of Ribs slightly more/ ✓ ℂ

Nightclubs

The Boardwalk   3524 Washington Boulevard, St. Louis, Missouri   314.533.5540

Located in the bustling theater district across from the Fox Theater, The Boardwalk provides great entertainment of its own. **Big-Name Jazz Groups** have done live recordings at this popular nightclub, and its **Excellent Sound System** blasts taped jazz on nights without live music. The Boardwalk is also a great spot for visitors and locals to mingle and cool out after a long day at the grind or sightseeing. Indeed, in the evenings after work, much of St. Louis's professional crowd gathers around the club's long octagon bar to relax or people-watch while enjoying the **Finger-Food Buffet**.

Cover charge / 30+ crowd/ ☐ ♗ 🎼

☆Gene Lynn's Cocktail Lounge & Restaurant 348 North Sarah, St. Louis, Missouri   314.652.6242

It's a Wednesday night, the house band is putting out **Great R&B Music**, the place is packed with a terrific-looking mature crowd of local regulars gathered around the bar, all glad that they made it through another "hump day." This is the kind of club you would want to own if you could: intimate, up-close personal, and fun! And with all the clubs in and around St. Louis, Gene Lynn's gets props for being relaxed, festive, and unpretentious. It's just large enough to hold the right amount of folk, most of whom know each other and happily welcome visitors to their fold. And then there's the tall and distinguished-looking proprietor, lounge singer, and host extraordinaire, Gene Lynn, who personally greets every patron who enters his club. If you are a lucky lady, he may even sing to you! Gene Lynn's features a **Soul Food Buffet** during its **Weekday Happy Hours** and serves bar finger-food after that.

35+ crowd/ ☐ 🍷 🎶

Ms. Whit's Candlelight Palace Lounge
9814 West Florissant, St. Louis, Missouri
314.867.9066

This rustic and comfortable lounge is one of St. Louis's favorite neighborhood bars catering to the mature over-35 crowd, and it's all because of Ms. Whit. With her ever-present sassy hat slightly tilted to one side, the proprietor of this establishment is a real live wire! And that's Ms. Whit to you, or to anyone else! She demands to be addressed in this way, not out of smugness but out of respect. It's the same respect she gives to every one of her loyal customers who has supported her in the near-decade she has been in the bar business. A hands-on entrepreneur who has owned a beauty and nail salon, a novelty shop, and a convenience store, Whit claims that the bar scene has been the most challenging of all her ventures, but it has also been the most rewarding. Her club is **Open Seven Nights a Week** (talk about challenges!). Ms. Whit herself deejays on Thursday through Sunday evenings, and the **Music is Pure R&B!** Need more excitement? Pit your skills against St. Louis's best at the Lounge's weekly electronic darts tournaments.

Mature crowd/ ☐ 🍷

WASHINGTON, D.C. & VICINITY

Fine Dining

☆B. Smith's   50 Massachusetts Avenue, N.E., Downtown, Washington, D.C.   202.289.6188

Located in the Grand Hall of Washington, D.C.'s beautifully refurbished Union Station, in what was once the suite where the Presidential party was received prior to train departures, is B. Smith's restaurant. Although the Washington location shares a name with its sophisticated sister establishment in Manhattan, the two are not identical twins. Like the capital city itself, B. Smith's of Washington is more formal. The grand room—with its high-vaulted ceilings decorated with gold leaf details, silver stenciling, and the Presidential seal—has been restored to its original grandeur. Faux leather-and-mahogany walls, spectacular period wall sconces, and brilliant chandeliers add warmth to the ambiance.

With her partners at Ark Restaurants, B. Smith's creator Barbara Smith has brought charm, sophistication, and "southern fare with New York flair" to an appreciative D.C.. Call it what you like, B. Smith's is quickly changing the face of fine dining in Washington with its introduction of what has become known as "Nouvelle Soul Food." **Mississippi Caviar** (black-eyed pea dip served with salsa and tortilla chips), **Grilled Cheddar Cheese Grits, Mudbugs** (Crayfish) **and Creole Gravy,** and **Grilled Chicken and Strawberry Salad** are great starts to dinner. **Virginia Trout with Spinach-and-Crab Stuffing, Bronzed Salmon with Potato Cake and Braised Greens, Grilled Lamb Chops with Wicked Greens and Smashed Potatoes,** and **Sliced Glazed Jerk Pork Tenderloin with Spicy Mango–Papaya Chutney** are just a few of the interesting entrees Smith offers her Washington guests. **Live Jazz** is featured on Wednesday, Thursday, and Saturday Evenings. And you thought D.C. was going to be boring!

$20+ ☎ ▢ ✓ ⓒ ⚱ ♫ 📷 ☕

"We selected Heart & Soul as the site for our wedding rehearsal dinner. Not only was the experience truly wonderful, Heart & Soul served some of the best fried turkey we have ever had!"
Johnetta & Melvin Hardy, Washingtonians

☆Georgia Brown's Restaurant   950 - 15ᵗʰ Street, N.W., Downtown, Washington, D.C.   202.393.4499

Bronze ribbons spin a graceful web across the ceiling while blond waves of maplewood surround diners at Georgia Brown's, **D.C.'s Most Popular Spot for Nouvelle Southern Cuisine**. Co-owned by William Jarvis, George Murray, and their partners at Capital Restaurant Concepts, Ltd., Georgia Brown's opened in the summer of 1993, providing excellent service and creative, delicious food in an inviting atmosphere.   Located just two blocks from the White House, this is one restaurant whose clientele crosses all racial, professional, and political lines. And all customers, whether they reside at 1600 Pennsylvania Avenue or make Washington east of the river their home, are treated with respect at Georgia Brown's.

Georgia Brown's extensive menu offers a range of tantalizing appetizers, from tender **Fried Chicken Livers and Sautéed Sea Scallops and Bacon to Smoked Fish Salad**. Among the restaurant's entrees, you'll find the excellent **Vegetarian Sampler** (which includes a tasty Black-Eyed Pea Cake), wonderful **Pan-Seared Sea Bass with Sautéed Crayfish**, **Barbecued Cornish Game Hen with Red Bliss Mashed Potatoes** (heavenly!), and **Carolina Shrimp and Grits** (spicy hot and lovin' it!). Georgia Brown's also offers an impressive wine list, and its dessert tray stars an absolutely sinful **Walnut-Topped Sweet Potato Cheesecake** (try it with a side of **Root Beer Ice Cream**). The **Sunday Jazz Brunch** at Georgia Brown's has become a Washington tradition.

$20+ ☎ ❐ ✓ ₵ ▯ ☕ V

☆Hibiscus Café   3401 K Street, N.W., Georgetown, Washington, D.C. 202.965.7170

Reservations are a must at the Hibiscus Café, a funky-yet-sophisticated little place hidden under the overpass at the base of D.C.'s trendy Georgetown neighborhood. Proprietor Jimmie Banks breathes life into this backdrop through reggae music, a **Nouvelle Caribbean Menu**, and enough ambiance for three restaurants. Adding to the exotic and whimsical atmosphere at Hibiscus Café are its handpainted entrance ways, squiggly neon lights, mismatched tables and chairs, and dramatic table settings. The walls proudly display an array of African masks and colorful Caribbean art. Nothing is spared a touch of creativity, making Hibiscus Café truly a unique dining event!

Sharon Banks, Jimmie's wife, gets all the credit for the exceptional food served at this restaurant. Recommendations for starters include the **Peppa Shrimp Hibiscus with Scotch Bonnet Peppers**, **Jerk Buffalo Wings with Pineapple Chutney**, and the **Shark and Bake** (hot bread pockets stuffed with shark and chutney). Spicy **Jerk Quail, Smoked Rack of Lamb, Seafood Creole over Pasta**, and **Grilled Salmon on Ginger Black Beans with Warm Avocado and Mango Vinaigrette** are a few entrees guaranteed to please. Save room for the **Ginger Bread Pudding with Currant Sauce.**

$20+ ☎ ☐ ✓ ℂ ⚱

☆Louisiana Café   713 Eighth Street, S.E., Capital Hill, Washington, D.C.   202.543.5400

Rose Plater's years of formal training at the Hyatt Corporation proved to be the perfect training ground for her most challenging project to date: managing the first-rate Louisiana Café. Lured away from corporate life by the Café's proprietor, Baton Rouge-born executive chef James Shivers, Plater swears that the smaller, more family-oriented atmosphere at her new digs is much more to her liking. The result? As one frequent patron noted: "The Louisiana Café is a spicy and sexy southern delight!" Indeed, the Café's handsome interior is a combination of exposed brick walls, double-clothed tables, natural lighting, beveled glass, framed African American art work, and colorful Mardi Gras masks. Upstairs features a baby grand piano and **Banquet Room** for private affairs.

The Louisiana Café takes its name seriously. **Oysters** are flown in daily from Alexander, Louisiana. The **Creole Gumbo** and **Shrimp Ettoufee** are spicy and deserving of praise, the **Catfish** is good every way they prepare it, and the fabulous **Sweet Potato Pecan Pie** and **Bread Pudding** are worth the visit alone! The **Sunday Champagne-and-Jazz Brunch** is well known throughout the city and offers a combination of Creole and traditional American classics including **Spiced Shrimp**, a "Made-to-Order" **Omelet Station, Blackened Fish**, and **Red Beans and Rice**. The price is a little steep, but worth it to enjoy such **Great Live Jazz** and top-notch cuisine.

$20+ Sunday Jazz Brunch $27.95+ / ☐ ⚱ ♫ 🍴 ☕

> "Gist Family Catering has a way of making you feel as though the food has been prepared especially for you." *Dr. Dorothy Height, President & CEO, National Council of Negro Women*

Casual Dining

☆Bailey's Café & Grille   1100 Wayne Avenue, Silver Spring, Maryland   301.495.4994

There's nothing like being in the right place at the right time! Emmanuel Bailey's first career was in finance, working at a bank located right next door to what was then T. J. Remington's Restaurant. Bailey was assigned to handle the restaurant's case when it went into arrears. Recognizing the location's potential, he jumped on the opportunity and turned it into one of the D.C. areas' premier restaurant/nightspots.

Bailey's upscale interior is framed on the outside by picture windows that offer a panoramic view of downtown Silver Spring. Inside, the spacious, wrap-around bar plays host to a professional after-work crowd. Sophisticated African American prints adorn a gold wall, providing the perfect backdrop for the most talented **Jazz, R&B, and Oldies Bands** in the area, which entertain at Bailey's Wednesday through Saturday Evenings.

First and foremost, Bailey's is a restaurant, offering an **Upscale Continental Menu** and a relaxed atmosphere for **Lunch** and **Supper-Club Dining**. Lunch selections range from the **Cajun Turkey Burger** with **Homemade Salsa on Grilled Pita to zesty Jambalaya** with **Shrimp, Scallops, and Chicken** over **Tricolor Fettucine**. The extensive dinner menu begins with **Caribbean Jerk Chicken Spring Rolls** and spicy **Jack Daniel's Buffalo Wings**, easing into **Rainbow Trout Stuffed** with **Crabmeat and Grilled New York Steak Topped with Herb Butter.** And if that isn't enough, the gracious wait staff strongly suggest a slice of luscious **Sweet Potato Cheesecake** to top off your meal! Twist my arm, please!

$20+ 🖥 ❏ ✔🍷 ♪🎼 🚗 ☕ **/ Late night music charge**

☆The BET SoundStage   9640 Lottsford Court, Largo, Maryland   301.883.9500

The BET (Black Entertainment Television) SoundStage Restaurant offers a **Visually Stimulating Dining Environment** through state-of-the-art video programming, an impressive collection of original works by African American artists, and a handsome, well-configured seating area. The patrons are the stars at this restaurant, and guests are given every opportunity to show off their talents. With mike in hand and cameraperson by his or her side, a master of ceremonies roves about the restaurant nightly, encouraging diners to come up onto the center stage and belt out an impromptu song. The emcee also seeks out birthday or graduation honorees, interviewing them on the spot and projecting their images and conversation across **50 In-House Video Monitors** for the entire restaurant to enjoy. Between interviews, music videos are broadcast for diners' viewing pleasure.

BET SoundStage offers an extensive menu featuring American and Caribbean Cuisine. Start your meal with **Coconut Shrimp with Pineapple Salsa, Zesty Onion Straws, Calypso Pea Cakes,** or a bowl of **Crab-and-Corn Chowder. Black Angus New York Strip Steak, Bourbon Street Salmon, Grilled Ginger Chicken with Mango Salsa,** and **Smothered Pork Tenderloin** over **Spicy Reggae Rice** are just a few of the entrees offered on the menu. **Sunday Brunch** at BET SoundStage includes **Champagne, Omelet and Meat-Carving Stations,** and all the **Strawberry Cobbler** and **Sweet Potato Pie** you can pile on your plate! Go on, enjoy—and worry about that diet tomorrow!

$15–$20   ☎ ▢ ▯ 📷 ☕

> "Republic Gardens is the kind of club where you may see your future wife walk by you at least 10 or 12 times a night, and it won't be the same woman each time!"
> *Charles "Chip" Jenkins, 1992 Olympic Gold Medalist*

☆ Bukom Café   2442 - 18th Street, N.W., Adams–Morgan, Washington, D.C.   202.265.4600

From the corner of 18th Street and Columbia Road, walk south to discover D.C.'s Adams–Morgan community: a melting pot of Ethiopian, West African, Caribbean, Italian, and modern American restaurants and bars. Adams–Morgan swings to an international beat nightly, and Bukom Café is a refreshing change of pace in a neighborhood known for its diverse offerings. Whether it's reggae, highlife, or soukous, the music and food at Bukom pays homage to the **real West African experience**.

A basket of tasty **Bukom Devil Wings** kick-starts what promises to be a too-much-fun evening. **Ecowas Okra Soup, African Curried Chicken, Oxtail Stew, Cassava Leaves and Beef, Egusi** (goat cooked in a broth of melon seeds, egusi, and spinach), and **Kumasi Nkatikwan** (groundnuts cooked with chicken) are just a few of the titillating dishes served at Bukom. Only problem is that it's so hard to enjoy the food when you can't stop **Dancing! Live Entertainment Tuesday through Sunday Nights**.

$15–$20 ☐ ✓ 🍷 🎵

☆Café Lautrec   2431 - 18th Street, N.W., Adams–Morgan, Washington, D.C.   202.265.6436

There's no way you can miss Café Lautrec. Smack-dab in the middle of Adams–Morgan's main drag, this restaurant is located beneath a 20-foot-high mural of French painter Henri de Toulouse–Lautrec. Inside, the long, narrow restaurant pays tribute to its namesake, with several framed posters by the artist hanging on the exposed brick wall. Outside, patrons can be found waiting patiently for one of Café Lautrec's outside tables so they can do some major people-watching!

In keeping with its theme, Café Lautrec serves **Light French Bistro Cuisine**. Le menu is long on **Cocktails** and **Specialty Coffees** like the **Café Lautrec, Triple Sec and Creme de Cacao**, the **Café Dagas,** and **Curacao and Cognac**. Hors d'oeuvres of **Pate Truffle, Escargots, Brie and French Bread**, and **Moules Provencale** (mussels in garlic and butter) bring a little of the Left Bank to Northwest D.C.. For your entree, select from **Lamb Brochette, Shrimp and Scallop Provencale, New York Strip à la Mountarde**, or **Chicken Bella Napoli**. In addition, Café Lautrec features the **Some of the City's Best Local Jazz Nightly**. On the weekends, R&B entertainer Johne Forges boogies his way into diners' hearts by tap-dancing up and down the length of the Café's long wooden bar. After his show, you're certain to join the scores of Washingtonians who have become life-long fans of Café Lautrec over the years. A votré santé!

$10–$15 ☐ 🍷 🎵

> "When I ordered the "Swamp Thing" [southern style greens tossed with shrimp, crawfish, and scallops] from B. Smith's award-winning menu, the name made me a bit skeptical. But after one taste, I became a believer!"   *Willie Jolley, Author of the Best Seller: It Only Takes a Minute to Change Your Life*

☆Fasika's   2447 - 18th Street N.W., Adams–Morgan, Washington, D.C.   202.797.7673

Since 1986, Fasika's has offered **Award-Winning Ethiopian Dining** in a handsome, bi-level setting surrounded by original paintings of Ethiopian leaders and countrymen, photos of beautiful native women, and exotic handicrafts and furnishings. Patrons can dine outdoors and watch the endless parade of Adams–Morgan revelers while enjoying traditional Ethiopian cuisine from large metal platters. Fasika's is known for its **Shrimp Royale**, **Yebeg Alecha** (braised lamb in green pepper sauce), **Doro Tibs** (chicken marinated in honey wine sauce), and **Yatakilt Wat** (vegetables in rich tomato sauce). **Live Ethiopian Music** is performed on Wednesday, Friday, and Saturday Evenings.

$10–$15 ☐ ✓ ℂ ⅊ 𝕒𝕛 𝔸

☆Florida Avenue Grill   1100 Florida Avenue, N.W., Washington, D.C.   202.265.1586

Florida Avenue Grill is arguably the **Most Famous Soul Food Restaurant in D.C.**, receiving Washingtonian magazine's "Cheap Eats Award" so many times, proprietor Lacey C. Wilson, Jr., has run out of wall space to display them. Maybe if he didn't have so many pictures of every famous person who has eaten there...well, forget it, there still wouldn't be any room! In any event, there are plenty of reasons why the Florida Avenue Grill has survived for 52 years. Since 1944, when Wilson's father first opened the restaurant and the days when Blacks had only limited dining options, the Florida Avenue Grill has been serving quality fresh foods, all made from scratch. Today, even with more choices available to us, the Grill is still a favorite Washington spot for the same reasons: great **Soul Food** and down-home ambience.

The food at the Florida Avenue Grill is uncomplicated and just plain good. **Breakfast** is served daily till 1pm. **Lunch Specials** for $3.99 range from the **Fried Whiting Sandwich** to

Golden Brown Fried Drumsticks. Dinner favorites include **Chitterlings, Meat Loaf, Beef Liver and Onions, Ham Hocks**, and **Short Ribs**. Long-time employees Matty and Pauline take turns making the Grill's signature **Potato Salad** (the way you would, if you had time!) But don't leave without having some of the **Banana Pudding**—oh, the calories of it all!

$10 ✓ℭ

☆**Heart & Soul Café   424 Eighth Street, S.E., Capital Hill, Washington, D.C.   202.546.8801**
        Down the street from the Capitol building is the Heart and Soul Café, with all the class and sass you would not expect from a neighborhood spot. Heart & Soul boasts a ultra-modern interior, a lively bar area where D.C.'s young professionals gather after work, and outdoor seating for dining under the stars. Proprietor Michael Hassan began his food service career in catering, but by 1994, he knew exactly the type of restaurant he wanted to open: one with an upscale menu and interior where he could showcase local artists, musicians, and all his favorite dishes.
        Heart & Soul Café's exciting and extensive menu offers "Soul Food with a Creole Flair": **Blackened Catfish, Grilled Salmon with Orange Pecan Sauce, Grilled Shrimp in Citrus Vinaigrette, Stuffed Tenderloin Pork Chops, Country-Fried Chicken, and Collard Greens and Cabbage** are just a few of the temptations awaiting you there. The Café is busiest during its by-now-famous **Sunday Brunch**. Monday nights are slated for **Poetry Readings and Political Discussions**, and Fridays feature **Straight-Ahead Jazz**.

$15–$20 ☐ ✓ℭ 🍴 🎶 🎵 ☕

Jinny French's Fine Southwestern and Southern Cuisine   1949 - 11th Street, N.E., Washington, D.C.   202.234.8790
        Proprietor Jinny French and her Washington, D.C.-based family lived in El Paso, Texas, for some time several years ago, and while there, they enjoyed the spices and flavors of southwestern cooking. After returning to D.C. and helping to establish one successful family restaurant (French's), Jinny's adventurous nature led her to want to try something different. The result was Jinny French's Fine Southwestern and Southern Cuisine, a casual restaurant that seats 90 comfortably. This new venture is managed by Jinny and

her daughter Jeanne Marie, who have successfully married the two cuisines together for an unique dining treat.

Breakfast at Jinny French's offers a choice between **Mexican Omelets, Steak and Eggs,** and **Ranch-Style Eggs**, along with side orders of **Chorizo Sausage, Tortillas, Southwestern Potatoes,** and **Casera Sauce.** **Southwestern Dinner Specials** include the **Southwestern Chicken Caesar Salad** (served in a tortilla shell), **Santa Fe Steak,** and **Spicy Texas Spareribs**. **Southern Dishes** include all the favorites we know and love, prepared the way only the French family knows how.

$10–$15 ❐ ✓ ℂ

☆The Islander Caribbean Restaurant & Lounge
1201 U Street, N.W., Washington, D.C.   202.234.4971

Everyone who is anyone in D.C. was in attendance. From the mayor to long-standing loyal patrons, it seemed the entire city came out in March 1997 to wish Addie and Ernest Green all the very best in their new U Street location. Their restaurant, The Islander, celebrated its grand re-opening with a huge buffet table overflowing with delicious island specialties, lots of champagne, and the Phantastic Steel Drum Band adding rhythmic island sounds to the festive atmosphere.

No doubt the success of The Islander is as much due to Addie Green's outgoing personality as it is to her wonderful Trinidadian recipes. Addie was the first Black woman in the D.C. area to open a Caribbean restaurant with a dining room, the first to organize the downtown Caribbean Carnival, and the first to cook on the mall and participate in the Smithsonian's annual Folklife Festival. With all of these firsts to her credit, it's no wonder Addie is considered the "First Lady of Caribbean Cuisine" in the D.C. area. And she in turn swears by her customers: "God sends the right people here to eat," she claims, "Therefore, my customers become more that just customers. They are now part of the family."

With her own children assuming various key responsibilities at the restaurant, Addie serves her other "family members" the best in Caribbean cuisine. **Whole Red Snapper, King Fish, Curried Shrimp, Calypso Chicken** (Addie's grandmother's recipe!), **Oxtail Stew**, and **Goat Roti** are just a few of The Islander's menu delights.

$10–$15 ❐ ✓ ℂ ⚲

Mango's 2017 - 14th Street, N.W., U Street Corridor, Washington, D.C. 202.332.2104

Fun, funky Mango's serves up **"Fusion Caribbean Cuisine"** nightly, from **Grilled Rainbow Trout over Black Beans and Herb Rice** with **Jade Salsa** to an **8-Inch Pizza with Pineapples and Roasted Red Peppers**. **Sunday Brunch** at Mango's offers a choice of **Oxtails with Lima Beans, Stewed Chicken,** or **Escoviche Fish** and **Fried Plantains**. Tuesday nights feature **Open-Mike Poetry Readings**, and late night Fridays are reserved for the **Hip-Hop/Reggae/R&B Classics Dance Parties**.

$15–$20 ☐ ✓ ₵ ᵽ ☕

Red Sea Restaurant 2463 - 18th Street, N.W., Adams–Morgan, Washington, D.C. 202.483.5000

Voted Among the "Fifty Best Restaurants" by Washingtonian magazine from 1982 to 1988, Red Sea offers **Traditional Ethiopian Cuisine** in a modest, clean environment at a fair price. Dishes are served on a communal plate, so be careful that your dinner companion doesn't reach over and try and grab that last shrimp! But don't worry, there's usually more than enough food to go around. Dine outside on the small deck in the summertime to enjoy **Doro Wat** (chicken marinated in lemon), **Yasa Wat** (fish stewed in a sauce of paprika, garlic, and onions), **Lega Tibs** (lamb chunks sautéed in spiced butter), or **Yetsom Wat** (vegetable sampler).

$15–$20 ☐ ✓ ₵ ᵽ 🚗

☆Shreveport Steakhouse 316 Massachusetts Avenue, N.E., Washington, D.C. 202.543.8613

This upscale, **Cigar Friendly**, **Creole Cuisine/ Steakhouse** just opened next to Union Station in January 1997.

$20+ ☐ ✓ ₵ ᵽ 🚗 🚗

☆The South African Café 1817 Columbia Road, N.W., Adams–Morgan, Washington, D.C. 202.332.0493

Inspired and encouraged by the success and acceptance of the many Ethiopian restaurants in the ethically diverse Adams–Morgan area, Cecilia Guyu Vilakazi opened the South African Café in January 1996 to introduce Washington diners to the unique cuisine and wines of her homeland. Originally from the port city of KwaZulu–Natal, Vilakazi arrived in the U.S. in the late Sixties. She attributes her interest in diverse cultures and cuisines to the influence of her parents, university professors specializing in anthropology and African Studies. Today, as restauranteur, caterer, and author of a cookbook on South African cuisine, Vilakazi enjoys sharing her favorite recipes and informing people about her native land. Her café holds the distinction of being the first South African restaurant and the first Black South African female-owned restaurant in the D.C. area.

The South African Café features an inventive mix of African, Malay, Indian, and Dutch Cuisines, a celebrated selection of **South African Wines**, and **Gourmet Coffees from Zimbabwe, Ethiopia, and Kenya**. The generous portions more than make up for the minimal decor. Patrons seated on the small outside patio on a warm spring night are in for a treat, with appetizers like the **South African Café's Pickled Fish, Peri Peri** (hot sauce) **Wings**, and a **Biltong** (dried strips of beef) **and Cheese Platter**. Entrees include **Bobotie** (South African-style meatloaf with dried fruit, curry spices, grated carrots, and apples), **Boerewors Platter** (grilled spiced sausage served with cornmeal and tomato-and-onion sauce), and **Vegetable Biryani** (rice and vegetables cooked in a curry sauce with grilled mushrooms basted in Peri Peri sauce). **Live Reggae and Jazz are Featured Friday through Sunday Evenings**.

$15–$20   ☐ ✓ ℂ ⌾ 🎵 ☙ 🐾

☆**Thompson Hospitality, L.P.**
T. J.'s Roadhouse
  12150 Central Avenue, Mitchellville, Maryland
   301.249.5508
  6040 Greenbelt Road, Greenbelt, Maryland
   301.982.7339
America's Best Diner
  2820 Columbia Pike, Arlington, Virginia
   703.521.1566
  2601 Virginia Avenue, N.W., Washington, D.C.
   202.965.1717 (Open 24hrs Weekends)
  541 Market Street, Leesburg, Virginia
   703.771.2250

Sharky's Seafood & Crab House
6091 Oxon Hill Road, Oxon Hill, Maryland
301.839.0324
8909 Central Avenue, Capital Heights,
Maryland   301.324.2200

Warren Thompson has always dreamed big, but surely even he couldn't have foreseen the day when he would own the second largest minority-owned franchised food operation in the United States. Or could he? Growing up in Windsor, Virginia, Thompson began mapping out his life's goals at the tender age of 12. He decided then that he was going to own a restaurant franchise like the one he and his family frequented on Friday nights. After graduating from business school, Thompson entered Marriott's "fast track" management program for formal hands-on training in the nuts and bolts of running a successful restaurant business. He quickly rose from assistant manager at a Roy Rogers restaurant to vice president of operations for Host Marriott's East Coast division. In 1992, at the age of 32, Thompson purchased 31 Bob's Big Boy restaurants from his former employer, and Thompson Hospitality was born.

Thompson Hospitality presently owns and operates over 20 restaurant units and holds dozens of government, business, and college food service contracts; it also manages the dormitories at George Mason University. Thompson's three exclusive restaurant ventures include **America's Best Diner**, which offer a menu and settings that are as All-American as their name implies, serving everything from the **Incredible Hubba Burger** (all the fixin's) to a terrific **Chicken Caeser Salad**, and **Double Chocolate Milk Shake**. **T. J.'s Roadhouse**, a fun, family-style restaurant and a steak lover's dream, serves U.S.D.A.–Choice aged and seasoned **Sirloin, Rib-Eye, Filet Mignon** and **T-Bone Steaks**. Thompson's two **Sharky's Seafood & Crab House** locations serve **Hot Crabs, Steamed Shrimp, Fried Catfish**, with **Fried Corn-on-the-Cob** (say what?!), ready for you to take-out and make it a Sharky's night!

America's Best Diner $10-$15 / T. J.'s Roadhouse $15–$20

Sharky's $10–$15 ☐ ✓ ⦅ 🎴 Beer & Wine served

Vivaldi's Restaurant   5507 Connecticut Avenue, N.W., Washington, D.C.   202.244.7774

Just a stone's throw away from Chevy Chase Circle is Vivaldi's, a small, casual bistro specializing in **Classic Italian Fare**. Named after the Italian composer, Vivaldi's is owned by Edward Hayes, an attorney who met his partner, Peruvian-born Yamil

Farach, when the latter sought Hayes's assistance in securing a restaurant deal. The two joined forces and began searching for a site with the following qualifications: located in a non-trendy neighborhood community, with ample off-street parking and available outdoor seating. (This may not sound like much, but off-street parking in D.C. is a major coup!) Their current location fit the bill.

The colorful, modern wall mural inside Vivaldi's depicts a famous Connecticut Avenue street scene, while the rest of the wall space is devoted to a revolving art gallery that features a broad range of original works by Peruvian, African, and Asian artists. The menu features **Chicken Milanese, Veal Picata, Shrimp Gamberi Diavolo** (shrimp in spicy marinara with linguine), **Blackened Scallops,** and great, cheesy **Pizzas**.

$15–$20   ☐   🎨 **Beer & Wine Served**

☆U-topia Bar & Grill   1418 U Street, N.W., Washington, D.C. 202.483.7669

Thursday and Sunday nights, U-topia lights up U Street with a menu of **Nouvelle International Cuisine**, a sophisticated, contemporary, and colorful interior featuring original paintings by local talents, and the best in **Live Jazz** from the Wayne Wilentz Trio. Ladies, don't resist if Moroccan-born owner Jamal Sahri grabs you by the hand for a twirl on the dance floor—his cha–cha is divine!

$15–$20   ☐   🍷🎵

Wilson's Grill   700 V Street, N.W., Howard University Vicinity, Washington, D.C. 202.462.3700

The smell of fried chicken hangs thick in the air at Wilson's, located right across the street from the Howard University Hospital, but that's a good indication that a real down-home meal is just a few moments away! Proprietor Joey Wilson worked for several years in his uncle's restaurant, D.C.'s renowned Florida Avenue Grill, learning the ropes and preparing himself for the day when he would realize the American Dream of owning his own place. That day came in April 1994. Today, Wilson's decor pays homage to every sport known to man and to the men and women who made those sports famous. Several athletes who have eaten at Wilson's have shown their appreciation by leaving an autograph or souvenir. Caps, banners, balls, assorted memorabilia, and photos of Redskins,

Orioles, and Bullets cover the walls and fill the nooks and crannies of the dining area.

Specializing in **Terrific Traditional Soul Food,** Wilson's is guaranteed to leave you full and happy. As one enthusiastic regular declared, leaving with his take-out order in hand: "I never get tired of eating at Wilson's!" Breakfast is legendary at Wilson's, but lunch and dinner is just as noteworthy. **Short Ribs of Beef, Smothered Pork Chops, that famous Pan-**Fried Chicken, **Chitterlings, Turkey Wings, and Meat Loaf** are a few of the daily dishes. **$10** ☐

"**Bukom Café was a wonderful, flavorful, and personally satisfying experience. Great food and great music!**" *Jon Hall, Public Information Director, Consumers Energy*

☆**Zed's 3318 M Street, N.W., Washington, D.C. 202. 333.4710**

Voted **One of Washington's 100 Best Restaurants** by *Washingtonian* magazine, Zed's brings "indescribably delicious" Ethiopian cuisine to a very grateful D.C. Metropolitan area. Proprietor Zed Wondemu opened her restaurant in 1987 in hopes of introducing and educating Capital diners to the joys of Ethiopian cooking, which she claims is "natural, fresh, and great nutrition for body and soul." And her restaurant, with its simply decorated interior highlighted by Ethiopian artifacts and pictures, offers a pleasant setting to enjoy it in. The tasty dishes coming out of Zed's kitchens are complemented by the friendly service offered by Wondemu and her staff, and three levels of dining allows the restaurant to host private parties without interrupting daily service.

Terrific food is what Zed's is all about! Its chefs avoid fat and use no pork in any of their recipes. Try the **Awazel Fitfit** (pieces of Injera bread soaked in red pepper sauce with beef), **Infillay**(strips of chicken sauteed with onions and seasoned butter), **Shrimp Tibbs** (shrimp sauteed with onion, fresh garlic and tomato), and a **Special Vegetable Dish** of cauliflower, stingbean, carrot, simmered in stewed tomato. All dishes come with **Injera** (Ethiopian bread), which serves as your fork. Of course, if you've just got to have a fork, Zed will find one for you, but when in Addis Ababa... Meals are also served communal-style on a large tray, so bring your gang along. If you're not into sharing, Zed can probably find you a plate as well, but again, don't let that stop you from trying some of the best Ethiopian food D.C. has to offer!

$15-$20 ☐ ✓ℂ ¶ 🍴

Cafeteria/Buffet-Style Dining

French's Fine Southern Cuisine   1365 H Street, N.E., Washington, D.C.   202.396.0991

You may remember John French and his daughter Sharon from the Lawry's Seasoning commercials a few years back. That national recognition brought many visitors to French's Fine Southern Cuisine. The walls of this restaurant are lined with photos of and acknowledgments from famous diners, all of whom sing the praises of the good food they enjoyed while there. What makes French's story unique is the fact that daughter Sharon lured her dad away from his executive position with the McDonald's Corporation to help her start the restaurant. Her persistence paid off, and the rest, as they say, is history. With mom Jinny and sister Jeanne Marie lending their capable hands, French's is proof that a family that stays together, makes great Peach Cobbler together!

As the name suggests, French's serves fine Southern cuisine, cafeteria-style, so of course, the portions are generous, but the quality of the food is high as well. **Chitterlings, Fried Chicken, BBQ Ribs, Smothered Steak, and Pork Chops** are among the many specials found in the buffet line daily. The spacious seating area provides a comfortable setting for family dining.

$10 ✓ℂ

Take-Out Dining

Ben's Chili Bowl   1213 U Street, N.W., Washington, D.C.   202.667.0909

Virginia Ali and her husband Ben opened Ben's Chili Bowl in 1958. Back then, U Street was for Blacks the most fashionable place to be in segregated D.C.. Recording artists like Nat King Cole and Billy Eckstine would often stop in for late-night breakfasts after playing a set at the Lincoln Theater located right next door. Then came the unrest of the Sixties and the construction obstacles of the subway system in the Eighties. Through it all, Ben's Chili Bowl weathered the storm. Today, U Street is enjoying a revival, and under the management of Ben Jr., Ben's Chili Bowl continues to attract visitors and locals alike to Washington's favorite late night spot.

They say Bill Cosby swears by Ben's **Half-Smokes**; other patrons go for the Chili Burgers. Whatever your taste, the Ben's Chili Bowl boast is that "the flavor is in the sauce!" **All-Beef Chili Dogs, Chili Con Carne with Cheese and Onions, Chili Cheese Fries**, and **Turkey and Veggie Burgers** are what Ben's is known for. Nowadays, **Breakfast** at Ben's is served only between 6am and 11am, but it's **Open Until 4am on Weekends**. And late night eaters still jam the place 'til closing!

$10

Blaze 1110 U Street N.W., Washington, D.C.
202.234.0361

Blaze, one of the newest additions to D.C.'s thriving "New U" Street business district, offers a neat, narrow, and delicious menu of **Barbecue Pork and Beef Ribs, Chicken**, and **Jumbo BBQ** or **Hot Wings**. The buy of the day is one of Blaze's Quarter-Pound **Chopped Chicken, Beef Brisket or Pork Sandwiches**, served with a side vegetable for only $3.25! P.S.: Unlike some other take-out joints, Blaze weighs the amount of meat on every sandwich, so you always get more than your money's worth!

$10 Slabs of Ribs slightly more / ✓ C

☆Creole Café 1339 H Street, N.E., Washington, D.C.
202.398.1652

Joan Bishop is passionate about four things: her family, her community, her city, and her cooking. Ever since she moved to D.C. from her homeland of Trinidad–Tobago, she dreamed of owning a restaurant. So, with her husband Arnim doing the cooking and her children baking the desserts, Joan opened Creole Café in 1993. Since then, she has used her small establishment not only to serve some of the best Caribbean food in the city, but to help enrich the H Street Corridor community she now calls her second home by feeding the homeless, lobbying for better parking, and assisting in efforts to clean up the neighborhood.

A visit to the Creole Café is a must stop in the D.C. area. It's strictly take-out, so carry home some **Curried or Stewed Chicken** or **Goat, Oxtails, Sword Fish, Roti, Stewed Rabbit**, or **Baked Chicken**. For dessert, any of Bishop's Cakes is sure to

please, whether it's the **Yellow Pound, Chocolate Marble, Spice Nut,** or **Pineapple Upside–Down.**
$10 ✓₵

☆**Delights of the Garden   2616 Georgia Avenue, N.W., Howard University Vicinity, Washington, D.C. 202.319.8747**

This is quite a story: Ten young men between the ages of 22 and 26, graduates of Georgetown University and Morehouse College, became frustrated when they couldn't find any restaurants that served the kind of healthy foods they desired. With money borrowed from their credit cards (hey, it worked for Robert Townsend, didn't it?), they opened their first Delights of the Garden restaurant in Atlanta, specializing in **Raw Vegan Cuisine.**   Other locations were later opened in Ohio and Washington, D.C.. Today, the Delights of the Garden chain is one-unit strong, serving the Howard University community. Matthew Tollin, one of the partners, explains the philosophy behind the restaurant's menu: "Vegan means no dairy or animal.   Food is uncooked and alive.   Since we are living beings, we should consume food that is alive, that emulates life."

The food served at Delights of the Garden may sound foreign to some, but the taste is pure pleasure due to the abundance of spices the chefs use to enhance the food's natural flavor. Try the **Veggie Tuna** (made from carrot pulp), **Seaweed Greens, Marinated Vegetables, Garden Supreme Pita,** and **Vegan Tacos. Thirst Busters** include **Banana, Mango Tango Delight, Peanut Punch,** and **Strawberry Twister Smoothies.**
$10 ✓₵

☆**Negril**
2301–G Georgia Avenue, N.W., Howard University Vicinity, Washington, D.C. 202.332.3737
965 Thayer Avenue, Silver Spring, Maryland 301.585.3000

Offering a welcome change of pace from fast food, Negril serves Caribbean take-out that is inexpensive and served in a cheerful, clean, well-organized environment. House specialties include tasty **Jamaican Patties** (beef and vegetable), **Curried Shrimp Roti, Oxtails, Escoveitched Red Snapper,** and **Vegetable Lasagna.**
$10 ✓₵

> "I never knew a cheesecake could be so addictive—
> forget delicious!—until I tasted the Sweet Potato
> Cheesecake served at Georgia Brown's!"
> *Monique Braxton, Anchor, NewsChannel 8*

Nightclubs

☆ The New Vegas Lounge   1415 P Street, N.W., Washington, D.C.   202.483.3971

The New Vegas Lounge is, quite frankly, a joint. It's off-beat, dark, and small, with no distinguishing features to lend any polish, and reminiscent of those roadside juke joints down in South. On weekends, it's usually full of loud-talking, beer-drinking regulars, jammin' to great **Live R&B**. That's when the house band, the Out of Town Blues Band, packs the house with college kids, diehard blues lovers, anyone who simply wants to have a good time. Led by Dr. Blues' on vocals, these boys will have the walls sweating with their Chicago and New Orleans Blues before the evening is through. There's no dance floor at the New Vegas Lounge, but that doesn't stop this crowd from dancing—in the aisles, at their tables, with the band, wherever! It's all about having a good time, and they know how to do it at the New Vegas Lounge!

Cover charge/ Bar food/ ☐ 🍷 🎵

☆Republic Gardens   1355 U Street, N.W., Washington, D.C.   202.232.2710

February 7, 1997, marked the first anniversary of the opening of Republic Gardens, the hottest club to hit D.C. in a long time. And the owners hosted quite a celebration! Everyone, but everyone, was there or trying to get into the party of the year! All **Four Bars** were three deep, and the kitchen was offering its best from the club's **First-Class Menu**, which includes an excellent **Lamb Stew, spicy Jerk Chicken, Jumbo Shrimp in Shallot Wine Sauce,** and **Crab Cakes**. (Light fares of salads and sandwiches are also available.) Upstairs, the party rocked to the music of the Shades Band. Deejays kept the crowd pumpin' to the **Best in Urban Contemporary Music** between sets.

This is truly a beautiful club, with sophisticated hand-hammered metal sculptures displayed at every turn, exclusively designed for Republic Gardens by Robert Cole. The attention to detail in the club's ambience, menu, and service is what sets it apart from all the rest. Well done, guys, well done!

Cover charge / 21+ crowd/ ☐ ✓ ℃ ⑨ 🎵 🎁

The Ritz Nightclub   919 E Street N.W. Downtown, Washington, D.C.   202.638.2582

"Ain't nuthin' but a party goin' on" at The Ritz! Its **Three Floors of Entertainment** feature something to suit almost anyone's groove, from **Hip-Hop, Reggae,** and **Live Jazz to R&B Classics.** The Ritz also attracts **Big-Name Live Acts** and is available for private affairs.

Cover charge/ 21+ crowd/ ☐ ⑨ 🎵 🎁

☆Takoma Station Tavern   6914 Fourth Street, N.W., Takoma Park, Washington, D.C.   202.829.1999

Bobby Boyd, Sr., has been part of the Washington, D.C. club scene forever. A great fan of jazz, he long dreamed of having his own club where he could showcase the area's finest talents. After opening Takoma Station in the early Eighties, he soon noticed that instead of attracting a traditional jazz clientele, the club began pulling in a younger crowd. Hey, if you can't beat 'em, join 'em!—and Boyd began adding **Progressive Jazz, Blues, Reggae,** and **Funk** artists to the club's line-up, along with **Straight-Ahead Jazz** performers. Soon, Takoma Station had established itself as **The Spot for Great Live Music in D.C.,** and it's been going strong ever since! Boyd's son David and his partners have now taken over the Station, and they continue to pack the house nightly.

The menu at Takoma Station features **American Cuisine** including **Crab Cake Platters, Catfish, Baby Back Ribs, Sandwiches, Salads,** and **Exotic Drinks.** Try a **Dirty Hawaiian** or an **Electric Tea** for a little added excitement!

Cover charge/ $10–$20 / ☐ ✓ ℃ ⑨ 🎵

Twins   5516 Colorado Avenue, N.W., Washington, D.C.
202.882.2523

Twins is one club in D.C. that attracts an **International Clientele** that crosses racial and economic boundaries, all for the love of good music. Twin sisters Kelley and Maze Tesfaye's successful-but-small jazz club may have a nice, quiet "neighborhood bar" feeling to it early in the week, but things heat up on the weekends. That's when the club packs in the crowds who come to hear **Great Straight-Ahead** or **Contemporary Jazz.** Nationally known artists such as the Roy Ayers Quartet, Jimmy McGriff, and vocalist Shirley Horn have performed at Twins. As a complement to the **World-Class Entertainment,** Twins also serves up a **Full Dinner Menu** featuring **Ethiopian, Italian, American** and **Caribbean Cuisine.**

Cover charge/ $10 Dinner menu/ ☐ ⏧ ♫♫

Caterers

Gist Family Catering Service   1642 Vermont Avenue, N.W., Washington, D.C.   202.387.1627

Willie Gist's earliest influences directing him into the food-service industry came from hanging around his mother in the kitchen of the family's home in Chester, South Carolina. Like many restauranteurs, he started his career as a dishwasher. By 1980, he had worked his way up to general manager at Beefsteak Charlie's restaurants; next followed six years as a unit manager for Wendy's. During these corporate years, Gist, a self-taught chef, catered many events in the D.C. area. In 1986, he established his own firm and start catering full-time.

Gist's big break came in 1990 when he catered an event for the National Coalition for Negro Women. That evening's success brought him other prestigious clients, including a contract to prepare and serve a formal dinner honoring newly elected South African President Nelson Mandela on his visit to the D.C. area. Gist Family Catering Service **Specializes in Southern Cuisine**, especially, **Cobblers, Fried Chicken, Potato Salad,** and **Fresh Greens.**

Good Food Services, Inc.   202.544.2003

John Goodwin, proprietor of Good Food Services, has built a client list that spans the entire East Coast. Whether his employees are laying out a corporate picnic spread on Hilton Head or staffing a cocktail reception in Manhattan, Goodwin's reputation as a capable **Full-Service Caterer** precedes him. That distinction is based on his commitment to provide the highest standard of food services and **Event Planning** expertise to his customers. Goodwin guarantees that he and his staff will do whatever is needed to ensure that your next affair will be "a spectacular event that will be remembered by all."

Good Food Services **Specializes in Seafood. Fabulous Maryland Crab Cakes, and Jumbo Shrimp** are a few ocean favorites to be found at a typical Good Food Services-catered affair. Of course, Goodwin's company will prepare any type of food you may desire, as well as ice sculptures and other decorations. Good Food can also provide **Professional Uniformed Staff**.

Kelsey Catering   202.526.8221

"Catering with a touch of class!" is how Irene Kelsey describes her **Full-Service Catering** firm established in 1987. **Specializing in Weddings and Dinner Parties**, Kelsey's proven catering team will design a menu exclusively for you featuring any type of cuisine desired ranging from a wide selection of international dishes to a down-home country dinner. **Cold Salmon with Dill, Crab Imperial, Stuffed Chicken Breast**, a mean **Apple Cobbler**, and a refreshing **Fruit Punch** are just a few of the items Kelsey Catering is known for.

Signature Events and Catering Affairs
1603 Piscataway Road, Clinton, Maryland
301.292.5735

Vincent Henderson is one of the only African American caterers in the country who has serviced the White House consistently over the years. His **Full-Service Catering and Event Planning** firm can provide for any type of affair. It specializes in continental cuisine ranging from **Nova Scotia Smoked Salmon, Maryland Crab Cakes,** and **Crawfish Monica** to **Baked Virginia Ham au Praline**. Henderson's signature dish is the "Tree of Life," a fresh seasonal and tropical fruit creation artfully arranged in the form of a tree.

BEST OF THE BEST

Best Ambiance
Hairston's – Atlanta
Showcase Eatery –
  Atlanta
Queen of Sheba – Dallas
Sauce – Detroit
Harlequin Café – Detroit
Edmund Place – Detroit
Reggae Hut – Houston
Georgia – L.A.
Hal's Bar & Grill – L.A.
Mobay – L.A.
Elephant Walk – L.A.
Savannah – Miami
Tap Tap – Miami
Dooky Chase's
  – New Orleans
Olivier's – New Orleans
T.J.'s Gingerbread House
  – Oakland
Bambou – New York
B. Smith's – New York/
  Washington, D.C.
Dayo – New York
Jezebel's – New York
Little Jezebel's Plantation
  – New York
Savannah Club –
  New York
BET SoundStage –
  Washington, D.C.
Georgia Brown's –
  Washington, D.C.
Hibiscus Café –
  Washington, D.C.

Best Breakfast
Beautiful Restaurant – Atlanta
Gladys' Luncheonette – Chicago
Izola's – Chicago
New Detroiter – Detroit
Betty's Restaurant –
  Ft. Lauderdale
Maxine's – Kansas City
Bahamian Connection – Miami
Jackson's Soul Food – Miami
Emily's Restaurant– New York
The Pink Tea Cup – New York
Lois The Pie Queen – Oakland
Florida Avenue Grill –
  Washington, D.C.

Best Sunday Brunch
Sylvia's – Atlanta/New York
McDonald's – Charlotte
C'est Si Bon – Chicago
The Retreat – Chicago
Dulan's Restaurant – L.A.
The Praline Connection –
  New Orleans
Café Beulah – New York
The Cotton Club – New York
The Shark Bar –
  New York/Chicago
B. Smith's – Washington, D.C.
BET SoundStage –
  Washington, D.C.
Georgia Brown's –
  Washington, D.C.
Louisiana Café –
  Washington, D.C.

Best Buffet
Satterwhite's – Atlanta
Chanterelle's – Atlanta
Steve's Soul Food –
  Detroit
Madison Kitchen/United
House of Prayer–
  Greensboro
Family Café – Houston
Houston's This Is It
  – Houston
Madry's Dash of Flavor –
  Kansas City
People's Bar-B-Q – Miami
Dooky Chase's –
  New Orleans
The Tourist Trap –
  New Orleans
Little Jezebel's Plantation
  – New York
Crown Cafeteria –
  St. Louis
French's Fine Southern
  – Washington, D.C.

Most
Romantic Setting
The Mansion – Atlanta
La Tesso Tana
  – Baltimore
Edmund Place – Detroit
Melange Café
  – Philadelphia
Bambou – New York
Jezebel's – New York

Best Corporate
Dining
Sylvia's – Atlanta
Army & Lou's – Chicago

Bazzell's – Chicago
Edmund Place – Detroit
Harlequin Café – Detroit
The Blue Nile – Detroit
Georgia – L.A.
Hal's Bar & Grill – L.A.
Harold & Belle's – L.A.
Savannah – Miami
B. Smith's – New York/
  Washington, D.C.
Café Beulah – New York
Georgia Brown's –
  Washington, D.C.

Best After-Work
Watering Holes
Flood's – Detroit
Niecie's Lounge – Kansas City
B. Smith's – New York
The Shark Bar –
New York/Chicago
Soul Café – New York
Zanzibar Blue – Philadelphia
Bailey's – Washington, D.C.

Best Party &
Banquet Facilities
Hairston's – Atlanta
The Mansion – Atlanta
Michael Jordan's Restaurant
  –Chicago
Salaam Restaurant – Chicago
Hayward's Pit Bar-B-Q –
  Kansas City
The Praline Connection Gospel
  & Blues Hall – New Orleans
B. Smith's –
  New York/Washington D.C.
Champagne – Philadelphia
Voyager South – St. Louis

Best Celebrity Spotting & People Watching
Georgia – L.A.
Savannah – Miami
Norma's on the Beach
  – Miami
Bambou – New York
Café Beulah – New York
The Shark Bar –
  New York/Chicago
Soul Café – New York
Sylvia's –
  New York/Atlanta

Best Live Music/ Nightspots
Café Echelon – Atlanta
The New Haven Lounge
  – Baltimore
Harvey's Garage
  – Charlotte
The Cotton Club
  – Chicago
Baker's Keyboard Lounge
  – Detroit
Flood's – Detroit
Ambiance – Houston
Midtown Live – Houston
5th Street Dick's – L.A.
The New Showcase
  Lounge – New Orleans
Zanzibar Blue –
  Philadelphia
Warmdaddy's –
  Philadelphia
Bailey's –
  Washington, D.C.
Bukom –
  Washington, D.C.

Café Lautrec –
  Washington, D.C.
New Vegas Lounge –
  Washington, D.C.
Republic Gardens –
  Washington, D.C.

Best Fried Chicken
Sylvia's – Atlanta/New York
Army & Lou's – Chicago
Frenchy's – Houston
Aunt Kizzy's Back Porch – L.A.
Mama Rosa Restaurant–
  Philadelphia
Jezebel's – New York
The Shark Bar –
  New York/Chicago
Powell's – San Francisco
Voyager South – St. Louis
Florida Avenue Grill –
  Washington, D.C.
Georgia Brown's –
  Washington, D.C.

Best Ribs
Tom's Place – Ft. Lauderdale
Dillard's Bar-B-Q – Durham
M & D's Café– Denver
Jada's–Detroit
Milt's Gourmet Bar-"B"-Que –
  Detroit
Harlon's Barbeque House–
  Houston
Gates Bar-B-Q – Kansas City
Luther's Finest – Kansas City
Intertsate Bar-B-Q–Memphis
Neely's Bar-B-Q Shop –
  Memphis
Everett & Jones – Oakland
Dwight's – Philadelphia

Mama Rosa Restaurant –
  Philadelphia
Reynolds' – St. Louis
Richard's Ribs – St. Louis
Big Nate's –
  San Francisco

Best Sweet Potato Pie

Sylvia's –
  Atlanta/New York
C'est Si Bon – Chicago
DC's Café – Dallas
Milt's Gourmet Bar-"B"-
  Que – Detroit
Aunt Kizzy's Back Porch
  – L.A.
The Praline Connection
  – New Orleans
Lois The Pie Queen
  – Oakland
Denise's Delicacies –
  Philadelphia
Moody's On The Pike –
  Philadelphia
Powell's – San Francisco
Richard's Ribs – St. Louis

Best Peach Cobbler

Beautiful Restaurant
  – Atlanta
Army & Lou's – Chicago
M & D's – Denver
Luther's – Kansas City
Papa Lew's Barbecue
  – Kansas City
Laurita's Café Soul
  – New York
The Shark Bar
  – New York/Chicago
Richard's Ribs – St. Louis

Best Jerk Chicken

Patti Hut – Atlanta
Chelsea Place – Atlanta
Jamaica Jamaica – Durham
Jerk Machine – Ft. Lauderdale
Reggae Hut – Houston
Coley's Kitchen – L.A.
Dayo – New York
Daphne's Caribbean Express
  – New York
Negril/Island Spice – New York
Rock 'N Reggae Café – Raleigh
The Islander
  – Washington, D.C.

Glossary

Ackee and Saltfish—Considered the national dish of Jamaica. Ackee is a bright-red tropical fruit, originally brought to the Caribbean from Africa in 1793. When ripened, it opens to reveal a soft white meat and three large black seeds; until it has ripened, it is considered uneatable and poisonous. Saltfish is a dried, salted fish, usually cod, that is always cooked with the skin on. To prepare this dish, ackee are carefully selected, cleaned, steamed, and sautéed with the fish, onions, and Jamaican pepper.

Blackened—A method of cooking whereby meat or fish are covered in a combination of Cajun spices, then seared in a pan until done, giving the appearance of being burnt.

Cajun Cuisine—"The Cajuns were the original Acadian immigrants who had come to Nova Scotia from France in 1620. Armed with their black pots, they were happy to live off the land. Cajun cuisine is characterized by the use of wild game, seafood, wild vegetation and herbs. Jambalaya, stews, gumbo, and stuffed vegetable dishes are all characteristics of the Cajun one-pot meals." (Reprinted from the menu at Bazzell's French Quarter Bistro, Chicago, Illinois)

Callaloo—The large green leaves of the taro root plant, "Jamaica's answer to collard greens!" (The Jamaican Café, Santa Monica, California)

Creole Cuisine—"Creole cooking reflects the diversity of Creole culture, combining elements from around the world: French, Italian, Spanish, and African....Those flavors are mingled with our abundant local vegetables and seafood. A masterful blending of varietal spices that have come to the port of New Orleans from around the world gives Creole Cuisine its distinctive complexion." (Olivier's Restaurant, New Orleans, Louisiana)

Escoveitch Fish—A popular island dish traditionally served for breakfast, Coley's Restaurant in Los Angeles serves it two ways. Their King Fish Escoveitch is prepared by "lightly frying the fish and smothering it with vinegar, onions, & hot pepper," or by sautéing the fish "in tomato sauce with a blend of herbs & spices."

Etouffe—"A light roux, chopped bell peppers, green and yellow onions, and celery added to a fresh homemade crawfish stock with a touch of tomato paste, flavored with basil, thyme, and garlic. Spicy boiled crawfish are added to the finished sauce. Served over rice." (Olivier's Restaurant, New Orleans, Louisiana)

Ginger Beer—"Freshly grated ginger, boiled, brewed with exotic spices. This very rich ginger taste is sure to clear up any sinus problems!" (Le Belle Caribbean, Oakland, California)

Gumbo—A derivative of the African word for okra, Gumbo is "a spicy soup consisting of crab, shrimp, oysters, chicken, sausages, ham and seasonings, simmered in a thick broth..." (Dooky Chase's, New Orleans, Louisiana)

Jambalaya—A one-pot dish made with chicken, shrimp, sausage, and spices, mixed or "jumbled" with rice.

Jerk—"A spicy marinade of seasonings unique to Maroon culture" (Coley's Restaurant, Los Angeles), what is known to the world as "jerk" seasoning is a combination of onions, thyme, Scotch Bonnet pepper, bird pepper, cinnamon, nutmeg, allspice, and scallions used to season various types of meats ("jerk chicken," "jerk beef," etc.).

Po-Boy—A large sandwich made with French bread and stuffed with fried oysters, shrimp, or catfish. As my father tells it, during the Depression, grocery stores were desperate to sell soda pops. To entice money-strapped customers, the stores offered a free sandwich with the purchase of every drink! Hence the name, "Po-Boy"!

Roti—"Lightly fried flour dough filled with fine ground split peas and greera (cumin powder). The fried dough is used as a 'Caribbean burrito' and wrapped around your choice of meat or vegetable." (Le Belle Caribbean, Oakland, California)

Smothered—The process of "sautéing and slowly cooking meats in a rich brown onion gravy so when it's time to serve, no knife is needed!" (Aunt Kizzy's Back Porch, Marina Del Rey, California)

Sorrel—A red plant that is a member of the Hibiscus family. The flowers are dried and soaked in water to produce a tart, scarlet-colored drink. Traditionally served during Christmastime in the Caribbean, Sorrel is now enjoyed all year 'round.

About the Author

Carla Labat was born and raised in New Orleans, a city rich in culture and no stranger to distinctive foods and great music. At age 12, her family moved to Dakar, Senegal, where her father served as Peace Corps director. During the five years she and her family lived in Africa, Carla gained an appreciation for the local cuisine and music. A year in a Swiss boarding school heightened her interest in international cultures and foods. After graduating from the University of Maryland, Carla moved to Manhattan where she pursued a career as a retail manager and accessories buyer for Bonwit Teller. While traveling in Europe and throughout the U.S. on buying trips, she was constantly being introduced to new restaurants and soon developed a reputation among friends and associates as a dining and travel connoisseur. Her own frustrations over not being able to identify or find restaurants, nightclubs, or caterers featuring African American, African, and Caribbean cuisine and music prompted her to pull together this unique guide. She spent four months on the road seeking out these establishments, sampling their food and entertainment offerings, and personally interviewing close to 300 owners, managers, chefs, and patrons. She currently lives in McLean, Virginia.

Order Form

✳ Fax orders: 703.448.6062
☎ Telephone orders: 703.448.6062
   Have your AMEX, VISA or MasterCard ready.
✉ Postal orders: Impressions Books, Carla Labat, P.O. Box 9622, McLean, Virginia 22102-0622, USA

I would like to order __ book(s) at $13.95 each. Please send:
Name: _____
Address: _____
City: _____ State: _____ Zip: _____
Telephone: _____

Please send ___ book(s) as a gift at $13.95 each.
Name: _____
Address: _____
City: _____ State: _____ Zip: _____
Telephone: _____

Sales Tax: Please add 4.5% for books shipped to Virginia addresses.

Shipping: Add $3.00 for the first book, $1.00 for each additional book. Allow 2-3 weeks for delivery.

Payment:
☐ Check: Make check out to Impressions Books
☐ Credit cards: ☐ AMEX ☐ VISA ☐ MasterCard
Card number: _____
Name on card: _____ Exp. Date: _____
Bill to address: _____
(if not the same as above)

703.448.6062 Call Now to Order!